Statistical Analysis Techniques, Volume 1

Statistical Analysis Techniques, Volume 1: Foundations and Basic Applications

BY

AZİZ AKGÜL

OSTIM Technical University, Türkiye

emerald
PUBLISHING

United Kingdom – North America – Japan – India – Malaysia – China

Emerald Publishing Limited
Emerald Publishing, Floor 5, Northspring, 21–23 Wellington Street, Leeds LS1 4DL

First edition 2026

Reprints and permissions service
Contact: www.copyright.com
Printed and bound by CPI Group (UK) Ltd, Croydon, CR0 4YY

British Library Cataloguing in Publication Data
A catalogue record for this book is available from the British Library

ISBN: 978-1-80592-342-8 (Print)
ISBN: 978-1-80592-341-1 (Online)
ISBN: 978-1-80592-343-5 (Epub)

INVESTOR IN PEOPLE

Contents

About the Author

Aziz Akgül, Ph.D., graduated from the Business Administration Department of the Turkish Military Academy and completed his MBA at the Middle East Technical University. He pursued further studies abroad, earning his M.S. degree from the US Naval Postgraduate School and his Ph.D. in Business Administration from the Faculty of Political Sciences at Ankara University.

Throughout his career, Professor Akgül has held numerous high-level positions, including Senior Advisor to the Prime Minister of Türkiye and President of KOSGEB (Small and Medium Enterprises Development Organization). He also served as a Member of Parliament, contributing to national economic and social development initiatives.

Currently, he is the Chairman of the Board of Trustees of the Turkish Foundation for Waste Reduction (TISVA) and a faculty member at OSTIM Technical University. His academic and professional expertise spans Business Administration, Operations Research, Statistical Analysis, the Defense Industry, and the socio-economic philosophy of Happytalism.

Professor Akgül has published 18 books and numerous scholarly articles, reflecting his lifelong commitment to education, social innovation, and public service.

Preface

The evaluation and interpretation of data in the social sciences play a crucial role in supporting effective decision-making processes.

In today's increasingly data-driven world, managers and policymakers rely heavily on empirical evidence to identify problems, understand underlying causes, and formulate strategic plans that align with organizational objectives and market dynamics.

Through careful data analysis, they can assess current performance, forecast future trends, and make informed decisions that improve operational efficiency and long-term competitiveness.

However, the accuracy and utility of these decisions are highly dependent on the proper collection, classification, and analysis of relevant data. The quality of research begins with defining the right problem and determining which variables are meaningful and measurable within the given context.

Pre-decision research must also include the selection of appropriate statistical tools and methodologies tailored to the nature of the data and the research objectives. Errors in this process—whether in data collection, sampling design, or analytical technique—can lead to distorted conclusions and misguided decisions.

Common pitfalls include selecting the wrong statistical model, ignoring assumptions underlying analytical tools, or overgeneralizing from limited datasets. Such issues highlight the need for a methodologically sound approach and a critical understanding of statistical inference in social science research.

This book has been prepared using a QR code approach to enhance the reading experience. I hope that it will contribute to academics, students, and all those interested in the subject—especially researchers working in all social sciences, particularly in business administration and economics.

I would like to take this opportunity to express my gratitude to Professor Murat Yülek for his invaluable support, and my sincere thanks to Halil Orhan, Elif Turgut, Uğurcan Gökcan, Tutku Güner, Esra Yılmaz, Filiz Gül, Handan Öztürk, Berkay Sünbül, Halil Fatih Akgül, and Aslıhan Köksal for their kind support, as well as to the Publication Commission of OSTIM Technical University and Emerald.

Aziz Akgül, Ph.D.

Chapter 1

Research Design and Planning

Objectives

- To support the effective design of research studies.
- To define the purpose of research.
- To translate the research purpose into a hypothesis.
- To determine the appropriate sample size for conducting research.

1.1 Introduction

No one would deny the importance of mathematics in science and its necessity for its accuracy. However, mathematics cannot produce correct answers from incorrect premises. When applied with accurate inputs, mathematics yields valid results; when applied to flawed inputs, the results will also be flawed.

Poorly designed research creates problems that no statistical method can resolve. Statistical analysis applied to a weak research design offers no benefit. Therefore, while preparing for a research study, the characteristics of the research topic, time constraints, financial resources, and available personnel must all be carefully considered and meticulously planned. Otherwise, the outcomes may be unreliable and result in wasted resources.

1.2 Description of the Purposes of Research

Key questions that should be addressed during research planning or while reviewing a research plan are summarized in Table 1.1.

Hence, the questions that need to be answered should be clearly defined before any work begins. Often, it is challenging to focus on a single question. For instance, someone asked to assess the effectiveness of a new method might ask, "Is the new method better than existing methods under these conditions?" Another question may concern potential undesirable effects. Additional relevant questions may also be posed.

Despite this, it is advisable to focus on a single main objective. Secondary objectives should be kept to a minimum and clearly defined.

Statistical Analysis Techniques, Volume 1, 1–21

Published under exclusive licence by Emerald Publishing Limited
doi:10.1108/978-1-80592-341-120261001

Table 1.1. Determination of Purposes While Planning a Research.

What is the main purpose of research?
Is the purpose clearly stated?
Is the purpose economically significant?
Are secondary purposes clearly stated?

It should also be taken into account whether the answer to the main question is of economic importance. For example, if the method being tested differs slightly from the standard method, the new method **may not be of economic significance**, as any difference in efficiency is likely to be small. As a result of the research, it can be seen that the new method **is statistically significantly superior to** the standard method but with a very small margin of economic superiority. Such an outcome is unlikely to change the practice.

1.3 Considerations in Research Design

The purpose of eliminating the sources of error in a research is to ensure that when a difference is detected between the groups, this difference comes from the applied factor, not from the heterogeneity of the subjects in the groups. It is not possible to carry out accurate statistical analysis without removing the said effect. For a reliable research, the points in Table 1.2 should be particularly provided.

Table 1.2. Factors to Consider in Research Design.

Making a good research design
Choosing an appropriate sampling method
Taking no sides
Carrying out the research under standard conditions
Using appropriate statistical methods
Finding the right size
Getting the measurements right
Identifying relationships between variables
Collecting accurate, reliable and complete data
Comparing comparable situations
Interpreting the results correctly
Eliminate errors caused by the measurer (interviewer, observer)
Moral issues

1.4 Determination of the Purpose of Research

As in laboratory experiments, the first step in business research is to pose the basic research question, i.e., purpose of the research. While the said question is called a **hypothesis** in general, it helps to determine important research **parameters** (such as the types of methods to be compared, the quality of the results to be evaluated, the number of subjects in each study group, the characteristics that the subjects to be included in the study must have).

The parameter measured to answer the most important question of the research for any problem of business is the key objective to be reached. Researchers should consider the following questions when determining key objectives:

Which objectives are important for the business?
Which of these objectives can be reasonably measured?
What challenges are there in practice, such as the size of the study group, the financial resources of the research, or the long-term monitoring of businesses/staff?

A research can be designed to answer the following question: "Does the A-type method or the B-type method provide better results when it is desired to employ the personnel working in a business more efficiently?"

1.5 Determination of the Hypothesis in Research

The researcher's problem is very similar to the court order process (Table 1.3). The absolute truth about whether or not the defendant committed the crime cannot be determined. Instead, the court starts hearings from the point that the defendant did not commit the crime on the assumption that he is **innocent** at the beginning. The court then decides whether there is sufficient evidence to reject the presumption of innocence of the defendant. Subsequently, the court may err by punishing the innocent defendant or not punishing a guilty defendant.

Similarly, the researcher begins with the assumption that there is no relationship between predictor and outcome variables in the population. Based on the data in the chosen sample, the researcher uses statistical tests to determine if there is sufficient evidence to reject the null hypothesis in favor of the alternative hypothesis. The standard for these tests is **the level of statistical significance.**

The majority of statistical decision-making involves testing hypotheses about population parameters. A **hypothesis** is a statement about the world to be tested. For example, it may be desirable to test the hypothesis that the population mean of men living in a town is 99% of the university graduates. The hypothesis can be proposed using the researcher's own knowledge, estimation or previous observations.

It is necessary to investigate the process of whether the data indicate evidence contrary to the hypothesis about the population parameter. If the data indicate

Table 1.3. Similarity Between Statistical Tests and Court Decision Process.

Court Order	Statistical Test
Innocence: The defendant did not extort money	*Null hypothesis*: There is no relationship between productive work and wages in mid-level managers
Crime: The defendant extorted money	*Alternative hypothesis*: There is a relationship between productive work and pay received
Standard of presumption of innocence: To be determined with sufficient evidence	*Standard of rejection of null hypothesis*: Alpha with statistical significance level
Correct decision: Arresting the one who extorted money	*Correct decision*: Concluding that there is a correlation between productive work and pay, which actually exists
Correct decision: Acquittal of an innocent person	*Correct decision*: Concluding that there is no correlation between productive work and pay, which does not actually exist
Incorrect decision: Arresting an innocent person	*Incorrect decision (Type I):* Concluding that there is a correlation between productive work and pay, which does not actually exist
Incorrect decision: Releasing the extortionist	*Incorrect decision (Type II):* Concluding that there is no correlation between productive work and pay, which actually exists

evidence contrary to the hypothesis, the hypothesis is rejected. If the data do not indicate evidence contrary to the hypothesis, the hypothesis is not rejected.

How is it decided whether data indicate evidence contrary to a hypothesis? We begin by accepting that the hypothesis is tentatively correct. It is then determined that the data set shows how likely it is that the hypothesis is true. If the data set shows a slight probability that the hypothesis is true, the data show the evidence contrary to the hypothesis. If the data set shows with a certain probability that the hypothesis is true, the data indicate that there is no evidence contrary to the hypothesis.

A good hypothesis should be based on a good research question, simple, clear, and pre-stated. The null hypothesis can be expressed by symbols such as:

$$H_0: \mu_1 = \mu_2$$

Here μ_1 and μ_2 signify the first and second population averages, respectively. The null hypothesis is that there is no difference between the two population averages in terms of the subject of interest. The null hypothesis states that there is no relationship between the predictive and outcome variables in the population from which the study group was taken.

Beginning with a statement that there is no correlation, statistical tests estimate the probability that the observed association is due to chance.

The purpose of these experiments is to test whether the observed results are consistent with the null hypothesis. If the obtained data are not consistent with the null hypothesis, the null hypothesis (H_0) is rejected in favor of the alternative hypothesis (H_A). The alternative hypothesis can be expressed as follows:

$$H_A: \mu_1 \neq \mu_2$$

While **one-tailed hypothesis** ($\mu_1 < \mu_2$ or $\mu_1 > \mu_2$) determines the direction of the relationship between the predictor and the outcome variable, **two-tailed hypothesis** only states that there is a relationship, not its direction. The one-sided hypothesis is that managers with more experience are more likely to succeed than those with less experience.

Estimating the differential success rate of more experienced managers to be more or less experienced than less experienced managers is a two-sided hypothesis. While one-tailed hypotheses allow studying a smaller number of subjects, one-tailed hypotheses are not always appropriate.

The one-tailed test is stronger than the two-tailed test because the value obtained as a result of a one-tailed statistical test does not have to be very large to be found significant.

On the other hand, when p_1 represents % of people who succeed in one year after type A training and p_2 represents % of people who succeed in one year after type B training, the null hypothesis and alternative hypothesis can be represented by symbols as:

$$H_0: p_1 = p_2$$
$$H_A: p_1 \neq p_2$$

Note that in the alternative hypothesis, the percentages are not equal to each other. This alternative hypothesis states that these two trainings will differ from each other in terms of one year success.

1.6 Determination of the Sample Size

When planning a research, the question of how many subjects are required immediately comes to mind. There are moral and statistical aspects to determining sample size.

If the sample size is too small or contains too many subjects, far from revealing the relationship or significant difference, the resources allocated for the research and the cost of the researchers cannot be supported. **Sample size is related to significance level, effect size, and power.**

1.6.1 Level of Significance

The level of significance is the rejection of the true null hypothesis (**Type I error**), which is called alpha (α) and is usually taken as 0.05.

The number of subjects (sample size) to be included in the research should be determined at the same time as the main objective of the study. At the end of any research, the data are analyzed and a **statistical** decision is made to reject or accept the research hypothesis. Since this decision is based on **probabilities**, it can be right or wrong. The relationship between the probable findings of the A- and B-type training research and the "**real**" is shown in Table 1.4. The purpose of this discussion is to draw conclusions that can be generalized to the whole population by using representative samples and results from properly applied training involving employees who meet the requirements of "real" research. However, since only one sample can be used, there is also the risk of getting wrong results.

In Cells A and D of Table 1.4, the results of the research are the same as the "real". In Cells B and C, the results of the research are not the same as the "real". In other words, there are errors. These two types of errors differ in their sources and results.

Table 1.4. Comparisons of Research Results and Reality.

	"Reality"	
Results of research	Trainings are different	Trainings are not different
	A	**B**
Trainings are different	True (correct-Positive)	**Type I** error (false-Positive)
	C	**D**
Trainings are not different	**Type II** error (false-negative)	True (correct-Positive)

As with court decisions, the investigator's decision may be wrong. Sometimes just by chance, the sample may not be representative of the population. Thus, the results obtained by using the example do not reflect the real situation in the population, causing an incorrect result.

If there is a difference between the trainings in the research and there is no difference in reality (**B cell**), then there is a **Type I error**. In these circumstances, the research results are falsely positive. In the example of Type A and Type B training, if the researcher concludes that there is a difference between the trainings in terms of achievement but there is no difference between the averages of success according to "real", **Type I error** was made. If there is no difference between the trainings in the study, but there is a real difference (C cell), it can be said that **Type II error** has been made. In these circumstances, the research results are falsely negative.

If the researcher concludes that there is no difference between the trainings in terms of success averages, and on the other hand, if one of the trainings creates a higher success average than the "real**", Type II error** has occurred.

Research can be falsely positive or falsely negative, either due to faulty methodology or for both reasons occurring by chance. Although methodological errors can be minimized by paying attention to the research design, chance errors cannot be eliminated completely. These errors, however, are predictable. The value indicating that the observed difference between the groups is not due to a real difference but to **Type I error** that occurred by chance is called **α significance level. 1-α** is the **reliability level** of the test and the probability of not rejecting the actually true null hypothesis.

The value indicating the probability of occurrence of **Type II error**, which consists of not finding a difference as a result of the research although there is a difference in reality, is also called **the beta level (β).** While researchers are planning their research, they also determine **alpha** and **beta** levels and show them in their research. **Alpha** level is generally set at 0.05. This means that the researcher accepts the probability of making **Type I error** with a 5% risk. The researcher should also predetermine the probability of making **Type II error**. In general, the probability of making a **beta** error is 0.20. In other words, there is a 1/5 chance of skipping an actual difference between groups. A study with a **beta** level of 0.20 has a statistical power of 0.80 or 80%. There is an 80% chance that such a study will reveal a certain difference in results between training groups.

The larger the sample size, the smaller the beta. Thus, the power of the test increases **1-β.**

Once the **alpha and beta** levels have been determined, the researcher must determine other important parameters to be used in the research before determining the sample size. The size of the difference in results between training groups is an important parameter. Since the difference between the training plans being compared is significant, the training should be chosen on the basis of knowledge. When deciding what difference is worth finding between the results, the researcher should consider one or more of the following questions:

When training this type of personnel, what difference in results would be significant for trainers or managers?
What difference does it make to a manager who complains about the consequences of failure?
What difference in results might justify the effectiveness that this training method has been used despite being more expensive and requiring larger facilities?

The three factors mentioned (acceptable levels of **Type I and Type II** errors and the expected size of the difference in results between groups) are inversely related to the required sample size, and reducing the acceptable **Type I and Type II** error will have the effect of increasing the required sample size.

In many researches, alpha is set at 0.05 and beta at 0.20 (power of 0.80). In a sense, these are optional values, and sometimes, different values can be used. For example, values in the range of 0.01–0.10 can be used for **alpha** while a common range of 0.05–0.20 for **beta**. Generally, the researcher should use a low **α level** to avoid **Type I error** and a low **β level** to avoid **Type II error.**

As the size of the expected difference in outcomes (e.g., mean achievement) between training groups decreases, a larger sample size is needed to find the difference. Conversely, the smaller the variability in outcome (e.g., the standard deviation of achievement), the fewer subjects are needed to demonstrate that there is a difference in outcomes between groups.

The sample size should be increased by the researcher when the chance of making **Type I error** is accepted as 1% instead of 5%. The smaller the significance level, the larger the sample is required. Similarly, if there is a decrease in the level of **Type II error**, which increases statistical power, more subjects are needed in the study.

Ideally, alpha and beta should be zero to eliminate the possibility of false-positive and false-negative results. Downsizing them often requires a larger sample size. However, while conducting the research, a sample size that will keep alpha and beta at acceptable levels without increasing the cost of the study too much should be selected.

The reason alpha is given more consideration than beta is because alpha has more serious consequences than beta. For example, alpha, which refers to giving up a known and effective training method and choosing a relatively unknown and actually not much better training method, has more serious consequences than beta, which refers to continuing to apply an existing known and relatively effective training method while neglecting a much better training method.

When it is desired to reveal the similarity rather than the difference between the two training methods; beta becomes more important than alpha.

1.6.2 Effect Size

The effect size indicates the difference between groups or the power of the correlation. If the effect is large, such as 90% less number of defective products in enterprises using the X-type production system, it is easy to detect in the sample. If the size of the correlation is very small, such as a 2% decrease in defective products, it is difficult to detect the effect in the sample.

Often, the researcher does not know the size of the correlation since the purpose of the research is to predict this. Instead, the researcher can predetermine the possible correlation size that can be obtained from the sample researched. Choosing the appropriate effect size is the most difficult part of determining the sample size. Researchers sometimes use previous researches or pilot researches to determine the appropriate effect size.

When there is no data on it to estimate the effect size, the researcher can choose the lowest effect size that is economically meaningful. A 10% reduction in the production of faulty products can be given as an example. A 1% reduction in the production of defective products is also important for the business. Thus, the determination of the effect size is completely up to the preference of the researcher. In the event that the number of subjects to be studied is limited, it should be evaluated whether it is reasonable for the researcher to study the limited subject in question.

Generally, in the *t*-Test comparing the mean of the two groups, the expected small effect is considered to be 0.2 of the standard deviation, the expected medium effect is 0.5 of the standard deviation, and the expected large effect is 0.8 of the standard deviation.

1.6.3 Power of the Test

Power is the probability of rejecting the null hypothesis. In other words, it refers to avoidance of **Type II** error. Generally, 80% is considered sufficient.

Beta is defined as the probability of not rejecting the null hypothesis that is actually false while **1-β** is the power of the test and **the probability of rejecting the null hypothesis that is actually false.**

It is desirable that the power of the test be higher. Of the two test techniques that test the same null hypothesis, the one with the higher power is preferred. The lower the alpha is, the higher the beta will be. Thus, the power of the test 1-β is reduced. **The higher the power, the bigger the sample is required.**

The researcher controls the **Type I** error by choosing the level of significance. He wants to take **Type II** error under control as well. Controlling **Type II** error is possible simply by changing the sample size. As the sample size increases, the probability of making **Type II** error decreases. However, it should not be forgotten that increasing the sample size increases the cost as well as it is time consuming. For this reason, we try to establish a sample size larger than the required minimum for a small **Type II** error.

The required minimum sample size can be determined with the help of prepared tables or by using computer programs such as "**Research**". Having an equal number of subjects in the groups usually provides the highest power value for the total subjects included in the study.

1.7 Determination of Sample Sizes in Different Researches

In analytical researches, the following steps are followed to determine the sample size:

The null and alternative hypotheses are defined. It is stated whether the alternative hypothesis is one-tailed or two-tailed.

Based on the type of predictive and outcome variables, **the statistical test to be used is chosen.**

Pretests or the effect size from previous researches (difference between the mean values of the outcome variable of the study groups) and **its prevalence** (standard deviation) are estimated. When the z-statistic is used, the effect size and prevalence are expressed in terms of p_6 as the percentage of outcome in one group and p_2 as a percentage of outcomes in the other group. When the correlation coefficient is used, the absolute value of the smallest correlation coefficient with the effect size is taken.

Depending on the importance of avoiding **Type I** and **Type II** errors, appropriate **alpha** and **beta** levels are determined.

The situation is somewhat different in descriptive studies, where the aim is to estimate the number of subjects required for the confidence interval based on the given confidence level and its sensitivity (width). Here are the steps to follow:

For binary (dichotomous) variables, the percentage of subjects is estimated for the variable of interest. For the continuous variable, its standard deviation is estimated.

The desired precision (width) is determined for the confidence interval. Confidence level (for example, 95%) is determined.

After determining the general elements, examples of sample size will now be examined.

1.7.1 Determination of the Sample Size in Experimental Researches where the t-Test is Applied

***t*-Test** is used to determine if the mean of a continuous outcome variable in one group is significantly different from that in the other group.

The research question is to compare the average amount of milk processed per minute by M1 and M2 type machines, which are a type of milk processing machine. In previous researches, the average milk processing capacity of a normal machine was 2.0 liters per minute and its standard deviation was 1.0 liters.

The researcher wishes to find a difference of 10% or more between the average milk processing capacities of the two machine types. Given alpha (two-tailed) = 0.05 and power = 0.80, what is the number of machines that should be selected for each group (M1 and M2)?

The required sample size is calculated as:

- *Null hypothesis*: The average amount of milk processed per minute by M1 and M2 type machines is the same.

- *Alternative hypothesis*: The average amount of milk processed per minute by M1 and M2 type machines is different.
- *Effect size*: 0.2 liters (10 × 2.0 = 0.2)
- *Standardized effect size*: To calculate the standardized effect size, the expected effect size is divided by the standard deviation of the outcome variable. In this example, the calculation is done as **"effect size/standard deviation= 0.2 liters/ 1.0 liters= 0.2"**.
- Alpha (two-tailed): 0.05, Beta = 1 - power = 1–0.80 = 0.20

In Table 1.5, the required number of machines is found by reading the standardized effect size 0.20 from the leftmost column, 393 which is the number at the intersection of alpha (two-tailed) = 0.05 and beta = 0.20 from top to bottom.

Such a large sample size may lead to reconsideration of the research design, for example, to consider a design that is repeated measurement.

1.7.2 Determination of Sample Size in Case-Control Studies where the t-Test is Applied

The research question concerns whether the amount of faulty production (in meters) in a fabric mill is related to employees' receiving specific training on the subject. The average error rate for the personnel who did not receive a specific training was determined as 200 meters/month and the standard deviation was determined as 20 meters/month. In the previous researches, a difference of +10 meters/month was detected between the personnel who received a certain training and the personnel who were not; in some researches, it was determined that there was no difference between them and even the amount of faulty production decreased in the personnel who did not receive a certain training.

Taking alpha (two-tailed) = 0.05 and beta = 0.10, how many trained and how many untrained personnel need to be selected to detect a difference of 10 meters/ month between groups?

The required sample size is calculated as:

- *Null hypothesis*: There is no difference between the average amount of defective production of personnel who have received certain training and those who have not.
- *Alternative hypothesis*: There is a difference between the average amount of defective production of personnel who have received certain training and those who have not.
- *Effect size*: 10 meters/month.
- *Standardized effect size*: (Effect size/standard deviation) = 10/20 = 0.5 (Here, it is assumed that the standard deviations for the amount of defective production are the same for those who received training and those who were not).
- Alpha (two-tailed): 0.05, Beta = 0.10.

Table 1.5. Required Sample Size When Using *t*-Test to Compare Means of Continuous Variables.

One-Tailed alpha =		0.005			0.025			0.05	
Two-Tailed Alpha =		0.01			0.05			0.1	
Beta =	0.05	0.10	0.20	0.05	0.10	0.20	0.05	0.10	0.20
Standardized effect size									
0.10	3563	2,977	2,337	2,599	2,102	1,570	2,165	1713	1,237
0.15	1,584	1,323	1,038	1,155	934	698	962	762	550
0.20	891	744	584	650	526	393	541	428	309
0.25	570	476	374	416	336	251	346	274	198·
0.30	396	331	260	289	234	174	241	190	137
0.40	223	186	146	162	131	98	135	107	77
0.50	143	119	93	104	84	63	87	69	49
0.60	99	83	65	72	58	44	60	48	34
0.70	73	61	48	53	43	32	44	35	25
0.80	56	47	36	41	33	25	34	27	19
0.90	44	37	29	32	26	19	27	21	15
1.00	36	30	23	26	21	16	22	17	12

In Table 1.5, the standardized effect size is found by reading 84 from the leftmost column, 0.5 from top to bottom, alpha (two-sided) = 0.05, and 84 at the intersection of beta = 0.10, and the number of personnel who have received 84 training and 84 who have not been trained. Two-tailed alpha was chosen because the researcher wanted the alternative hypothesis to be two-tailed. In other words, the state of being trained is associated with both low and high defect production.

1.7.3 Determination of Sample Size in Cohort Studies where the t*-Test is Applied*

Z-statistic is used to compare the percentages of subjects in each of the two groups with dichotomous outcomes. The z-statistic is similar to the Chi-Square test, with one difference: the z-statistic can be one one-tailed or two-tailed whereas the chi-square is always two-tailed.

The research question is about whether elderly people who smoke are more likely to get skin cancer than nonsmokers. When previous researches were examined, the probability of developing skin cancer in elderly nonsmokers was determined as 0.20 in 5 years. Taking alpha (one-tailed) = 0.05 and power = 80%, how many smokers and how many nonsmokers should be studied to determine whether the odds of developing skin cancer in older smokers are at least 30% at 5 years?

The required sample size is calculated as follows:

- *Null hypothesis:* Elderly smokers and nonsmokers are equally likely to develop skin cancer.
- *Alternative hypothesis:* Elderly smokers and nonsmokers have a different probability of developing skin cancer.
- *Effect size:* p_1 (percentage of subjects expected to have a certain risk factor in one group - probability in smokers) = 0.30, p_2 (probability of nonsmokers expected to have a certain risk factor in the other group) = 0.20. The smallest of these values is 0.20 and the difference between them (p_1–p_2) is 0.10. In general, p_1 is the percentage of subjects expected to have an outcome in one group, while p_2 is the percentage of subjects expected to have an outcome in the other group. In case control studies, p_1 represents the percentage of cases with a predictive variable, while p_2 represents controls with a predictive variable.
- Alpha (one-tailed) = 0.05, Beta = 1–0.80 = 0.20.

In Table 1.6, the required number of 231 smokers and 231 nonsmokers is found by taking 0.20 from the leftmost column, the expected difference 0.10 and reading 231 from top to bottom [the figure at the intersection of alpha (one-tailed) = 0.05 and beta = 0.20].

1.7.4 Determination of Sample Size in Case-Control Studies Where z-Statistics is Applied

Assume a case-control study is planned to investigate whether not getting a good undergraduate education is associated with managerial failure. In a small pilot study, it was found that about 30% of successful managers do not have a good undergraduate education.

Suppose the researcher is interested in revealing an odds ratio (OR) of 2.5 or more for being an unsuccessful manager associated with not getting a good undergraduate education, given alpha (one-tailed) = 0.025 and power = 90%. How many subjects are needed?

The required sample size is calculated as follows:

- *Null hypothesis*: The percentage of people (cases) who do not have a good undergraduate education and are unsuccessful managers is the same as the percentage of people who are successful managers (controls) who do not have a good undergraduate education.
- *Alternative hypothesis*: The percentage of people who do not have a good undergraduate education and are unsuccessful managers is different from the percentage of people who are successful managers who do not have a good undergraduate education.
- *Effect size*: p_2 (percentage of controls expected to have the risk factor) = 0.30, p_1 (percentage of cases expected to have the risk factor) = $[OR \times p_2/(1-p_2 + OR \times p_2)] = [(2.5 \times 0.3)/(1\text{–}0.3 + 2.5 \times 0.3)] = 0.75/1.45 = 0.52$.

The smallest of these values is 0.30, and the difference between them (p_1–p_2) is 0.20.

- Alpha (one-tailed) = 0.025, Beta = 1–0.90 = 0.10.

In Table 1.6, the required 124 cases and 124 controls are found by reading 124 from the leftmost column by taking the expected difference of 0.30 and the expected difference of 0.20 from top to bottom with the lower digit [alpha (one-tailed) = 0.025 and the figure at the intersection of beta = 0.10].

1.7.5 Determination of Sample Size in Cross-Sectional Studies where Correlation Coefficient is Applied

Assume the research question of whether not being able to make a decision quickly (indecision) and being successful in management is inversely related is being examined. The researcher believes that those with higher indecision will have lower success in management. In a previous research, a low correlation (−0.20) was found between indecision and success in management. The researcher

Table 1.6. Required Sample Size for Each Group When Using z-Statistics to Compare Percentages of Binary Variables.

Top number:		Alpha =	0.05 (one-tailed)		or	Alpha =	0.10 (two-tailed);		Beta = .20	
Middle number:		Alpha =	0.025 (one-tailed)		or	Alpha =	0.10 (two-tailed);		Beta = 0.20	
Bottom number:		Alpha =	0.025 (one-tailed)		or	Alpha =	0.05 (two-tailed);		Beta = 0.10	
	Expected difference between $p1$ and $p2$									
Pick the smaller from $p1$ and $p2$	0.05	0.1	0.15	0.2	0.25	0.3	0.35	0.4	0.45	0.5
0.05	342	110	59	38	27	21	17	13	11	9
	434	140	75	49	35	27	21	17	14	12
	581	187	100	65	46	35	28	22	19	15
0.1	539	156	78	48	33	25	19	15	12	10
	685	199	99	62	43	31	24	19	16	13
	916	266	133	82	56	42	32	25	21	17
0.15	712	197	95	57	38	28	21	16	13	11
	904	250	120	72	49	35	27	21	17	14
	1,210	334	161	96	65	47	35	28	22	18
0.2	860	231	108	64	42	30	23	17	14	11
	1,093	293	138	81	54	38	29	22	18	14
	1,462	392	184	108	72	51	38	29	23	19

(Continued)

Table 1.6. *(Continued)*

0.25	984	258	119	69	45	32	24	18	14	11
	1,249	328	152	88	58	41	30	23	18	14
	1,672	439	203	117	77	54	40	30	24	19
0.3	1,083	280	128	73	47	33	24	18	14	11
	1,375	356	162	93	60	42	31	23	18	14
	1,840	476	217	124	80	56	41	31	24	19
0.35	1,157	295	133	75	48	33	24	18	14	11
	1,469	375	169	96	61	42	31	23	18	14
	1,966	502	226	128	82	56	41	30	23	18
0.4	1,206	305	136	76	48	33	24	17	13	10
	1,532	387	173	97	61	42	30	22	17	13
	2,050	518	231	129	82	56	40	29	22	17
0.45	1,231	308	136	75	47	32	23	16	12	9
	1,563	391	173	96	60	41	29	21	16	12
	2,092	523	231	128	80	54	38	28	21	15
0.5	1,231	305	133	73	45	30	21	15	11	-

expects that it will be at least as relevant in this research. Given alpha (one-tailed) = 0.05 and beta = 0.10, how many managers are needed?

The required sample size is calculated as follows:

- *Null hypothesis:* There is a correlation between not being able to make a quick decision and being successful in management.
- *Alternative hypothesis:* There is no correlation between not being able to make decisions quickly and being successful in management.
- *Effect size*: = Absolute value, |−0.2 | = 0.2 is taken.
- Alpha (one-tailed) = 0.05, Beta = 0.10

Taking r = 0.20 from the leftmost column in Table 1.7, 211 managers are needed, which is the figure at the intersection of alpha (one-tailed) = 0.05 and beta = 0.10 from top to bottom.

Table 1.7. Required Sample Size When Using Correlation Coefficient (r).

One-tailed alpha =	0.005			0.025			0.05		
Two-tailed Alpha =	0.01			0.05			0.1		
Beta =	0.05	0.1	0.2	0.05	0.1	0.2	0.05	0.1	0.2
R									
0.05	7,118	5,947	4,663	5,193	4,200	3134	4,325	3424	2,469
0.1	1,773	1,481	1,162	1,294	1,047	782	1,078	854	616
0.15	783	655	514	572	463	346	477	378	273
0.2	436	365	287	319	259	194	266	211	153
0.25	276	231	182	202	164	123	169	134	98
0.3	189	158	125	139	113	85	116	92	67
0.35	136	114	90	100	82	62	84	67	49
0.4	102	86	68	75	62	47	63	51	37
0.45	79	66	53	58	48	36	49	39	29
0.5	62	52	42	46	38	29	39	31	23
0.6	40	34	27	30	25	19	26	21	16
0.7	27	23	19	20	17	13	17	14	11
0.8	18	15	13	14	12	9	12	10	8

1.7.6 Special Situations in Determining Sample Size

Sample size determination techniques for logistic regression and nonparametric tests are not available or difficult to use. In such cases, the researcher may determine the sample size by accepting that simpler analyzes will be applied. At this stage, actual research may have a slightly different power. When planning analysis with logistic regression, the approximate sample size can be estimated using the *t*-Test.

Categorical variables have a similar problem. When the number of categories is six or more, it can be considered as a continuous variable since the distribution is close to normal in ordinal variables. In other cases, the categorical variables should be paired to establish the hypothesis.

1.7.7 Determination of Sample Size in Descriptive Researches

In descriptive researches, there are no predictor and outcome variables. Therefore, concepts such as statistical power, null hypothesis, and alternative hypothesis are not applicable here. Instead, the researcher uses statistical techniques to present information about the population, as well as calculating descriptive statistics such as arithmetic mean and percentages.

Sometimes at the end of the research, in the descriptive search of **"What is the percentage of older workers in the business that get sick?"** the analytical questions such as **"What are the predictors of getting sick in older workers?"** are asked. In this case, the sample size should also be determined for the analytical research.

In descriptive studies, **the confidence interval,** which is usually a range for the sample mean or percentages, is specified. The confidence interval can simply be expressed as a measure of precision for sample estimates. While estimating the sample size in descriptive research, the researcher determines the desired confidence level and the width of the confidence interval.

1.7.7.1 Determination of the Sample Size of Descriptive Research with Continuous Variables

If the studied variable is a continuous variable, the confidence interval around the mean value is indicated.

The researcher wishes to determine the average bread consumption per capita in an urban area within a 99% confidence level and a confidence interval of ± 60 grams. In a previous research, the standard deviation of bread consumption in a similar city was determined as 600 grams. What sample size should it be?

$$\text{Standard deviation (SD) of the variable} = 600$$

$$\text{Total width of consumption} = 120 \text{ grams (above 60 grams and under 60 grams)}$$

$$\text{Thus, standardized width of gap} = (\text{total width/SS})$$

$$= 120 \text{ grams}/600 \text{ grams} = 0.2$$

Table 1.8. Sample Size of Descriptive Study With Continuous Variables.

Standardized Confidence Interval Width	Confidence Interval		
	90%	95%	99%
0.1	1,083	1,537	2,665
0.15	482	683	1,180
0.2	271	385	664
0.25	174	246	425
0.3	121	171	295
0.35	89	126	217
0.4	68	97	166
0.5	44	62	107
0.6	31	43	74
0.7	23	32	55
0.8	17	25	42
0.9	14	19	33
1	11	16	27

Confidence level = 99%.

After reading the standardized width 0.2 in the far left column of Table 1.8, 664 people with the required sample size are determined by coming down from the 99% confidence interval.

1.7.7.2 Determination of Sample Size of Descriptive Researches with Binary (Dichotomous) Variables

In a descriptive research of the binary variable, the results can be expressed as a confidence interval around the predicted percentage for one of the states taken by the subjects. For such a confidence interval, the estimated sample size can be determined as:

Assume the researcher wants to evaluate the impact of a new training seminar aimed at improving customer engagement. Based on a pilot study, he expects 80% of customer-facing staff will have a positive result. How many of these staff members are required to estimate the 95% confidence interval at a sensitivity of 0.80 ± 0.05 of the test?

The expected percentage = 0.20. If the percentage of staff with the expected qualification (0.80 here) is greater than half, the planned sample size is estimated from the expected percentage with negative test results. Here this is 0.20%.

Total width = 0.10(below 0.05 and above 0.05) Confidence interval = 95%

After reading 0.20 and 0.10 widths in the leftmost column in Table 1.9, the middle number for the 95% confidence interval in the table shows the number of personnel dealing with 246 customers, which is the required sample size.

Table 1.9. Sample Size in Descriptive Studies With Binary (Dichotomous) Variables.

				Top number: 90% confidence interval Middle number: 95% confidence interval Bottom number: 99% confidence interval	
Expected Percentage (p)	Total Width of Confidence Interval				
	0.10	0.15	0.20	0.25	0.30
0.10	98	—	—	—	—
	139	—	—	—	—
	239	—	—	—	—
0.15	138	62	—	—	—
	196	88	—	—	—
	339	151	—	—	—
0.20	174	77	43	—	—
	246	110	62	—	—
	425	189	107	—	—
0.25	203	91	51	33	—
	289	128	73	47	—
	498	221	125	80	—
0.30	228	101	57	37	26
	323	144	81	52	36
	558	248	139	90	62
0.40	260	116	65	42	29
	369	164	93	60	41
	638	283	160	102	71
0.50	271	121	68	44	31
	384	171	96	62	43
	664	294	166	107	74

1.7.8 Determination of Sample Size in Repeated Measurements

Repeated measurements can be made in cohort and experimental studies. The outcome variable is the difference between these two measurements, and the *t*-Test is used to compare the mean value of this difference in the two groups. This technique requires a smaller sample size, as it reduces the prevalence of the outcome variable. The sample size of this type of *t*-Test is done as described previously. However, here the standardized effect size is the change in variable divided by the standard deviation of that change.

Recall the example where the required sample size was calculated for applying a *t*-test in an experimental study. There it was determined that 393 subjects for each group were required. Now, assume that the *t*-Test is decided to be applied by taking the before-after measurement values and considering the amount of milk processed per minute in two types of machines. The researcher wants to determine that the amount of milk processed per minute by M1 compared to M2 could be 200 ml more. In a pilot study, the standard deviation of the change in milk processed per minute was only 250 ml. Given alpha (one-tailed) = 0.05 and beta = 0.20 how many machines are required?

The required sample size is calculated as:

- *Null hypothesis*: The change in the average amount of milk processed per minute by M1 type machines and the change in average amount of milk processed per minute by M2 type machines are the same.
- *Alternative hypothesis*: The change in the average amount of milk processed per minute by M1 type machines and the change in the average amount of milk processed per minute by M2 type machines are different.
- *Effect size*: 200 ml.
- *Standardized effect size*: (Effect size/standard deviation) = 200 ml/250 ml = 0.8.
- Alpha (two-tailed) = 0.05, Beta = 1−power = 1−0.80 = 0.20.

In Table 1.5, the number of machines required for each group is found as 25 instead of 393 by reading the standardized effect size from the leftmost column as 0.80, from top to bottom alpha (two-tailed) = 0.05 and 25 at the intersection of beta = 0.2

Chapter 2

Sample Selection

Objectives

- To evaluate sampling types.
- To use random number table in sample selection.
- To choose a random sample and random groups.

2.1 Choosing the Appropriate Sampling Method

Sampling methods are categorized into two main groups as probable and non-probable sampling methods. Probable sampling methods are methods in which the subjects are known from the population and can be selected with equal probability. They are categorized into four groups as follows:

- Simple Random Sampling,
- Stratified Random Sampling,
- Cluster Sampling,
- Systematic Sampling.

In simple random sampling, all individuals in the population are listed and numbered. Then, the individuals selected in the sample are selected by using the "**Random Numbers Table.**"

Stratified sampling method should be used when there is heterogeneity between strata and homogeneity within strata. If the studied variable differs according to any characteristic of the individuals in the population, such as education, age, gender, and socioeconomic level, then the individuals in the population should be stratified according to this characteristic first. Then, enough subjects from each stratum should be selected by simple random sampling method.

In the cluster sampling method, the sampling unit is not a single person but a group or cluster. When forming clusters, it is preferable that the clusters be of the same size or very close to each other.

It is desirable to have a small number of units in the cluster. In case the cluster contains units with different characteristics, the sampling error becomes smaller.

Statistical Analysis Techniques, Volume 1, 23–30

Published under exclusive licence by Emerald Publishing Limited
doi:10.1108/978-1-80592-341-120261002

Systematic sampling is a method used when the population is large.

The methods in which the subjects are not selected from the population with a known probability method and with equal chance are called **non-probability sampling methods.** Examples are the selection of the experimental animals in a cage, the selection of volunteers, and the random selection of a certain number of individuals from a population. **Non-probability sampling methods are not scientific and should not be used unless necessary. Generalization to the population should not be made when it is necessary to use it.**

2.2 Random Sampling and Random Number Table

The purpose of the statistical process is to use samples to obtain conclusions about the population. Statistical judgment is best achieved when probability sampling is used. **Simple random sampling** is the most suitable for our purpose among the probability sampling types. Random sampling provides the following:

- The purpose of random sampling is to ensure each individual has an equal chance of being selected.
- Selections from the population are made independently of each other. The selection of one subject does not affect the selection of the other.

Selecting every fifth person is not truly random. If we know that the fifth staff member has been selected, we know that the fourth staff member was not selected. Thus, the samples are not selected from the population independently of each other. The selection of every “k" name in a list is called **systematic sampling.**

Sometimes the population is divided into groups called **strata**. A **stratified random sample** is formed by combining random samples taken from the said strata. This sampling is especially used when the researcher wishes to recruit sufficient numbers of subjects from certain strata. The population of employees in enterprise X are categorized into four strata, based on education level and gender. These can be female employees with a university degree, female employees without a university degree, male employees with a university degree, and male employees without a university degree. When 50 employees from each stratum are randomly selected, a stratified random sample of 200 workers is obtained.

Thus, it can be ensured that the employees are distributed to in-service training groups by using a method that will ensure that the two groups are similar in experimental research. The characteristics of the employees that may affect the results of the research are spread over the whole research group. In modern research, the selection of study groups must be made at random. In this method, since the choice is based on probability, it is not affected by the manager’s or employee’s preferences.

The dismissal of each employee is handled independently from the dismissal of the other employee. In other words, the allocation of employees to in-service training groups does not affect each other. For example, if there are two in-service training groups that can be distributed in equal sample sizes for non-university graduate employees, the probability of each employee to be included in one of the training groups is 50%. Such a selection can be made simply by **flipping a coin**. For example, if head comes in, the employee is placed in the type A training group, and if tail comes in, it is placed in the type B training group. When dividing employees into training groups, the coin flip method may not be given much credit. Therefore, in the case of a complete list of population, researchers use a more reliable **random number table**. The random number table is designed to provide the following:

- In any given state of the table, the probability of each of the numbers 0–9 occurring is 1/10.
- The probability of a number occurring anywhere on the table is independent of the occurrence of another number on the other side of the table.

Random sampling occurs when each subject is chosen with equal probability (chance) from the population of interest. For this to be possible, there must be a complete list of those in the population.

Then, the random number table can be used to obtain the desired size of random sampling.

Assume we want to randomly select a sample of 10 employees from an employee population of 21 employees in Table 2.1. First, each employee is given two consecutive two digit numbers. Then, as desired, for example, a starting point is determined by putting the tip of the pen on a number by closing the eye. It is very important that the starting point is chosen in such a way as to avoid taking sides.

In this example, it is moved to the right and the first two digits are 47. Since the number 47 was given to B. Sargın, the person in question is the first subject to be sampled. When you move to the right in the random numbers table, the next two-digit number is 45, and this number is ignored since it belongs to B. Sargın, who was selected before. The next two-digit number is 49 and H. Erin is the second subject in the sample. Continuing in this way, 10 employees are chosen. The random numbers and the selected employees are given in Table 2.2.

2.3 Random Selection of Groups

In order to avoid biased comparisons that may arise from the preferences of employees and managers, the distribution to training groups should be made independently by chance. The purpose of the random selection is to determine the comparison groups using the **Random Number Table** in order to ensure that the training groups are "**equal**" in terms of their main or basic characteristics.

Whether the selected sample is random or not, randomness should be ensured when allocating employees to different training groups. Assume there is a population of 21 employees in Table 2.1. Assume that eight of the employees in question are intended to be distributed to the first group (**Type A**), eight to the

Table 2.1. Employee Population and Related Numbers.

Employees	**Given Number**
Z. Doğru	00–03
A. Meydaneri	04–07
Ş. Kılıç	08–11
Y. Eroğlu	12–15
M. Toprak	16–19
E. Tunç	20–23
i. Bağdu	24–27
S. Günay	28–31
D.Baran	32–35
N. Varlı	36–39
T. Kalcı	40–43
B. Sargın	44–47
H. Erin	48–51
H. Güler	52–55
B. Çelik	56–69
T. Diktaş	60–63
B. Yücel	64–67
S. Gülen	68–71
L. Mini	72–75
A. Öztürk	76–79
G. Güzel	80–83

second group (**Type B**), and five to the third group (**Type C**). In order to make this distribution, a two-digit number is selected for each employee. By ignoring the same repeated numbers, each employee has a number of his own. Then, the eight employees with the highest number are divided into the first group, the next eight employees with the largest number are divided into the second group, and the five employees with the smallest number are divided into the third group.

Suppose you randomly select the number in Column 4 and Row 12 of **the Random Number Table** as the starting point. Starting from this point, the two-digit numbers selected from the random numbers table are given to the employees in Table 2.1 in order. For Z. Doğru, 44 is selected. Now, going down, 76 is given to A. Meydaneri. Continuing like this, the numbers and persons in Table 2.3 are selected. The underlined numbers were neglected because they were given to another subject before.

Table 2.2. Selected Random Numbers and Resulting Random Sampling.

Random Number	Sampled Employee
47	B. Sargın
45	None (B. Sargın is reselected)
49	H. Erin
86	None (no patient number is 86)
38	N. Varlı
15	Y. Eroğlu
18	M. Toprak
98	None (no patient number is 98)
73	L. Mini
45	None (B. Sargın is reselected)
80	G. Güzel
50	None (H. Erin is reselected)
93	None (no patient number is 93)
33	D. Baran
92	None (no patient number is 92)
50	None (H. Erin is reselected)
86	None (no patient number is 86)
61	T. Diktaş
76	A. Öztürk

Random numbers and the groups obtained are given in Table 2.4.

After the selection of the training groups using the Random Numbers Table, demographic and educational characteristics between the groups can be compared to assess their equivalence. If employees are truly randomly selected, groups can be expected to be similar in terms of demographics and education.

As seen in Table 2.5, both education groups are similar in terms of gender, experience, previous education, etc.

If it is desired to have a similar number of employees with important characteristics in each training group, these characteristics can be explained in the random application process.

For example, employees who have a certain experience in the formation of **Type A** and **B** training groups can be distributed equally in both training groups. For example, assume that out of every four employees with 10 years of work experience, two are assigned to **Type A** and two to **Type B** training groups. While the order of the two trainings given to four employees is random, as a result of

Table 2.3. Sample Employees and Their Selected Random Numbers.

Employees	Given Number
Z. Doğru	44
A. Meydaneri	76
Ş.Kılıç	57
Y. Eroğlu	97
M. Toprak	61
E. Tunç	55
I. Bağdu	86
S. Günay	8
D. Baran	1
N. Varlı	46
T. Kalcı	94
B. Sargın	47
H. Erin	68
H. Güler	63
B. Çelik	28
T. Diktaş	*47 46*,41
B. Yücel	6
S. Gülen	37
L. Mini	96
A. Öztürk	92
G. Güzel	*92.51*

the research, the number of experienced employees in each research group is equal. This distribution of employees is called **random blocking.**

The purpose of random selection of the employees in the blocks is to protect the subgroups of employees who are important as education against unbalanced training practices.

2.4 Randomization as an Alternative to the Random Sample Assumption

Statistical tests and confidence intervals make the random sampling assumption. **It is wrong to show random sample selection as a sample selection that can be said to be suitable from as many existing subjects as is usually done. In random sample**

Table 2.4. Sample Employees, Their Sorted Random Numbers, and Grouping.

Group 1		Group 2		Group 3	
Employees	**Random**	**Employees**	**Random**	**Employees**	**Random**
Y. Eroğlu	97	M. Toprak	61	S. Gülen	37
L. Mini	96	Ş. Kılıç	57	B. Çelik	28
T. Kalcı	94	E. Tunç	55	S. Günay	8
A. Öztürk	92	G. Güzel	51	B. Yücel	6
İ. Bağdu	86	B. Sargın	47	O.Baran	1
A. Meydaneri	76	N. Varlı	46		
H. Erin	68	Z. Doğru	44		
H. Güler	63	T. Diktaş	41		

selection, the population list from which the sample will be selected must be known in detail.

Assume the sample of 100 employees from the population of newly trained employees is randomly selected. This means that the samples consisting of every 100 people selected from the population list have an equal chance of being selected.

In most researches, it is not possible to obtain random sampling, as there is no complete list of the population. In this regard, we cannot obtain a random sample of men working in the electrical repair business in Türkiye. Because there is no list of Turkish men working in electrical repair work. The best course of action here is not to take sides in the selected sample. **The sample should reflect as accurately as possible the population for which generalizations will be made.** Statistical techniques can still be used if the nonrandom sample is able to represent the population accurately and if the sample selection is not biased.

The uncertainty created by selecting a part of the population (the sample) instead of taking the whole population is called sampling error. In addition, the researcher's measurement error, classification, or other systematic errors are also important. For this reason, appropriate measurement is important in statistical studies in terms of carefully chosen research design, carefully done research and control of systematic errors.

As a result of the difficulty of obtaining a random sample, **randomization** is preferred in sample selection. Randomization is the practice of not taking sides in the sample selection. Taking sides is a systematic error that distorts the results and limits the validity of the results. Taking sides can be done consciously or unconsciously. During the research, it is ensured that other elements are equal in the comparison between the groups by means of techniques such as non-partisanship, blinding, and selection of the control group.

Table 2.5. Basic Characteristics of Employees Subjected to Distribution in Types A and B In-Service Training Trial.

Characteristics	Type A Training Group	Type B Training Group
Gender (male)	79	81
Age avg. (Year)	36	32
Experience (Year)	10	10
Health conditions	Normal	Normal
Previous in-service training	None	None
Attention to work	Normal	Normal

Randomization is the selection of employees into two training groups using a certain chance mechanism. For example, a coin can be tossed for this. When the tail comes, employee is allocated to first group; when the head comes, he is allocated to the second group. However, in order to eliminate the effect of external factors, the education groups should be similar in terms of characteristics such as age, gender, race, and education level that may affect the results.

Ideally, the two training groups are more likely to be similar when groups of sufficient size are used to select at least 100 employees for each of the two training groups. If the groups are few, randomization may produce dissimilar groups. As the number of employees in groups decreases, the chances of obtaining dissimilar groups increase.

Researchers should always check that groups are equal in terms of characteristics that are important. If randomization has resulted in the formation of dissimilar groups, re-randomization should be done if possible. Even if the groups are small, taking sides is prevented by randomization in the selection of employees into groups.

Chapter 3

Organization and Presentation of Data

Objectives

- To establish the relationship of different measurement units and statistical analyses.
- To interpret frequency distribution tables.
- To interpret information through various plots.

3.1 Unit of Measurement of Variables

The raw material of research is data. To obtain data, researchers need to measure the characteristics of people or other entities.

Four types of measurement methods can be specified to measure variables: nominal, ordinal, interval, and ratio.

Before starting to evaluate the data, it is necessary to determine by which type of measurement each variable is expressed. This assessment helps to choose which type of analysis to choose.

3.2 Scales in Characters Indicated by Count

Count-based variables may be either categorical or ordinal.

3.2.1 Nominal Scale

Nominal scale is the classification of received responses or measurements. Nominal variables are also called categorical or qualitative variables. Examples of these variables can be given in Table 3.1.

For nominal data, mode is the appropriate measure of central tendency. The arithmetic mean and median are not used with these data, and the measures of dispersion such as variance, standard deviation and standard error are not used.

Statistical Analysis Techniques, Volume 1, 31–62

Published under exclusive licence by Emerald Publishing Limited
doi:10.1108/978-1-80592-341-120261003

Table 3.1. Examples of Categorical Data.

Variant	Category
Work experience	1: Yes
	2: No
Gender	1: Male
	2: Female
Level of education	1: Primary school
	2: Middle school
	3: High school
	4: University
Marital status	1: Married
	2: Single

3.2.2 Ordinal Scale

Ordinal scale is the ranking of the naming scale in a certain way or according to a certain criterion. Ranking can be done from best to worst or from worst to best.

In ordinal data, shown in Table 3.2 arithmetic mean, mode or median can be calculated as measures of central tendency, as well as measures of dispersion such as variance, standard deviation and standard error. However, in such data, mainly mode and median can be used. **When there are six or more categories in ordinal data, it can be considered as data obtained by measurement.**

3.3 Scales in Characters Indicated by Measurements

Data obtained by measurement can be divided into two groups as interval and ratio.

3.3.1 Interval Scale

In the interval scale, both measurements can be listed and the interval between two measurements can be measured. Although the intervals between the units in the interval scale are equal, there is no proportionality between the measures.

A temperature of 10 degrees is not twice as much as a temperature of 5 degrees. In other words, when the thermometer rises from 5 degrees to 10 degrees, the air temperature does not increase twice. The zero point on the thermometer does not indicate the absence of air temperature.

Table 3.2. Examples of Ordinal Data.

Variant	Category
Work skill status	1: Bad
	2: Good
	3: Perfect
Agreeing with friends	1: Can't get along at all
	2: Can get along very little
	3: Can get along moderately
	4: Gets along very well
Propensity status	1: I Support a lot
	2: I Support
	3: No idea
	4: I Do not support
	5: I Do not support at all.

Arithmetic Mean, Median, and **Mode** can be used as measures of central tendency.

3.3.2 Ratio Scale

On a ratio scale, the zero point is a true value and indicates that something is not happening. There is also proportionality between the measurements. For example, 2 meters is 2 times 1 meter, 10 meters is 5 times 2 meters.

- Weight.
- Height.
- Expenditures.

In proportional scale data, arithmetic mean, median, and mode can be calculated as measures of central tendency, as well as measures of dispersion such as variance, standard deviation, and standard error.

The monthly salary is a proportional value. However, if the monthly salary is measured as sufficient and insufficient for the minimum subsistence for research purposes, it becomes a categorical variable.

Proportional metrics can be converted to nominal or ordinal metrics, as in the case of the monthly wage. Here, there may be psychological reasons underlying the dichotomous distinction. However, when there is no specific reason, it is not appropriate to convert interval or proportional measurement to ordinal or nominal measurement because it causes loss of information.

3.4 Organization of Data

In the first step of data organization, the following procedures are important for evaluating statistical assumptions before more complex statistical analyses:

- Initial analysis of each variable
- Data cleaning
- Review of data quality
- Identification of data changes
- Determination of the sample

Whether the data are gathered around large values or are evenly distributed can be revealed by the frequency distribution, which includes certain classes and frequencies.

The amount of information detail to show in frequency tables depends on the nature of the data and the purpose of the research. Very detailed frequency tables should be avoided. The goal is to summarize the data, not to specify every detail. In some cases, you may need to do several frequency distributions to get the final frequency distribution.

In some cases, data analysis may end as a result of frequency distribution evaluation. Maybe you can get the answer to your research question as a result of these evaluations. If the research question (purpose) is to "**determine the position level of the majority of the employees included in the study at the time of the review,**" in a survey involving 189 employees, it is possible to answer this through a frequency table.

Incorrect data entry, wrong elegant coding and missing data entry are most clearly seen in frequency tables. In this respect, frequency tables, histogram, stem and leaf, stemmed box plot are useful for basic statistical analysis.

3.5 Frequency Tables

The data set is organized as values or categories, and when these are explained with headings, the resulting data representation is called **table**. A researcher begins to build the table by distributing the data, in other words, counting the frequency of each value or category.

3.5.1 Frequency Table for Nominal and Ordinal Variables

For nominal and ordinal variables, the categories should be listed in a natural order, if possible, and frequencies should be specified for each category. Table 3.3 shows such a situation. The data set used in the creation of the said table is given in Table 3.4.

The following results were obtained in a research conducted in order to measure the knowledge of XYZ Inc. employees about whether the business they

Table 3.3. Unevaluated Data Set.

Research Result Groups	**Frequency**
Level 0 (no information on whether the business was affected by the crisis)	8
Level 1 (estimates business May have been affected by the crisis)	94
Level 2 (knowing that the business is affected by the crisis)	50
Level 3 (Doesn't know if the business has a plan to get out of the crisis)	15
Level 4 (knowledge of part of the crisis recovery plan)	7
Level 5 (knowledge of the entire crisis recovery plan)	9
Level 6 (full knowledge of whether the business was affected by the crisis and the recovery plan)	6
Total	189

work for was affected by the current economic crisis, whether the business has a plan to get out of this crisis, and their interest in these issues.

3.5.1.1 Data Input Format in SPSS and Obtaining Frequency Tables

In order to create the tables using the SPSS for Windows statistical program, the data must be entered into SPSS on the "**newdata**" screen. In the SPSS file, the columns show the variables and the rows show the subjects or events evaluated.

In a study, the elements to be examined are called "**variables**". These can be specified in different ways, such as age, gender, monthly salary, and educational background.

While opening the SPSS file, it may be useful to define the variables used in the study in the first step to prevent possible data entry errors that may occur later. The researcher can change the variable name later or change it later if he/she wishes. If variables are not given a name, SPSS automatically names them as **"var00001, var00002... variable 1, variable 2.."**

On the said screen, the data are entered as follows:

In order to print the label of each phase and the "**level**" selected as the variable name, SPSS displays the "**data view**" data entry screen in the lower left corner of the screen. If the "**variable view**", which is on the left side of it and is inactive, is activated, information such as the name of the data, data type, data width, etc. is written. (In previous versions, this was done by entering the "Data" command group and selecting the "**Define Variable Properties**" subcommand.) The rectangle under the "Name" is given a variable name with 8 characters. The name chosen here is "**level**".

Table 3.4. Entering Data on the Knowledge Level of the Personnel on the Impact of Crisis and Crisis Exit Plans of the Business into SPSS

No	Level
1	Level 0
2	Level 0
3	Level 0
4	Level 0
5	Level 0
6	Level 0
7	Level 0
8	Level 0
9	Level 1
10	Level 1
11	Level 1
12	Level 1
13	Level 1
14	Level 1
15	Level 1
16	Level 1
17	Level 1
18	Level 1
19	Level 1
20	Level 1
21	Level 1
22	Level 1
23	Level 1
24	Level 1
25	Level 1

Then, "**Type**" is selected using the mouse and the data type is selected. Then, using the mouse, write the relevant data width and the desired widths after the comma in the rectangle below the "**Width**", "**Decimal**" expressions, respectively. To the right of this is the phrase "**Label**". "**Label**" variables are a data label used when more explanation is needed. In this example, as "**Label**", the statement "the level of knowledge of the personnel about whether the business they work for was affected by the economic crisis and whether the enterprises have a plan to get out of this crisis" was written, which further explains the "**Level**" variable.

To label the values in the data set, when the "**Values**" to the right of "**Label**" is clicked with the mouse, the value to be labeled is written in the "**Value**" part, and the label of the value is written in the "**Value Label**" part. Value tags are common names that describe groups of values within a variable and can be up to 60 characters long. Any sign that is not used in the variable name can be used in the value labels.

Although labeling of a variable is not important for statistical analysis, labels facilitate interpretation during the evaluation of data and the tabular and graphical representation of its outputs.

The "**level**" variable, which is ordinal, can be defined as a numerical variable by giving values from 1 to 7, respectively, to the personnel levels in Table 3.3. When "**Level0**" is given a value of "**1**", the data entry is as follows: "**1**" is written in the "**Value**" section of the "**Value Labels**" window that appears when "**Values**" is opened. Then, the point of the mouse is brought to the "**Value Label**" section, "**Level0**" is typed, and then the "**Add**" button is pressed to enter the label list. After completing "**Level6**" by typing "**7**" value, "**OK**" button is pressed. "**Missing**", "**Columns**", "**Align**" and "**Measure**" information about missing data, column width, which side of the column (left, middle, right) the data are wanted to be aligned with (left, middle, right) and which scale the data are measured (ordinal, nominal) on the right of the "**Values**" command. After entering the relevant information, the "**Data View**" box is selected from the lower left corner of the screen, and it will be returned to data entry screen.

After the variable definition, labeling, and data entry are completed, Table 3.4 is obtained showing the data entry format with its labels.

In order to obtain the frequency table, the **"Analyze/Descriptive Statistics/Frequencies"** menu is selected from the SPSS peak commands. In the "**Frequencies**" window, the "**level**" variable, which is in the source variable list and whose data we entered before, is transferred under "**Variable(s)"** by using the arrow in between. "**Display frequency tables**" are preselected (default). By pressing the "**OK**" button, the frequency table of the "**level**" variable is obtained as in Table 3.5.

In Table 3.5, the frequency table of the variable named "**level**", which is the label of "**Knowledge Level of the Personnel on the Impact of the Crisis and Crisis Exit Plans of the Business**", is given. Value labels are given in the first column in the table in question, and the number of personnel at each level is given in the "**Frequency**" column. In the "**Percent**" column, the calculated percentages are given, including two personnel whose level is not specified. In the "**Valid percent**" column, the calculated rates are given after the two personnel are subtracted. These percentages should be used in assessments. In the "**Cumulative percent**" column, the cumulative percentages calculated based on the rates in the "**Valid percent**" column are shown.

Opposite the "**Missing System**" in the table, empty cells in the numerical data are shown, and "loss due to the system" is called the value. The missing values in

Table 3.5. **SPSS** Frequency Table for Knowledge Level of the Personnel on the Impact of the Crisis and Crisis Exit Plans of the Business.

		Frequency	Percent	Valid Percent	Cumulative Percent
Valid	Level 0	8	4.2	9.2	4.2
	Level 1	94	49.7	49.7	54
	Level 2	50	26.5	26.5	80.4
	Level 3	15	7.9	7.9	88.4
	Level 4	7	3.7	3.7	92.1
	Level 5	9	4.8	4.8	96.8
	Level 6	6	3.2	3.2	100
Missing total	Total system	189	99	100	
		2	1		
		191	100		

question are values that are not specified to which phase they belong to or are not actually and may also occur as a result of incorrect data entry. In the level example, the cells were left blank by not specifying the level of the two personnel (Table 3.5). These missing values can be removed by using the "**cut**" command from the "**Edit**" window after marking them with the mouse.

In some cases, personnel may choose not to answer certain questions, or the researcher may not want to include some personnel, for example, those at Level 1, in the investigation of business information. In this case, "**user missing**" value is in question. For this purpose, under the "**Missing**" command in the "**Variable View**" command in the lower left corner of the data entry screen, up to three values that are optionally undesirable can be written into the "**Discrete missing values**" boxes, as well as the lower and upper limits of the data that will not be included in the evaluation. It can be determined or both of the above selections can be made together. In the example of business information, if "**2**" is written in the first "**Discrete missing values**" box, in case the personnel at Level 1 are not considered to be examined, the frequency table will be like Table 3.6.

In the "**Percent**" column in Table 3.6, the percentages calculated by taking into account "**Level 1″,** which were not included in the analysis, are given. In the "**Valid percent**" column, the rates calculated after subtracting the personnel at "**Level1**" are given. These percentages should be used in assessments.

Normally, there should be no "**missing**" value in the research (Table 3.7). However, "**user missing**" may be found depending on the status of the search. In this regard, it is necessary to check the accuracy and reliability of the data before starting the statistical analysis.

Percentages related to the ordinal data in the example of the **Knowledge Level of the Personnel about the Impact of the Crisis and Exit Plans of the Business** are useful in terms of facilitating the interpretation of each category. When Table 3.7, which is the final frequency table containing all the data and without missing values, is examined, it can easily be said that most of the personnel are gathered at "**Level 1**″ and "**Level 2**″.

3.5.2 Frequency Table for Interval and Rational Variables

Sorting the values in ascending order or descending order in interval and proportional data is the first step in creating a table. Then the data are entered into SPSS as seen in Table 3.8. The data entry table in question, in which the personnel ages of the MN enterprise, which has 113 personnel, is given, is called the work table.

In Table 3.8, the data are listed, and for this, **"Data/Sort Cases"** is selected from the SPSS top commands. From the source variable section, the "**age**" variable is brought under "**Sort by:**". Then, the order that ascends or descends under "**Sort Order**" can be sorted by choosing the "**Ascending**" or "**Descending**" command as desired.

"**Analyze/Descriptive Statistics/Frequencies Variable (age)/OK**" commands are used in SPSS to obtain Table 3.9, which is a classified frequency table. If the

Table 3.6. SPSS Frequency Table Obtained When "Level 1" is Not Considered for Knowledge Level of the Personnel on the Impact of the Crisis and Crisis Exit Plans of the Business.

		Frequency	**Percent**	**Valid Percent**	**Cumulative Percent**
Valid	Level 0	8	4.2	8.4	8.4
	Level 2	50	26.5	52.6	61.1
	Level 3	15	7.9	15.8	76.8
	Level 4	7	3.7	7.4	84.2
	Level 5	9	4.8	9.5	93.7
	Level 6	6	3.2	6.3	100
Missing total	Total level 1	95	50.3	100	
		94	49.7		
		189	100		

Table 3.7. SPSS Frequency Table for the Knowledge Level of the Personnel about the Impact of the Crisis and the Exit Plans of the Business.

		Frequency	Percent	Valid Percent	Cumulative Percent
Valid	Level 0	8	4.2	4.2	4.2
	Level 1	94	49.7	49.7	54
	Level 2	50	26.5	26.5	80.4
	Level 3	15	7.9	7.9	88.4
	Level 4	7	3.7	3.7	92.1
	Level 5	9	4.8	4.8	96.8
	Level 6	6	3.2	3.2	100
	Total	189	100	100	

difference between the minimum value and the maximum value is greater than 15, it can be said that classifying the data before the final frequency table is made is beneficial for ease of interpretation.

Ages range from 29 to 78 in Table 3.10. For this reason, grouping the data makes it easier to evaluate the data.

After the ages and frequencies are entered as seen in Table 3.10, the values in the frequency column should be weighted.

For this, "**Analyze/Descriptive/Statistics/Frequencies/Age**" command is selected from SPSS top commands. After the weighting process is completed, the age classification process should be done. For this, "**Transform/recode**" is selected from SPSS top commands. In the window that opens, coding can be done "**Into Same Variable**" on the same variable or "**Into Different Variable**" on a different variable.

In our example regarding ages, "**Into Different Variable**" was chosen since the classification would be made within a different variable. When the "**Recode Into Different Variables**" window is opened, the "**age**" variable is checked from the variable source list and transferred under "**Input Variable → Output Variable**" using the arrow. At this time, the text of the "**Name:**" and "**Label:**" sections under the "**Output Variable**" become darker with the "**Old and New Values**" key and become ready to be processed. The name of the new variable "**class**" is written under "**Name:**" and the "**Change**" button is pressed. In the "**Label**" part, "**Classified Ages**" can be written, which is more descriptive of the variable.

The coding process is completed by specifying the new and old values in the window obtained by pressing the "**Old and New Values**" button. Here, the top "**range**" is selected. The first value "**25 through 29**" is written. Then, the first code "**1**" is written opposite "**Value:**" under "**New Value**". Meanwhile, the text of the "**Add**" button becomes darker. The expression "**25 through 29 →1**" is displayed by using the said key. This process continues until the entire coding process is

Table 3.8. Entering the Ages of the Personnel Working in the MN Enterprise into SPSS.

	Age
1	29
2	30
3	30
4	32
5	33
6	34
7	34
8	35
9	36
10	36
11	37
12	37
13	38
14	38
15	39
16	39
17	39
18	39
19	39
20	40
21	40
22	40
23	40
24	41
25	41

completed. By pressing the "**Continue**" and then the "**OK**" keys, a variable with the name "**class**" and containing the codes is obtained.

To label the codes in the "**Class**" variable, "**Variable View**" is selected in the lower left corner of the SPSS data entry screen. After typing "classified ages" under "**Label**", double-clicking under "**Values**" opens with the mouse. Here, "**1**″ is written in the "**value**" rectangle and "**25-29**″ in the "**Value Label**" part. At this time, the "Add" part becomes active. By pressing the said key, the phrase

Table 3.9. SPSS Frequency Distribution Table of Ages of Personnel Working in MN Enterprise.

Age					
		Frequency	**Percent**	**Valid Percent**	**Cumulative Percent**
Valid	29	1	0.9	0.9	0.9
	30	2	1.8	1.8	2.7
	32	1	0.9	0.9	3.5
	33	1	0.9	0.9	4.4
	34	2	1.8	1.8	6.2
	35	1	0.9	0.9	7.1
	36	2	1.8	1.8	8.8
	37	2	1.8	1.8	10.6
	38	2	1.8	1.8	12.4
	39	5	4.4	4.4	16.8
	40	4	3.5	3.5	20.4
	41	2	1.8	1.8	22.1
	42	12	10.6	10.6	32.7
	43	7	6.2	6.2	38.9
	44	6	5.3	5.3	44.2
	45	6	5.3	5.3	49.6
	46	5	4.4	4.4	54
	47	8	7.1	7.1	61.1
	48	7	6.2	6.2	67.3
	49	4	3.5	3.5	70.8
	50	3	2.7	2.7	73.5
	51	1	0.9	0.9	74.3
	52	1	0.9	0.9	75.2
	53	3	2.7	2.7	77.9
	54	3	2.7	2.7	80.5
	56	3	2.7	2.7	83.2
	57	2	1.8	1.8	85
	58	1	0.9	0.9	85.8
	59	1	0.9	0.9	86.7
	60	3	2.7	2.7	89.4
	61	1	0.9	0.9	90.3
	62	1	0.9	0.9	91.2
	63	1	0.9	0.9	92

(Continued)

Table 3.9. *(Continued)*

	Age			
	Frequency	**Percent**	**Valid Percent**	**Cumulative Percent**
66	1	0.9	0.9	92.9
69	1	0.9	0.9	93.8
70	1	0.9	0.9	94.7
71	2	1.8	1.8	96.5
73	1	0.9	0.9	97.3
75	1	0.9	0.9	98.2
77	1	0.9	0.9	99.1
78	1	0.9	0.9	100
Total	113	100	100	

"**1 = "25-29"** is included in the list. The same process is continued until the whole labeling process is completed. Then, the operations are confirmed by using the "**Continue/OK**" button. Thus, after explaining how the "**class**" variable in Table 3.10 is created, the SPSS top command "**Analyze/Descriptive Statistics/ Frequencies**" is selected to create the final frequency table in Table 3.11. In the window that opens, the "**class**" variable from the source variables is transferred under the "**Variable(s)"** by using the arrow in between, and the "**OK**" key is pressed.

You can access the video "Obtaining Frequency Tables" by scanning the QR code.

Table 3.10. The Age Distribution of Employees Working at MN Company in SPSS Grouped Format.

	Ages	Frequencies	Group
1	29	1	25–29
2	30	2	30–34
3	32	1	30–34
4	33	1	30–34
5	34	2	30–34
6	35	1	35–39
7	36	2	35–39
8	37	2	35–39
9	38	2	35–39
10	39	5	35–39
11	40	4	40–44
12	41	2	40–44
13	42	12	40–44
14	43	7	40–44
15	44	6	40–44
16	45	6	45–49
17	46	5	45–49
18	47	8	45–49
19	48	7	45–49
20	49	4	45–49
21	50	3	50–54
22	51	1	50–54
23	52	1	50–54
24	53	3	50–54
25	54	3	50–54
26	56	3	55–59
27	57	2	55–59
28	58	1	55–59
29	59	1	55–59
30	60	3	60–64
31	61	1	60–64
32	62	1	60–64
33	63	1	60–64

(Continued)

Table 3.10. *(Continued)*

	Ages	Frequencies	Group
34	66	1	65–69
35	69	1	65–69
36	70	1	70–74
37	71	2	70–74
38	73	1	70–74
39	75	1	75–79
40	77	1	75–79
41	78	1	75–79

Classified Frequency Table of Ages is given in Table 3.11. In the table in question, 11 classes with 5-year intervals were created. Although there is a 25-year-old teenager and a 79-year-old in our example, the top class started with 25 and the bottom class ended with 79 so that the classes would be 5 years apart. The purpose of this is to ensure that the class range is equal and the lower limit is a multiple of 5. Knowing the percentages in the frequency table is helpful for evaluation.

As can be clearly seen from Table 3.11, the majority of the personnel in the sample are between the ages of 40–49. When the cumulative percentages are analyzed, it is seen that more than 80% of the personnel working in the MN enterprise are 54 years old or younger.

While making classification, most of the researchers use the multiples of five to determine the class range so that the numbers can be evaluated more easily. The class range can be found by dividing the difference between the minimum and maximum values of the data set by the number of classes. In the age example, the grade range would be 78–29 = 49/11 grade = 4.45–5.

In the classification, care should be taken that the classes do not overlap, the class width is equal, and there is no open-ended classification. On the other hand, there is a difference of opinion among the **authorities** regarding the number of classes. In addition to those who recommend 10–15 classes, there are also those who recommend 6–15 classes, 8–15, and 5–20 classes. Too little or too many classes negatively affect the frequency distribution. Classes with frequency distributions covering all data and not overlapping should be created. Although there may be a loss of information as a result of grouping, summarizing the data provides ease of interpretation.

The final display of the data in the SPSS output in Table 3.11 varies according to the rules determined by the journals or the institutions where the thesis is made. Table 3.12 is just a variation of the frequency distribution of the age of the

Table 3.11. Classified Frequency Table of Ages of Personnel Working in MN Enterprise.

		Frequency	Percent	Valid Percent	Cumulative Percent
Valid	25–29	1	0.9	0.9	0.9
	30–34	6	5.3	5.3	6.2
	35–39	12	10.6	10.6	16.8
	40–44	31	27.4	27.4	44.2
	45–49	30	26.5	26.5	70.8
	50–54	11	9.7	9.7	80.5
	55–59	7	6.2	6.2	86.7
	60–64	6	5.3	5.3	92
	65–69	2	1.8	1.8	93.8
	70–74	4	3.5	3.5	97.3
	75–79	3	2.7	2.7	100
	Total	113	100	100	

Table 3.12. Frequency Distribution Related to Ages of the Personnel Working in MN Enterprise (N = 13).

Age	Frequency	Percentage
25–29	1	0.9
30–34	6	5.3
35–39	12	10.6
40–45	31	27.4
45–49	30	26.5
50–54	11	9.7
55–59	7	6.2
60–64	6	5.3
65–69	6	5.3
70–74	4	3.5
75–79	3	2.7
Total	113	100

personnel working in the MN enterprise, which can be included in a research report.

Whenever you need to present your data in tabular form, you should mention it in the research text. The table should contribute to explaining the main points discussed in the research.

3.5.3 Consideration in the Preparation of Tables for Research Reports

- Some factors that should be considered during the presentation of the tables in the research reports are as follows:
- Tables should be as simple and easy to read as possible.
- The title should appear above the table in such a way as to clearly and fully show what the table represents.
- The unit of measurement of the data must be specified.
- Totals should be stated if appropriate.
- Where appropriate, each row and column in the table should be named clearly and precisely.
- Codes, abbreviations and symbols should be written below the table.
- If the data are not original, it should be written below the source table.
- Considering the old issues of the journals in which the research will be published, the requirements of the journal or the criteria determined by the relevant university should be complied with.
- A table is unnecessary if table information can be better expressed in words.

3.6 Graphs

Tables are sometimes not explanatory enough. For this reason, graphs can effectively show frequency distributions. Graphs are useful in terms of giving an idea in general terms and in a short time.

3.6.1 Bar Charts

A bar chart is suitable for graphing nominal and ordinal data. When such graphs are made, category labels are usually indicated in a systematic order on the horizontal axis while vertical bars are drawn to represent the frequency or percentage associated with each category. If the category labels are long, the bar may be drawn horizontally. Between the bars is a range that reflects the property of the ordinal or nominal variable. The spacing and bar width are left to the discretion of the researcher, and once specified, the spacings and widths should be equal within themselves.

After entering the data to be graphed, "**Graphs/Bar**" is selected from the SPSS overhead commands. In the "**Bar Charts**" window, "**simple**" is selected if a bar chart of a single variable is to be taken, "**clustered**" if multiple variables are to be charted, and "**stacked**" if more than one variable is to be displayed on the same bar.

"**Values of individual cases**" is selected if the individual values of the subject measurements are to be seen, and "**Summaries for groups of cases**" if the variables are to be seen one by one.

In the new window, when a bar graph is desired to be drawn for the data about the level of knowledge of the company, given in Table 3.4, after selecting "**Simple/Summaries of groups of cases**", the "**Define**" button is pressed. In our example, the "**Bar Represent**" part is reached since the graphic is intended to be expressed in terms of the number of personnel at the levels in terms of information about the business they work for. If the bars are desired to show percentages, the "**% of cases**" option is checked. Then, the "**level**" variable is transferred to the "**Category Axis**:" from the source variables. By pressing the "**Titles**" button, the main title is specified under "**Title**", a subtitle is specified under "**Subtitle**" and a footnote is specified in the "**Footnote**" section, and the figure is obtained by pressing "**Continue**" and then "**OK**" buttons.

Alternatively, "**Analyze/Descriptive Statistics/Frequencies/Variable(s)/Charts/Bar charts/Continue/OK**" commands can be used to obtain the bar chart.

After the figure appears on the screen, new arrangements can be made on it by following the "**Edit Content/In Separate Window**" (or double-clicking on the shape) commands. Adjustments on the axes of the shapes can be made using the "**Chart/Axis**" commands on this newly opened window. "**Category/OK**" is selected when you want to make adjustments on the X-axis, and "**Scale/OK**" is selected when you want to make adjustments on the Y-axis. Final arrangements are given in Fig. 3.1.

If "**Format/Swap Axes**" is selected in the new window opened from "**Edit**", it converts a shape with categories on the horizontal axis into a shape with categories on the vertical axis and vice versa (Fig. 3.2). "**Chart/Legend/Legend Title**" commands can be selected and it can be explained what the bars show on the vertical axis.

Using the data in Fig. 3.1, the pie chart in Fig. 3.3 is obtained by selecting "**Gallery/Pie**" while in the "**SPSS Chart Editor**". When "**Chart/Options/Summary Statistics and Case Values**" is selected on the plot in question, the frequencies along with the phases are displayed. When you want to see the percentages, "**Percents**" is also selected.

When the marital status and educational status of the employees are added to the data in Table 3.4, Table 3.13 is obtained.

A bar chart can be drawn considering the knowledge level and marital status. For this purpose, after selecting "**Graphs/Bar/Clustered/Summaries for groups of cases/Define/N of cases**", "**level**" to "**Category axis:**", "**civilized**" variable to "**Define Clusters by**" and click "**OK**". After these processes, Fig. 3.4 is obtained. Fig. 3.5 is obtained after the **"Graphs/Chart Builder/Bar Charts/Marital Status Stack Color"** commands are followed and the level is set to x using the aforementioned data.

Following"**Window/Dataentryscreen/Graphs/Line/Multiple/Define/Category Axis (level)/Define Lines by (marital)/OK**" commands using the data in

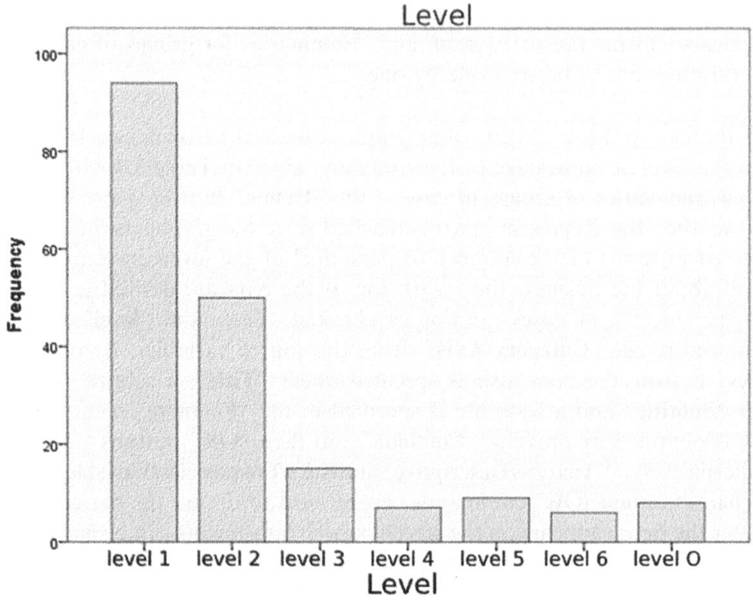

Fig. 3.1. Bar Chart of the Knowledge Level Data of the Personnel About the Business They Work

Table 3.13 ("**level**" and "**marital**" variables together), the line graph in Fig. 3.6, which is especially used in time-dependent evaluations, is obtained; the area graph in Fig. 3.7 is obtained by following "**Gallery/Line/Drop-Line/Replace**"-commands and "**Graphs/Chart Builder/Line Charts/Gallery/Marital Status Set Colour**" and by setting the level x axis the "**Point-Line**" graphic in Fig. 3.8 and following commands "**Mixed/Replace/Series Displayed as 'Line'/OK**" are entered to obtain the mixed graphic in Fig. 3.9.

"**Edit/Series/Transpose Data**" commands are selected to change the variables in the rows and columns of the graphics. Among the shapes, the most suitable for the purpose of the researcher can be used.

3.6.2 Histogram

Histograms are suitable for interval and ratio data, and sometimes ordinal data when the number of categories is greater than 6. It's helpful to look at the Histograms for a normal distribution fit. These charts are similar to bar charts. But there is no spacing between the bars. The area of each bar represents frequency or percentage. For this reason, the total area of each histogram is 100%.

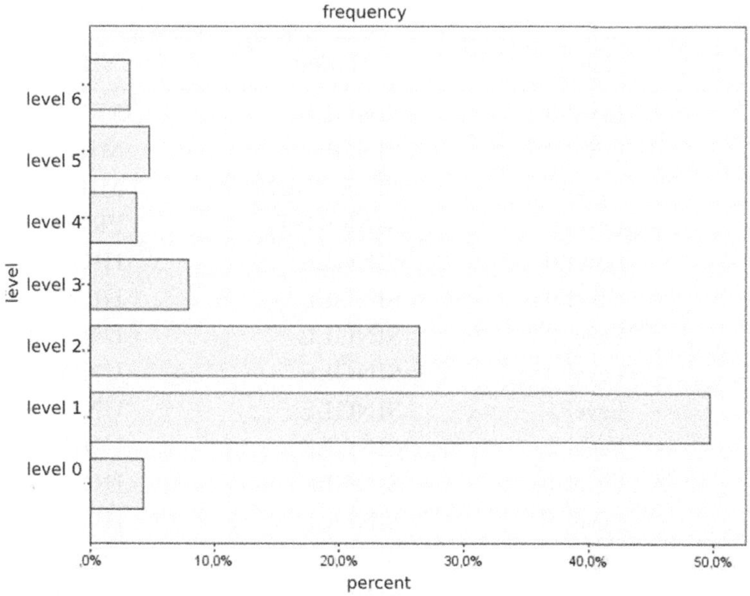

Fig. 3.2. Bar Chart of the Knowledge Level Data of the Personnel About the Business They Work.

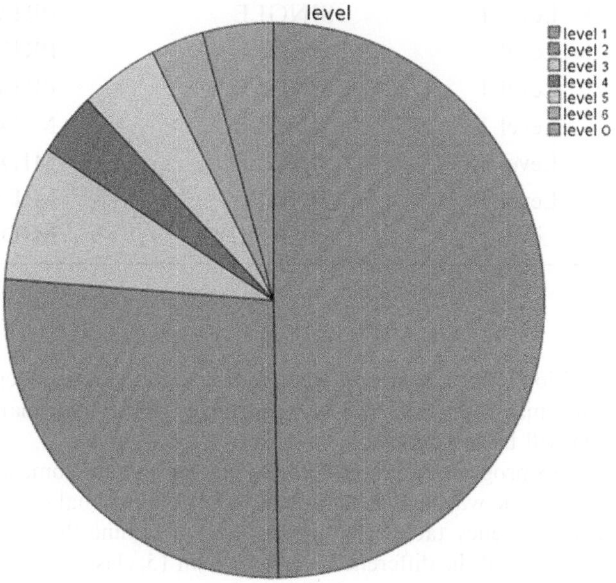

Fig. 3.3. Pie Chart of Knowledge Level Data of the Personnel About the Business They Work.

Table 3.13. Marital Status and Educational Status of the Personne.

	Level	Marital	Education
1	Level 0	SINGLE	MIDDLE
2	Level 0	SINGLE	MIDDLE
3	Level 0	MARRIED	MIDDLE
4	Level 0	MARRIED	PRIMARY
5	Level 0	SINGLE	HIGH
6	Level 0	SINGLE	HIGH
7	Level 0	SINGLE	UNIVERSITY
8	Level 0	SINGLE	UNIVERSITY
9	Level 1	SINGLE	UNIVERSITY
10	Level 1	SINGLE	UNIVERSITY
11	Level 1	SINGLE	HIGH
12	Level 1	SINGLE	HIGH
13	Level 1	SINGLE	HIGH
14	Level 1	SINGLE	PRIMARY
15	Level 1	SINGLE	PRIMARY
16	Level 1	SINGLE	PRIMARY
17	Level 1	SINGLE	PRIMARY
18	Level 1	SINGLE	PRIMARY
19	Level 1	SINGLE	PRIMARY
20	Level 1	SINGLE	PRIMARY
21	Level 1	SINGLE	PRIMARY
22	Level 1	SINGLE	MIDDLE
23	Level 1	SINGLE	MIDDLE
24	Level 1	SINGLE	MIDDLE
25	Level 1	MARRIED	MIDDLE

The first decision in histogram construction is related to the number of bars. If too few bars are made, the data will be aggregated; while if too many bars are made, the data will be too detailed.

Although SPSS programs are useful in making histograms, some adjustments may be necessary. The warning about interval and proportional data during the construction of frequency tables also applies here. Examine the minimum and maximum values, and if the difference is greater than 15, classify the data. Try to

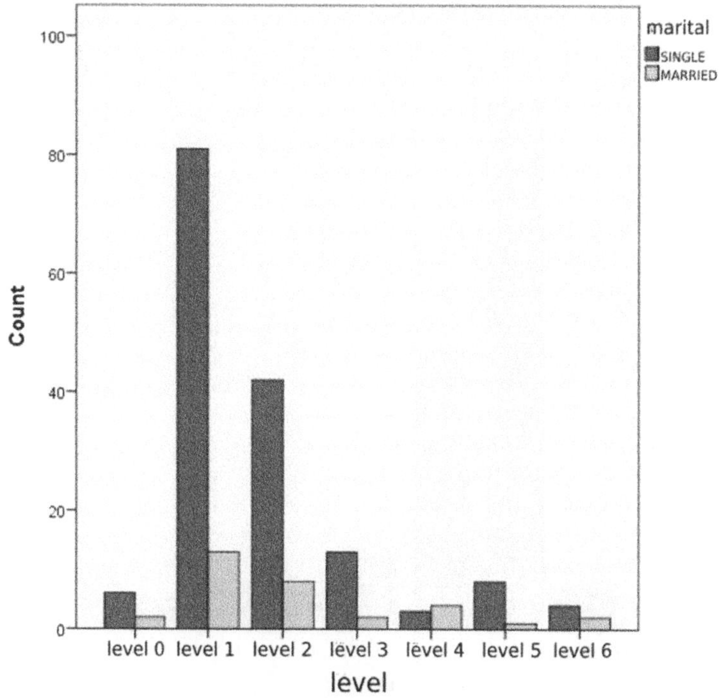

Fig. 3.4. Knowledge Level of the Personnel About the Business They Work

choose the range and starting point divisible by 5. Histograms usually have 5–20 bars.

After determining the number of bars in the histogram, the second decision is about the height of the vertical axis. If the chart is made on the horizontal axis, some authors suggest the height of the vertical axis as approximately half the width while others suggest approximately two-thirds or three-quarters of the width. The reason for these recommendations is to create different effects by changing the height of the graph.

Histogram drawing in SPSS can optionally be done using the "**Analyze/Descriptive Statistics/Explore/Dependent List (level)/Plots/Histogram/Continue/OK**" commands, as well as the "**Graphs/Histogram/Variable (level)/OK**" commands. Or it can also be obtained by selecting the "**Analyze/Descriptive Statistics/Frequencies/Variable(level)/Charts/Histogram/Continue/OK**" commands. Since the "**Graphs**" command series is used in the construction of the bar graph, the first way will be followed in the example histogram drawing in order to show the new method.

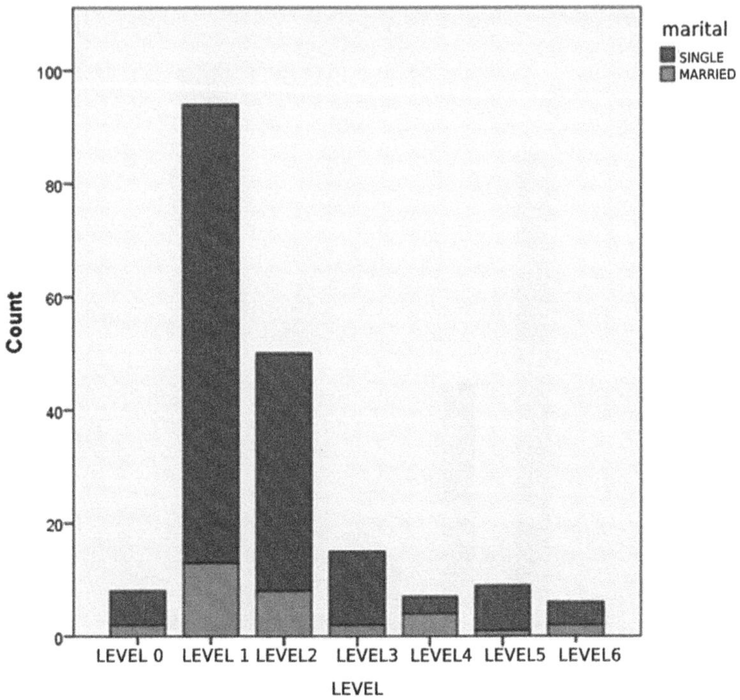

Fig. 3.5. Knowledge Level of the Personnel About the Business They Work.

If the variables used in the SPSS data set are used as they are, without classification, like the age data in Table 3.8, the variable used in the histogram will be transferred to the "**Dependent List**" following the "**Analyze/Descriptive Statistics/Explore**" commands and displayed under "**Display**". After selecting "**Plots**", "**Plots/Histogram/Continue/OK**" commands are selected. By using the "**Edit**" command and then its sub-commands, desired additions and changes can be made on the histogram. For example, if you want to see the normal distribution curve on the histogram, "**Edit/SPSS Chart Object/Open/Chart/Options/Normal Curve/OK**" commands are used.

If the variable used in the SPSS data set is classified as in Table 3.10, the "**frequency**" variable, which shows the frequency of occurrence, should be weighted. For this, using the "**Data/Weight Cases/Weight cases by**" commands, the "**frequency**" variable is transferred under the "**Frequency Variable**" and the "**OK**" key is pressed. The same procedure applied to the Table 3.8 data to obtain the histogram is repeated here as well.

Adjustments on the axes of the figures can be made using the "**Edit/SPSS Chart Object/Open/Chart/Axis**" commands. "**Interval/OK**" is selected when it is

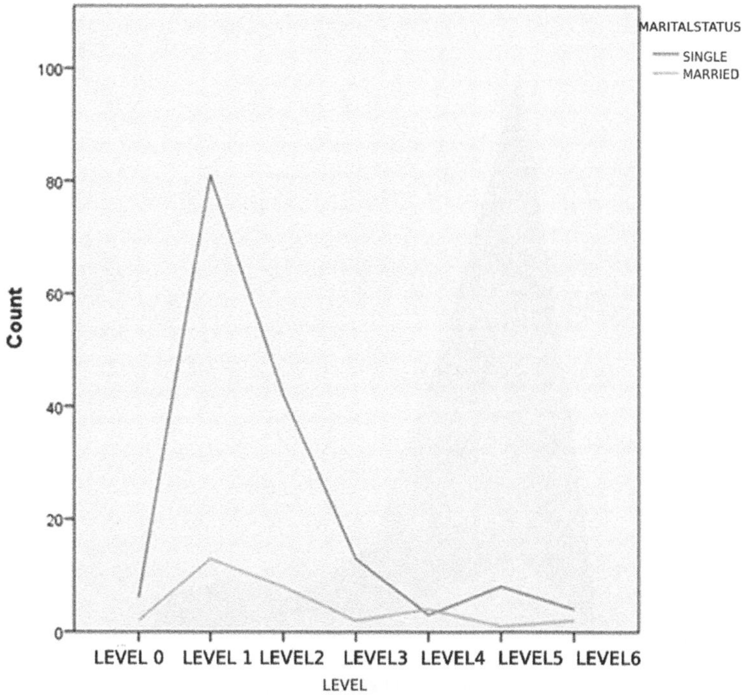

Fig. 3.6. Knowledge Level of the Personnel About the Business

desired to make adjustments on the *X* axis. If adjustments are requested on the *Y* axis, "**Scale/OK**" is selected. The histogram of age data is given in Fig. 3.10.

3.6.3 Stem and Leaf Plot

The way the data is presented close to the histogram is the **Stem and Leaf Plot.** The plot in question gives more information about the actual values than the histogram. The histogram shows the number of cases falling within a certain range in the form of a bar chart. However, the details of the values in these ranges are not known. For example, there may be four people in the range of 0–30. The histogram does not show how many of them are 25, whether they have a value of 22 or not.

In the Stem and Leaf Plot, both a graphic image like a histogram and this detail can be easily seen. As with the histogram, the length of each line gives the number of subjects falling within a certain range. However, the actual numerical value of each subject is shown in the stem and leaf plot. In this case, each of the observed values is divided by the number of stems and leaves. **The Stem and Leaf Plot is usually used in 10-unit intervals.**

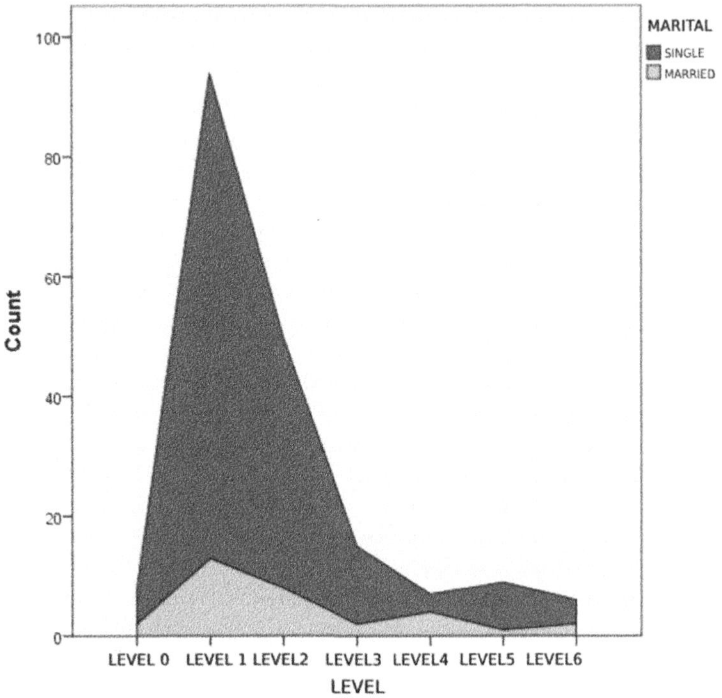

Fig. 3.7. Knowledge Level of the Personnel About the Business.

By using the data set in Table 3.8, the stem and leaf plot in Fig. 3.11 can be obtained. For this, after selecting the **"Analyze/Descriptive Statistics/Explore"** commands from SPSS commands, the "**age**" variable is transferred under the "**Dependent List**". Then, by selecting "**Plots**" under "**Display**" and using "**Plots**" button, "**Stem and Leaf/Continue/OK**" under "**Descriptive**" is selected and the graphic in Fig. 3.11 is obtained. In the figure in question, "**Frequency**" means Frequency and "**Stem & Leaf**" means Stem and Leaf, and stem two and leaf nine for the number 29.

In Fig. 3.11, the line "5.00 3.002344" indicates that there are five values between 30–34, namely 30, 32, 33, 34, and 34. The third line from the top, "12.00 3.566778899999," indicates that there are 12 values between 35–39, namely 35, 36, 36, 37, 37, 38, 38, 39, 39, 39, 39, and 39.

In the last line of the stem and leaf plot in Fig. 3.11, the extreme values are given in the "**Extremes**" line. In our example, these values are 69, 70, 71, 73, 75, 77, and 78. Evaluation can be made by comparing the data in Fig. 3.11 with the data in Table 3.9.

If the data set to be plotted stem and leaf consists of small numbers such as 0.1, the leaves of the said plot are represented by zeros. If the data set to be

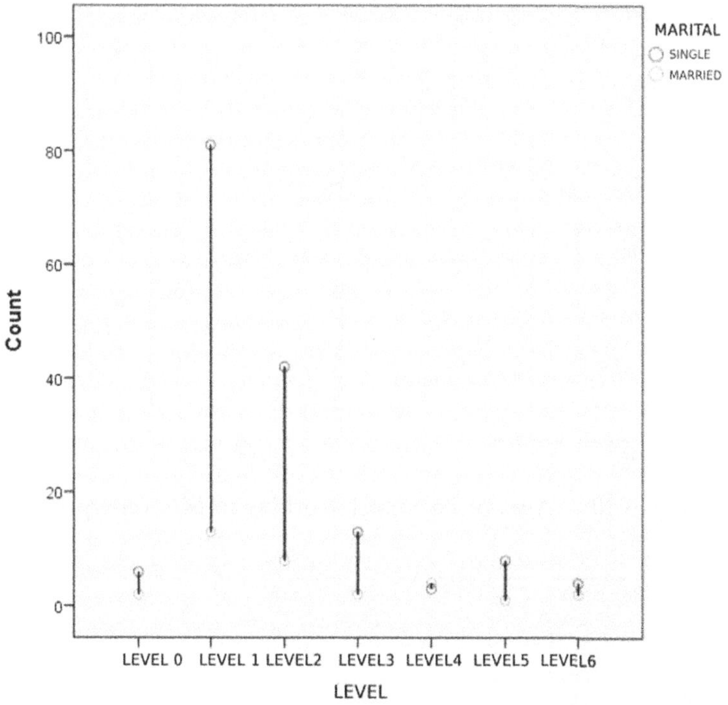

Fig. 3.8. Knowledge Level of the Personnel About the Business.

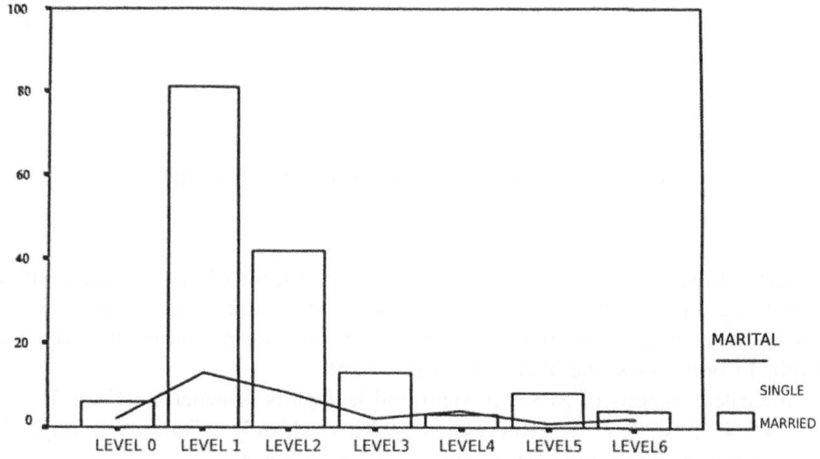

Fig. 3.9. Knowledge Level of the Personnel About the Business.

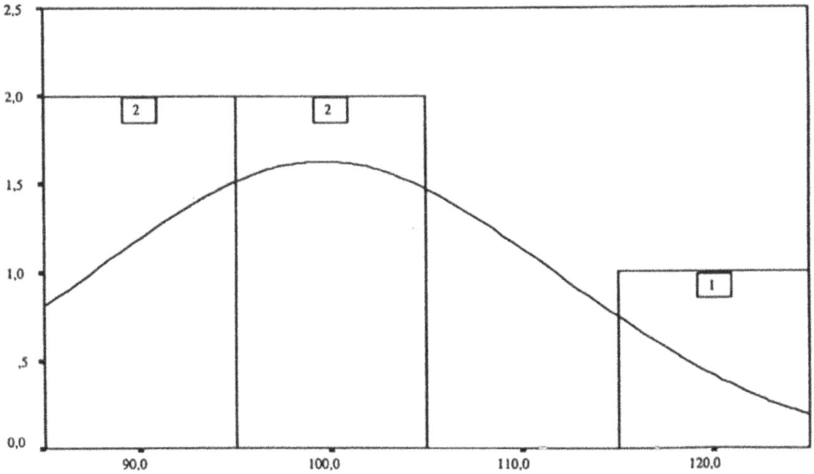

Fig. 3.10. Ages of Personnel Working in MN Enterprise.

```
AGE Stem-and-Leaf Plot

 Frequency    Stem &  Leaf

   1,00        2 .  9
   5,00        3 .  02344
  12,00        3 .  566778899999
  31,00        4 .  0000112222222222222333333444444
  30,00        4 .  555555666667777777788888889999
  11,00        5 .  00012333444
   7,00        5 .  6667789
   6,00        6 .  000123
   1,00        6 .  6
   8,00 Extremes    (>=69)

 Stem width:      10
 Each leaf:       1 case(s)
```

Fig. 3.11. Stem and Leaf Plot of Age Data.

plotted with stem and leaves consists of large numbers such as 100, the graphic display is given at intervals of 100 and decimal and hundredth values are seen. At this point, in both cases, it is not possible to read the real numbers from the graph. In both cases, the histogram is preferable.

In earlier versions of SPSS, in stem and leaf plots in general, "*": 0–1, "t": 2–3, "f ': 4–5, "s": 6–7, ". ": Represents 8-9 leaves. If only "*" and "." if any, the leaves represent the ranges "0–4" and "5–9", respectively.

"**Stem width**" at the bottom of the graphs means the stem range, and "**Each leaf**" means that the subjects in each leaf are shown one by one.

3.6.4 Simple Scatter Plot

Histogram, stem and leaf plots help evaluate a variable. It does not give information about the relations of two variables with each other. For this, a "Simple Scatter Plot" should be used, which shows one variable on the *X*-axis and the other variable on the *Y*-axis and indicates the distribution of each value. This type of plot is important when repeated measurements are taken on the same subject because there are two values for each subject in the plot. In this respect, the number of defective parts produced by the same people in the first and second weeks and given in Table 3.14 will be used.

The scatter plot obtained by considering the number of defective parts produced by a working group of 30 people in the first and second weeks is given in Fig. 3.12. To obtain the aforementioned Simple Scattering Plot, the "**Graphs/Scatter/Simple**" commands are followed, and the relevant variables are transferred to the "**Y-axis (one week)"** and "**X-axis (two weeks)**" boxes, and the "**OK**" button is selected.

In Fig. 3.12, defective production values extend diagonally from the lower left corner to the upper right corner of the plot. Such a situation indicates that there is a positive relationship between the values. In other words, the low value on the *X*-axis appears to be related to the low value on the *Y*-axis and vice versa. If a high value on one axis was associated with a low value on the other axis, it turned out that there was a negative correlation between the values. In this case, the dots on the plot would show going from the upper left corner to the lower right corner. When there was no relationship, the dots were spread out in the middle of the plot like on a target.

Although the **Simple Scatter Plot** shows a positive relationship between the first and second week values related to defective production, it does not show how strong this relationship is. For this, the correlation coefficient, which will be explained in the following sections, must be calculated.

3.6.5 Box Plot

A box plot is a type of chart that uses descriptive statistics based on percentiles. The length of the figure is the interval between quarters. In other words, the box starts at the 25th percentile and ends at the 75th percentile. These percentiles are sometimes called **Tukey's hings**. The box provides information on the central tendency and prevalence of the middle 50% of the distribution, as shown in Fig. 3.13.

While the histogram and the stem and leaf plot are used to evaluate the closeness of the observed values, the extreme values besides the sharp peaks; the box plot shows the distribution of the data, proportionally the data within the 25th and 75th percentiles, and marking the extreme deviations from the group. The middle 50% is shown as a box, while the median of the distribution is a line passing through the middle of the box.

Table 3.14. Number of Defective Parts Produced by the Same Personnel in the First and Second Weeks.

	One week	Two weeks
1	90	88
2	94	90
3	100	96
4	106	100
5	110	106
6	114	110
7	120	110
8	112	106
9	108	104
10	104	100
11	92	90
12	94	92
13	100	96
14	106	100
15	110	106
16	114	112
17	118	114
18	114	114
19	106	100
20	108	100
21	92	94
22	94	96
23	98	100
24	104	104
25	108	110
26	118	120
27	120	120
28	110	112
29	104	110
30	106	112

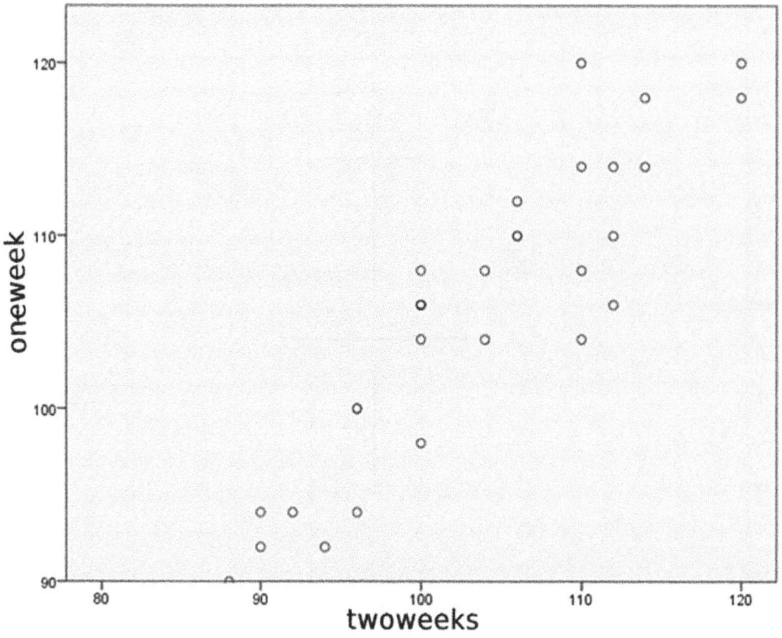

Fig. 3.12. Scatter Plot of Defective Parts Produced by the Same Personnel in the First and Second Weeks.

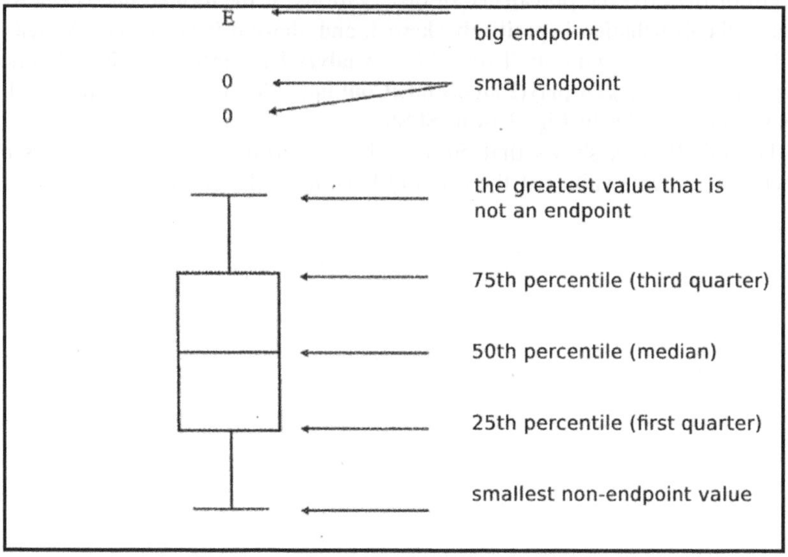

Fig. 3.13. Schematic Illustration of Creating Box Plot.

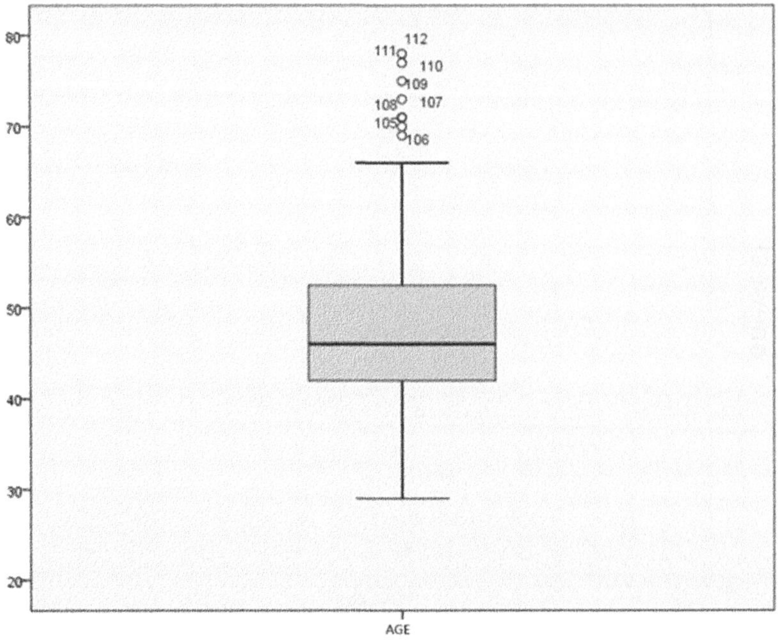

Fig. 3.14. Age Distribution of Personnel Working in MN Enterprise.

From the median, it is possible to determine the central tendency and from the length of the box, the prevalence of observations. **If the median line is below the center, the distribution is positively skewed, and above it is negatively skewed.**

Using the age data in Table 3.8, "**Analyze/Descriptive Statistics/Explore/DependentList(age)/Display(Plots)/Plots/Continue/OK**" commands are used to obtain the box plot in Fig. 3.14 in SPSS.

The middle box shows that 50% of the age grouped around 50 years old. There are extreme values at the top and bottom of the box plot.

Chapter 4

Descriptive Statistics

Objectives

- To valuate measures of central tendency.
- To assess measures of dispersion.

4.1 Descriptive Statistics

Descriptive statistics are a graphical or numerical summary of data. Like an arithmetic mean, a line chart is a descriptive statistic. Although frequency tables and graphs are useful tools for summarizing and displaying data, some calculations and considerations are also required. After the data are collected, their central tendency, dispersion, skewness, and steepness are investigated.

Most descriptive statistics are simple and easily understandable. What is important, however, is the conclusions and interpretations drawn from these statistics. It is possible to obtain these statistics in SPSS in different ways. The data set in Table 3.8 in the third section will be used in the explanations here.

Descriptive statistics, in the SPSS statistical package program, "**Analyze/DescriptiveStatistics/Descriptives/Variable(age)/Options/(desireddescriptivestatistics)/Continue/OK**"or"**Analyze/DescriptiveStatistics/Frequencies/Variable(age)/Statistics/(desired descriptive statistics)(descriptivestatistics)/Continue/OK**"or"**Analyze/DescriptiveStatistics/Explore/DependentList(age)"/Display(statistics)/Statistics/Descriptives/Continue/OK**" commands.

When the first of these commands is applied using the age data in Table 3.8 in the third section, SPSS output is obtained in Table 4.1, when the second of the commands is applied, in Table 4.2, and when the third one is applied, in Table 4.3.

Statistical Analysis Techniques, Volume 1, 63–73

Published under exclusive licence by Emerald Publishing Limited
doi:10.1108/978-1-80592-341-120261004

You can access the "Descriptive Statistics" video by scanning the QR code.

4.2 Measures of Central Tendency

Measures of central tendency show where the data distribution is aggregated. Measures of central tendency to be explored in this book are the arithmetic mean, median, mode, and geometric mean. It is possible to obtain measures of central tendency from SPSS using two essentially different chains of command.

The first of these is to use the commands "**Analyze/Descriptive Statistics/ Frequencies/Variable(age)/Statistics/CentralTendency/Continue/OK**".

The second is the use of "**Analyze/DescriptiveStatistics/Explore/DependentList (age)/Display(Statistics)/Statistics/Descriptives/Continue/OK**" commands.

Also,"**Analyze/DescriptiveStatistics/Descriptives/Variable(age)/OK**" can be selected if only arithmetic mean, standard deviation (SD), and minimum and maximum values are being searched.

4.2.1 Arithmetic Mean

Arithmetic mean is the most widely used measure of central tendency. The arithmetic mean is used for data that has a reasonably symmetrical distribution, has measured interval and ratio variables, is not skewed, and has a single mode. It can also be applied to ordinal data in many cases.

Since the arithmetic mean is affected by every value in the data set, it is not a suitable descriptive statistic for censored situations where all values in the data set are not known. The arithmetic mean is sensitive to extreme values. It is possible to reduce the effect of outliers in a data set by increasing the sample size. For this reason, the arithmetic mean should not be used if extreme points are present in small samples.

Table 4.1. Descriptive Statistics of Age Data.

	N	Range	Mean	Std.	Variance	Kurtosis	
	Statistic	Statistic	Statistic	Statistic	Statistic	Statistic	Std. Error
Age	113	49	47.6283	10.1473	102.968	1.06	0.451
Valid N (listwise)	113						

	N	Minimum	Maximum	Sum	Mean	Skewness	
	Statistic	Statistic	Statistic	Statistic	Std. Error	Statistic	Std. Error
Age	113	29	78	5,382	0.9546	1.021	0.227
Valid N (listwise)	113						

Table 4.2. Descriptive Statistics of Age Data.

Statistics		
Age		
N	Valid	113
	Missing	0
Mean		47.63
Std. error of mean		0.955
Median		46
Mode		42
Std. deviation		10.147
Variance		102.968
Skewness		1.021
Std. error of skewness		0.227
Kurtosis		1.06
Std. error of Kurtosis		0.451
Range		49
Minimum		29
Maximum		78
Sum		5,382
Percentiles	25	42
	50	46
	75	52.5

4.2.2 Median

Median can be used for interval, ratio, and ordinal data. Since the median is not sensitive to outliers, it can be used in symmetrical or unsymmetrical distributions, especially when the data is skewed and in open-ended data where the entire data set is unknown. However, it is not suitable for nominal values.

Although the median can be used with any shape of distribution, it is most often used in ordinal data or quantified data with a much skewed distribution.

4.2.3 Mode

Mode is the most repeated value or category. It can be used as a rough measure of central tendency in interval, ratio, and ordinal variables. Since the arithmetic mean and median are not suitable for nominal data, mode is a suitable measure of central tendency for nominal data.

Table 4.3. Descriptive Statistics of Age Data.

Case Processing Summary

	Cases					
	Valid		**Missing**		**Total**	
	N	**Percent**	**N**	**Percent**	**N**	**Percent**
Age	113	100%	0	0%	113	100%

Descriptives

Statistic				**Std. Error**
Age	Mean		47.63	0.955
	95% confidence interval for mean	Lower bound	45.74	
		Upper bound	49.52	
	5% trimmed mean		47.06	
	Median		46	
	Variance		102.968	
	Std. Deviation		10.147	
	Minimum		29	
	Maximum		78	
	Range		49	
	Interquartile range		11	
	Skewness		1.021	0.227
	Kurtosis		1.06	0.451

When used in nominal data, it is called a **modal category**. Thus, the category with the highest number of answers emerges. Mode applies mainly to **dimodal** distributions that have two modes. Mode can be useful as it shows where the distribution stacks up.

4.2.4 Geometric Mean

Geometric mean is mainly applied to logarithmically measured data. Because each measure of central tendency has a different meaning, it is not always necessary to choose only one of the above-mentioned criteria. Sometimes, it can be helpful to introduce different aspects of the distribution. In a study investigating the delay in responding to applications, mode is 1 hour, the median value is 4 hours, and the arithmetic mean time is 10.6. What central tendency measure(s) should be used in this example? If there is a significant difference between **the Median** and **the Arithmetic Mean**, it may be helpful to include both in research reports.

4.2.5 Trimmed Mean and M-Estimators

Arithmetic Mean is affected by very marginal extreme values. A value that deviates greatly from the group deviates the central measure. The median, which is connected to the main body of the data set, is not affected by the extreme values. However, there are good estimators that show the center of the distribution more reliable than these and provide more reliable information about what kind of population the data are from.

Before M-estimators can be evaluated, the lower and upper-end values in the data set must be determined. The SPSS output in Table 4.4 by using the "**Analyze/Descriptive Statistics/Explore/DependentList(age)/Display(Statistics)/Statistics/Outliers/Continue/OK**" commands of SPSS package program obtained. After examining the values here, M-estimators can be evaluated.

One of these estimators is the **Trimmed Mean.** When Trimmed Mean is calculated, the values are divided into those that are included in the average and those that are not. Thus, Trimmed Mean can be treated as weighted average with a weight value of "**0**" and "**1**" for the values, depending on whether it is included in the calculation of the mean. For example, a 5% smoothed average takes the average of the middle 90%, discarding the lower and upper 5% of the rowed values.

Generally, **Trimmed Mean**, while avoiding extreme values such as the median, is more reliable than the **Median** because it is not calculated based on one or two values in the middle. Since the upper and lower 50% of the values are neglected in the median calculation, the median is the 50% trimmed mean. "**Analyze/Descriptive Statistics/Explore/DependentList(age)/Display(Statistics)/Statistics/Descriptives/Continue/OK**" commands are selected to obtain the corrected average in SPSS. This SPSS output is given in Table 4.3.

Table 4.4. Outliers of Age Data.

			Case Number	Value
Age	Highest	1	113	78
		2	112	77
		3	111	75
		4	110	73
		5	109	[a]
	Lowest	1	1	29
		2	3	30
		3	2	30
		4	4	32
		5	5	33

a. Only a partial list of cases with the value 71 are shown in the table of upper extremes.

In trimmed mean, some of the lower and upper values are excluded. In order to eliminate this drawback and reduce the effect of extreme values, calculations made by giving less weights to extreme values are called **M-Estimators**.

Since the values are given different weights, different M-estimators have emerged. In fact, the arithmetic mean is also an M-estimator calculated by giving a weight of "**1**" to all values.

M-estimators used by SPSS; Huber, Hampel, Tukey, and Andrew. M-estimators are good alternatives to Arithmetic Mean and Median. The Huber M-estimator is preferred when the distribution is close to normal but not recommended for extremes.

SPSS's M-estimators are obtained by selecting "**Analyze/Descriptive Statistics/Explore/Display(statistics)/Statistics/M-Estimators/Continue/OK**". The SPSS output obtained when these commands are selected is given in Table 4.5.

4.3 Measures of Dispersion

Measures of dispersion must be used together with the arithmetic mean. Because, while two data sets have the same arithmetic mean, they can be of different dispersion. SD, standard error (SE), width, quartile, and coefficient of variation were examined as measures of dispersion.

Measures of dispersion, like measures of central tendency, can be obtained mainly in three ways:

First, the commands "**Analyze/Descriptive Statistics/Frequencies/Variable (age)/Statistics/Dispersion/Continue/OK**" can be used.

Table 4.5. M-Estimators of Age Data.

	Case Processing Summary					
	Cases					
	Valid		Missing		Total	
	N	**Percent**	**N**	**Percent**	**N**	**Percent**
Age	113	100%	0	0%	######	100%

	M-Estimators			
	Huber's M-estimator[a]	**Tukey's Biweight[b]**	**Hampel's M-Estimator[c]**	**Andrews' Wave[d]**
Age	45.84	44.78	45.42	44.76

a. The weighting constant is 1,339.
b. The weighting constant is 4,685.
c. The weighting constants are 1,700, 3,400, and 8,500.
d. The weighting constant is 1,340*pi.

Second, the commands "**Analyze/Descriptive Statistics/Explore/DependentList (age)/Display(Statistics)/Statistics/Descriptives/Continue/OK**" can be selected.

Third, the commands "**Analyze/DescriptiveStatistics/Descriptives/Variable (age)/Options/Dispersion/Continue/OK**" can be used. The said measures of dispersion are given in Table 4.1, Table 4.2 and Table 4.3.

4.3.1 Standard Deviation

SD shows how far the observations diverge from the mean. In other words, it expresses how widespread is among the subjects (individuals).

The most important reason why variance is not used as a measure of dispersion is that the square of the data unit, such as the square millimeter, should be used instead of the millimeter. Therefore, the SD is used instead of the variance.

It is necessary to look at the data to determine whether the SD is large. If the data are given in 100s, the SD of 729 is large. However, this SD is considered small if the data are given in 10,000.

SD is meaningful when the distribution is symmetrical and has a single mode, as in the Arithmetic Mean. For this reason, as a general rule, it is appropriate to use SD for normal or near-normal distributions from which the arithmetic mean can be calculated.

The SD can be roughly estimated by dividing the difference between the maximum and minimum values in the distribution by four. In any distribution, 75% of the observation values are always within the range of mean ± 2 SDs.

In a normal distribution, 68% of the observation values are in the range of "1" SD, 94% of them are in the range of "2," and 99% of them are in the range of "3" SDs.

4.3.2 Standard Error

The SE is the SD of the means in the sampling distribution. It shows the dispersion between the **means** in the samples to be selected.

Should SD or SE be used in research reports? The SD should be used because SE is a function of sample size. Thus, the error can be reduced by increasing *n*. By definition, SE is about means. It's not about the subjects.

The width (mean ± 2SE) covers approximately 95% of the sample means. But it does not cover 95% of the observations on the subjects. The mean ± SD is required for this.

4.3.3 Range

The simplest measure of dispersion is range. The range, which tends to increase with sample size, is very sensitive to extremes mainly used to get a quick idea of dispersion.

In a research, when it is desired to give a range value, it is more appropriate to give the minimum and maximum values without subtraction.

4.3.4 Quartiles and Percentiles

Quarter and percentiles represent any point relative to other points in the dispersion. The 25th percentile is called the first quartile, the 50th percentile second quartile, or more commonly known as the median and the 75th percentile third quartile. Quarter and percentiles represent a point, not a range.

The 25th percentile is the value where 25% of the observations fall below this and above 75%. At the 50th percentile, 50% (half) of the values are below this value and 50% are above this value.

4.3.5 Interquartile Range (IQR)

First quartile is 25th percentile; the third quarter is the 75th percentile. The interquartile range is the range between the third quartile and the first quartile.

To determine the first quartile, the median of the dispersion must first be determined. The first quartile is the value in the middle of all values below the median. The third quartile is the value in the middle of the values above the median.

Quarter, percentile and interquartile range, in SPSS statistical package program "**Analyze/DescriptiveStatistics/Frequencies/Variable(age)/Statistics/Quartiles/Percentile(80)/Add/(90)/Add/Continue/OK**"

or

"**Analyze/DescriptiveStatistics/Explore/DependentList(age)/Display(Statistics)/Statistics/Percentiles/Continue/OK**" can be obtained using commands.

When the first of these commands is applied using the age data in Table 3.8 in the third section, the SPSS output in Table 4.6 is obtained, and when the second one of the commands is applied, the SPSS output in Table 4.7 is obtained.

Table 4.6. Interquartile Range of Age Data.

	Statistics	
Age		
N	Valid	113
	Missing	0
Percentiles	25	42
	50	46
	75	52.5
	80	54.4
	90	61.6

Table 4.7. Percentages of Age Data.

		Percentiles						
		5	**10**	**25**	**50**	**75**	**90**	**95**
Weighted average (definition 1)	Age	33.7	37	42	46	52.5	61.6	71
Tukey's Hinges	Age			42	46	52		

4.3.6 Coefficient of Variation

It is used to compare the SDs obtained by researchers examining the same variable. The coefficient of variation is calculated with the formula CC = SS/ ART.AVG (100).

Chapter 5

Normality Analysis and Assessment of Assumptions

Objectives

- To determine data randomly.
- To analyze the normal distributions.
- To apply tests about distributions.

5.1 Random Variable

Most statistical evaluations require the use of randomly assigned subjects. **The random variable** consists of values that are obtained as a result of a chance mechanism. For example, regarding the determination of monthly income levels, if the monthly income of randomly selected people is obtained, the random variable can be found from the monthly income values formed from the said measurements. As we do not know what their monthly income will be before the selection is made, it is called **random selection** because the measurement value is obtained as a result of a selection with the chance factor.

The variable of monthly income levels is called a **continuous** random variable since it can take every value in two intervals, while the variable of the number of children is a **discrete** random variable because it cannot take dotted values in two intervals.

Statistical estimation and statistical tests are processes of obtaining results by drawing samples from the population. These processes work best when the sample is representative of the population. The best form of probabilistic sampling is random sampling.

Random sampling cannot be used in many studies because the complete list of the population may not always be known. For this reason, hypothesis testing and statistical estimates can be made using nonrandom samples, as long as the sample selection is not biased. However, whether the sample is randomly selected or not, the random numbers table must be used when the subjects are selected into different groups.

Statistical Analysis Techniques, Volume 1, 75–119

Published under exclusive licence by Emerald Publishing Limited
doi:10.1108/978-1-80592-341-120261006

5.2 Randomness Test in One Group (Wald–Wolfowitz Runs Test)

The Wald–Wolfowitz Runs Test, which can be applied to a group, is a randomness test. Does the value of an observation affect the following observation? No influence means that the sequence is random. This situation can also give an idea about independence.

5.2.1 Randomness Test for Continuous Variables

Sequences are the order in which observations are taken, and the order of values is important when recording the age or gender of customers in a bank queue. The test mainly examines whether something extraordinary happened during the unfolding of events. For example, if we assume that any cut point (or calculated arithmetic mean) we set for the age of customers in a bank queue, as 50,

46 58 35 22 55 68 70 14 30 31 90 60 58 52

Up to five arrays mentioned above can be created. The total number of sequences is indicative of randomness. Too few sequences or too many sequences imply dependency between observations. **The Wald–Wolfowitz Runs Test** converts the total number of sequences into a Z-statistic with an approximate normal distribution.

In order for **Runs Test** to be applied, the variable must be dichotomous. When the arithmetic mean (47,6283) is given as the cut-off point for the age variable in Table 3.8 in the third section, which is a continuous variable, 69 cases below the mean and 44 cases above the mean are observed.

In order to test the **randomness hypothesis**, the output in Table 5.1 is obtained by using the **"Analyze/Nonparametric Tests/Legacy Dialogs/Runs/Test Variable List(age)/Cut Point(Mean)/OK"** commands to apply the sequence test to the variable in question.

Since the observed significance level is very small (0.00005), the randomness hypothesis is rejected. In this case, it can be stated that the data were not obtained randomly. However, in order to be a sample application, the data will be accepted as randomized data, and statistical analyzes will be made using the data in question.

5.2.2 Randomness Test for Discrete Variables

As an example of the discrete variable, by examining the weather reports in the last 20 days of March, it is stated whether it rains (1) or not (2) as follows:

2 1 1 1 1 1 1 1 2 1 2 1 1 1 1 1 1 1 2 2

Table 5.1. Randomness Test in a Group With Continuous Data.

Runs Test	
	Age
Test value[a]	47.63
Cases < Test value	69
Cases >= Test value	44
Total cases	113
Number of runs	2
Z	−10.484
Asymp. Sig. (2-tailed)	0

[a]Mean.

In order to apply the sequence test in testing the hypothesis (randomness hypothesis), whether it rains on any given day or not has an effect on whether it rains on the next days, after the data are entered, the output in Table 5.2 is obtained by using the **"Analyze/Nonparametric Tests/Runs/Test Variable List (rain)/Cut point/Custom(2)/OK"** commands.

By scanning the QR code, you can access the "Randomness Test in Continuous Variables" video.

Since the observed significance level is above average (0.5324), the randomness hypothesis is accepted. In this case, it can be said from these data that rainy or nonrainy days do not affect the precipitation in the following days.

Table 5.2. Randomness Test in a Group With Discrete Data.

Runs Test	
	RAIN
Test value[a]	2
Total cases	20
Number of runs	7
Z	−0.624
Asymp. Sig. (2-tailed)	0.532

[a]User-specified.

The cut-off point can be determined by the researcher (Custom "2"), as in the discrete variable above, or mean, median, and mode can also be selected for the continuous variable.

5.2.3 Independence

The concept of independence can be applied to random variables as well as events. If the $\mathbf{X}_1$ variable values do not give an idea about the $\mathbf{X}_2$ variable values, or vice versa, the variables $\mathbf{X}_1$ and $\mathbf{X}_2$ are independent of each other.

Suppose that by choosing a random employee from Enterprise X, the monthly health expenditure is determined. Likewise, let's assume that monthly health expenditure is determined by selecting a random employee from Enterprise Y. Thus, values were obtained for two independent random variables in Enterprise X and Enterprise Y. Just as knowing the monthly health expenditure of the employee in Enterprise X does not give any idea about the monthly health expenditure of the employee in Enterprise Y, knowing the monthly health expenditure of the employee in Enterprise Y gives no idea about the employee in Enterprise Z.

On the other hand, let's assume that by randomly selecting an employee, the monthly health expenditure is determined in the first month and the monthly health expenditure of the same employee is determined again one month later. Here, dependent random monthly health expenditure variables (monthly health expenditure in the first month and monthly health expenditure in the second month) were obtained for the first and second months. Knowing the monthly health expenditure for the previous month can give an idea of the next monthly health expenditure. The monthly health expenditure value in the first month gives information about the monthly health expenditure value in the second month.

The assumption about independent observations is one of the most violated assumptions in many studies. The consequences of violating independence cannot be neglected. If dependent values are used in a statistical process that requires independent observations, very serious errors will occur.

In SPSS, the independent variable takes different names such as "**factor**", "**independent variable**" or "**grouping variable**".

5.3 Normal Distribution

The characteristic of the distribution is very important when performing statistical analysis. Because in order to apply parametric tests, the distribution must be normal or close to normal.

Sometimes, it can be said that the data are not normal without making any evaluation in the population values. Since normal distributions are continuous, you will quickly realize that if the random variable values are discrete, the distribution is not perfectly normal. Since the cars in the provinces are only expressed as integers, it cannot be assumed that they are normally distributed. However, since the number of cars has a wide range of values. If they are symmetrical and have a single mode, it can be assumed that they are distributed close to normal. The discrete variable, which consists of several different values and whose value range is very small, cannot even be said to be distributed close to normal.

The application of many statistical analyses requires a normal distribution of data. In other words, data requires a measured, continuous, ratio, or intermittent form of measurement **because the normal distribution is continuous.** However, as mentioned earlier, when the ordinal data set has more than six categories, it can be used in parametric test analysis by being treated as an intermittent measurement.

Moreover, the range of possible values in a data set (the number of distinct values the variable takes, not the number of samples) can be very small. For example, it may consist of only five different values such as 12, 14, 15, 16, and 17. Since such a data set will be far from normal, it should be investigated whether the data are only symmetrical, especially by using the **Fisher Skewness Coefficient.**

The economic or medical normality or abnormality of the data should not be used to determine normal or non-normal distributions. A random variable cannot be said to have a non-normal distribution because it contains economically or medically abnormal values. Statistical normality refers to a certain type of distribution and has nothing to do with economic or medical normality.

Although the hourly wage values of employees in any sector are not economically normal, they may be close to normal in statistical terms. While hourly wage values are normal for employees of another sector, they may show a statistically non-normal distribution. Statistical normality does not imply that the random variable is economically normal.

Most of the random variables used in various studies have a distribution such as a normal distribution. Normal distributions are continuous distributions with bell-shaped frequency curves.

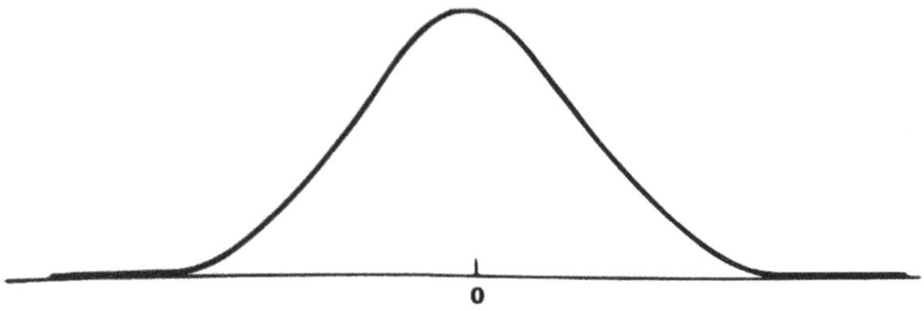

Fig. 5.1. Standard Normal Distribution.

The standard normal distribution has a mean of 0 and a standard deviation (SD) of 1 and has a "bell-shaped" frequency curve as in Fig. 5.1. Normal distributions with a mean other than 0 and an SD different from 1 are standard non-normal distributions and are the most common form of distribution in practice.

The shape of the standard normal distribution is illustrated as in Fig. 5.1.

However, most of the normal distributions encountered in practice are non-standard normal distributions. Like standard normal distributions, nonstandard normal distributions illustrate in different curve shapes depending on their SD although they are symmetrical and have single modes (Fig. 5.2). The larger the SD is, the more common and less steep normal distribution is obtained.

Normal distributions with the same SD but different means will have different places even though they have similar normal distribution curves as in Fig. 5.3.

The arithmetic mean shows the center of the standard normal distribution in Fig. 5.4. Other things being held constant, it measures the situation of typical people as it is illustrated in the figure.

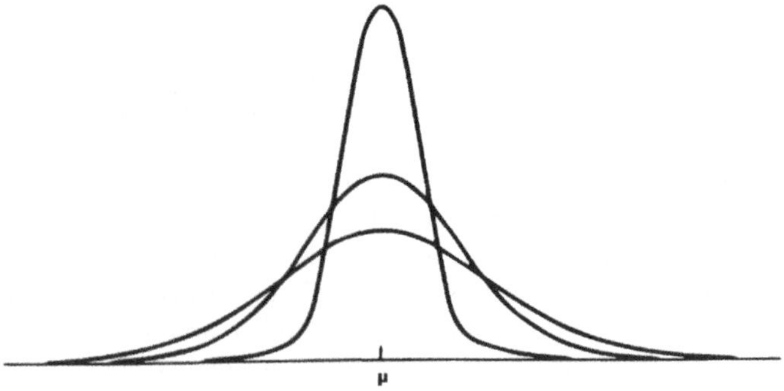

Fig. 5.2. Normal Distributions With Same Mean Different Standard Deviation.

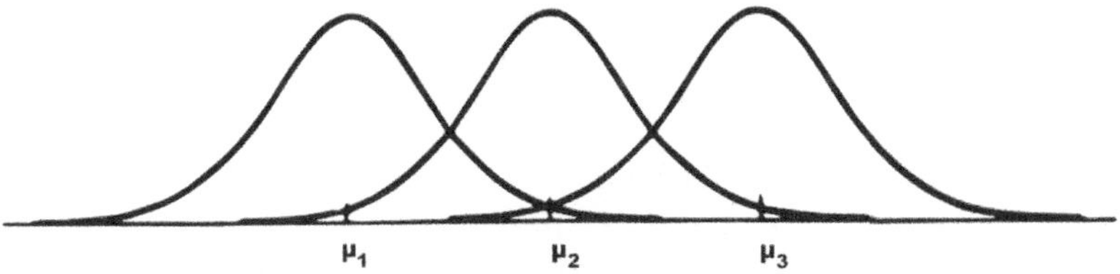

Fig. 5.3. Normal Distributions With Same Standard Deviation and Different Mean.

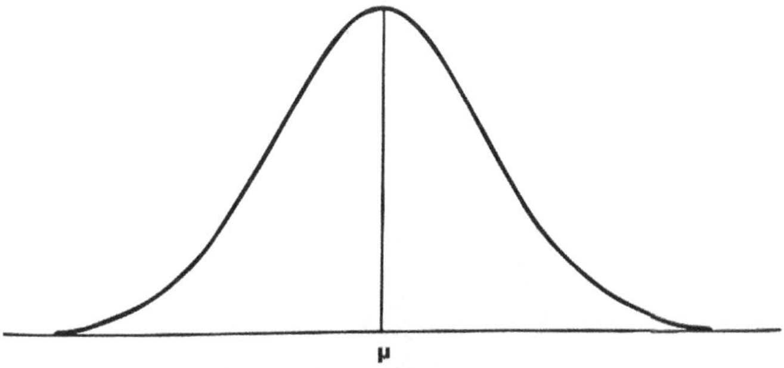

Fig. 5.4. Normal Distribution (Arithmetic Mean).

Contrary to variance, SD is preferred because it uses the simple form instead of the square of the measurement unit, and it measures the dispersion in the normal distribution as illustrated in Fig. 5.5.

To explain the normal distribution curve, only two values are needed—the arithmetic mean and the SD. These are technically known as parameters describing the normal distribution.

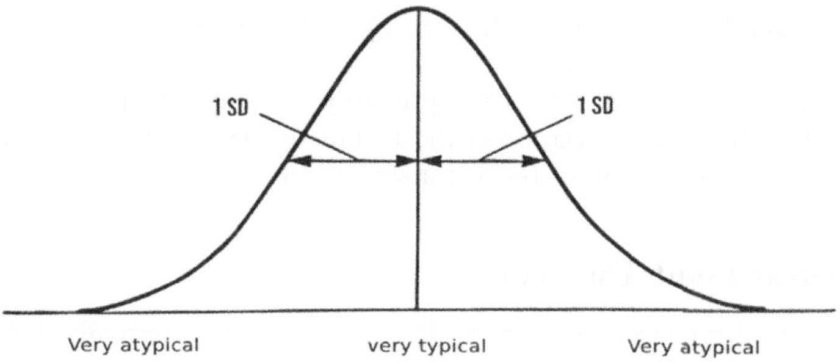

Fig. 5.5. Normal Distribution (Standard Deviation).

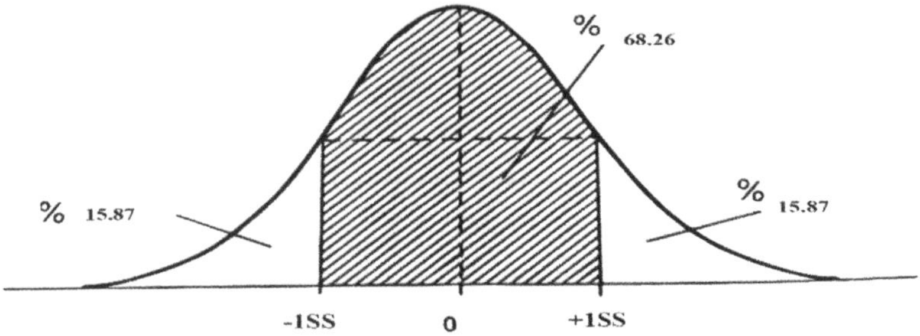

Fig. 5.6. Normal Distribution (Percentage of Area at ±1 Standard Deviation From the Mean).

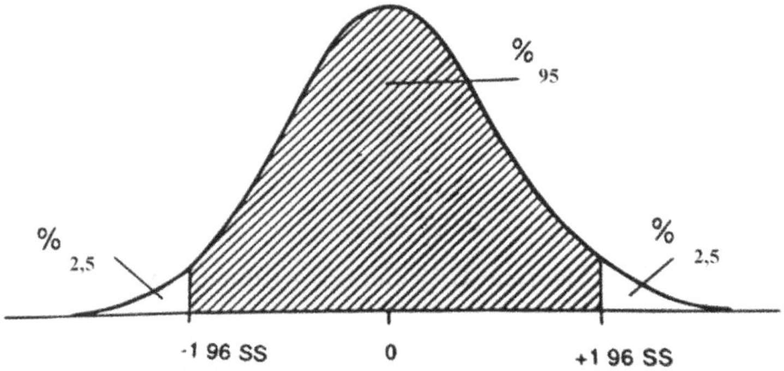

Fig. 5.7. Normal Distribution (Percentage of Area ±1.96 From the Mean).

Since the normal distribution shows a well-defined and simple shape, many aspects are known about it. For example, as seen in Fig. 5.6, 68.26% (approximately 2/3) of the values are 1 SD above and below the mean. Because the curve is symmetrical, 15.87% of the results are 1 SD greater than the mean and 15.87% are 1 SD less than the mean.

As it can be observed in Fig. 5.7, probably 95% (approximately all) of the values fall within ±1.96 deviation of the arithmetic mean and 99% of the values are within ±2.58 deviation of the arithmetic mean.

5.4 Central Limit Theorem

Most statistical processes assume that the sample mean is normally distributed. If the sample is based on a normally distributed population, the sample mean will be normally distributed. As observed in many studies, what should be done when samples are taken from non-normal populations? **The central limit theorem**, which is one of the most important results of statistics, is mostly applied. This theorem enables the application of a statistical technique that requires the normal distribution of sample means to non-normal data. The central limit theorem can be expressed as follows:

When sufficiently large random samples are selected from an infinitely large population with finite variance, the sample mean has an approximately normal distribution.

How big is "**sufficient size**" in the central limit theorem? It depends on how unordinary the population is. **If the population is continuous, unimodal, and approximately symmetrical, a sample size as small as 5 may be large enough. If the population is much skewed, a sample size of 30 or larger may be required**. The further away the population is from normal, the larger sample size is required.

Since researchers generally do not know the distributions of the populations they sample, they evaluate how similar the population distributions are to the normal distribution using the samples they have taken. These analyzes can be made using the histogram and other normality analysis techniques, which will be explained later.

Sample size should be taken into account when making normality assessments. If the sample is large (e.g., $n \geq 25$), the normality curve in the histogram should be bell-shaped. In other words, the histogram of the sample must be symmetrical and unimodal to be compatible with normality.

If the sample size is quite small (for example, $n \leq 10$), a skewed histogram does not necessarily mean that it is not compatible with a normal population. Too much skewness makes the assumption of normality questionable. On the other hand, a sample can be obtained from the normal population but with a histogram far from the normal.

This situation can be avoided by increasing the sample size. The histogram is not suitable for evaluating the normality of observations less than 5.

Let us consider some examples in which the Central Limit Theorem is taken into account when performing normality analyses.

Example 1:

After entering the data on the quantity of goods marketed by 20 personnel working in the marketing department of an enterprise into SPSS as in Table 5.3, using the required commands for histogram and stem and leaf plot given in the third section, the histogram in Fig. 5.8 and the stem and leaf plot in Fig. 5.9 are obtained.

When stem and leaf plot of the mentioned data are examined, it can be stated that they are clearly skewed and are not compatible with the sample obtained from the normal population. However, since the population is continuous, unimodal, and approximately symmetrical and the sample size of the data obtained by measurement is sufficient, the Central Limit Theorem allows this non-normal distribution to be considered as a near-normal distribution, making it reasonable to use it in parametric statistical applications.

Table 5.3. Entering the Amount of Goods (kg) Marketed by Marketing Personnel to SPSS.

	Amount
1	31
2	36
3	31.2
4	24.2
5	36
6	36.8
7	25.7
8	42.8
9	22
10	32.1
11	28
12	30
13	42.6
14	23.1
15	30.4
16	23.7
17	33.8
18	25.2
19	41.9
20	20.6

Example 2:

When the histogram in Fig. 5.10 of the seniority years of 31 employees in Enterprise A given in Table 5.4 and the stem and leaf plot given in Fig. 5.11 are examined, the data are considered close to normal for the reason explained in Example 1.

Example 3:

When the histogram in Fig. 5.12 and stem and leaf plot in Fig. 5.13 of the repair times (min) of 29 technicians given in Table 5.5 are examined, the data are considered close to normal due to the reason explained in Example 1.

Example 4:

When the histogram in Fig. 5.14 and the stem and leaf plot in Fig. 5.15 of the data on the number of days that 10 employees come to work late in a month, given in Table 5.6 are examined, it is seen that they imply data that are far from

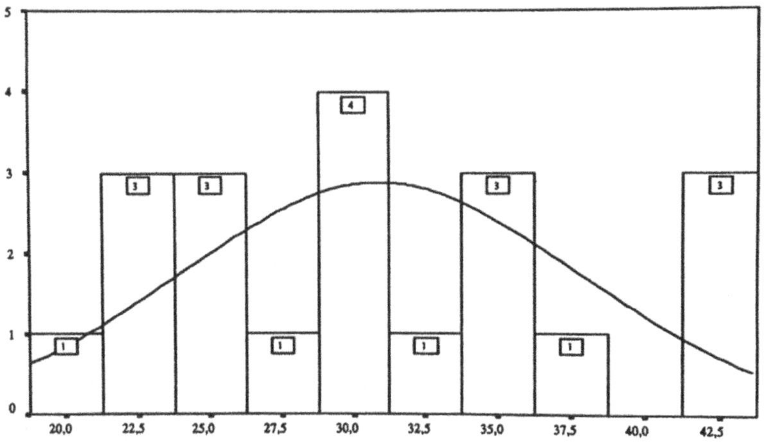

Fig. 5.8. Histogram of the Amount of Goods Marketed by Marketing Personnel.

```
AMOUNT Stem-and-Leaf Plot

 Frequency    Stem &  Leaf

     5,00        2 .  02334
     3,00        2 .  558
     6,00        3 .  001123
     3,00        3 .  666
     3,00        4 .  122

 Stem width:    10,00
 Each leaf:      1 case(s)
```

Fig. 5.9. Stem and Leaf Plot of the Amount of Goods Marketed by Marketing Personnel.

normal because this sample consisted of only three numbers such as 2, 3, and 10. For this reason, the data set in question is considered far from normal.

Example 5:

When the histogram in Fig. 5.16 and the stem and leaf plot in Fig. 5.17 are examined, it is observed that the data regarding the excused leave periods of 19 employees in Enterprise K given in Table 5.7 imply a far from normal data because this sample consisted of only 1, 2, 3, 4, 5, and 6 values. Since the value range is small, the assumption of normality is not valid for the data set in question. The sample is skewed and far from normal.

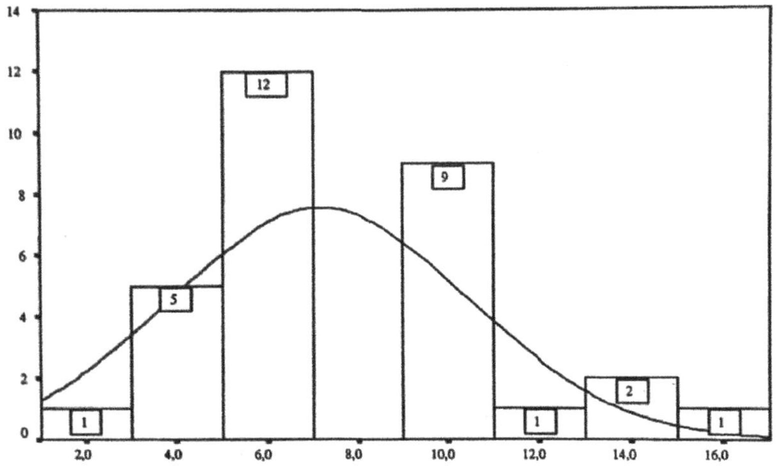

Fig. 5.10. Histogram of Years of Seniority Data.

Table 5.4. Entering Seniority Data Into SPSS.

	Seniority
1	2
2	3
3	11
4	3
5	3
6	4
7	4
8	14
9	13
10	10
11	5
12	15
13	5
14	5
15	9
16	5
17	6

Table 5.4. *(Continued)*

	Seniority
18	6
19	6
20	6
21	6
22	6
23	6
24	6
25	9
26	9
27	9
28	9
29	9
30	9
31	9

```
SENIORITY Stem-and-Leaf Plot

 Frequency   Stem & Leaf

     ,00       0 .
    4,00       0 . 2333
    6,00       0 . 445555
    8,00       0 . 66666666
    8,00       0 . 99999999
    2,00       1 . 01
    1,00       1 . 3
    1,00       1 . 4
    1,00 Extremes    (>=15)

 Stem width:    10,00
 Each leaf:      1 case(s)
```

Fig. 5.11. Stem and Leaf Plot of Senior Years Data.

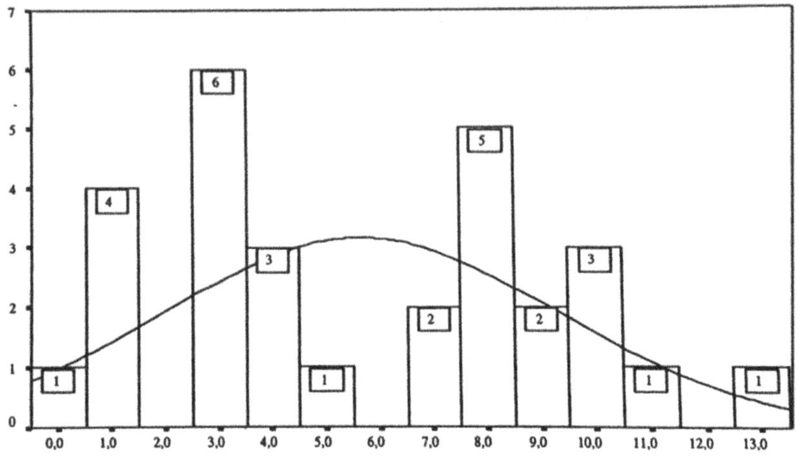

Fig. 5.12. Histogram of Times of Repairing Machines by Technicians.

```
TIME Stem-and-Leaf Plot

Frequency    Stem &  Leaf

  5,00        0 . 01111
  9,00        0 . 222222333
  1,00        0 . 5
  4,00        0 . 6777
  6,00        0 . 888889
  3,00        1 . 001
  1,00        1 . 2

Stem width:     10,00
Each leaf:      1 case(s)
```

Fig. 5.13. Stem and Leaf Plot of Technicians Times of Repairing Machinery.

Table 5.5. Entering Repair Times Into SPSS.

	Time
1	8.6
2	2.9
3	8.1
4	11.4
5	9.9
6	10.4
7	2.6

Table 5.5. *(Continued)*

	Time
8	10.2
9	3.7
10	3.8
11	8
12	7.8
13	1
14	7.3
15	2.5
16	7.7
17	5
18	8.9
19	1.1
20	2.5
21	2.6
22	3.7
23	1
24	8.3
25	0.4
26	2.8
27	6.8
28	12.9
29	1.4

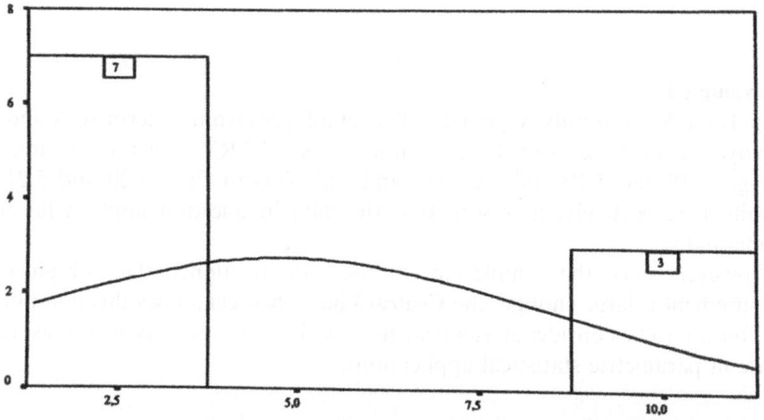

Fig. 5.14. Histogram of 10 Employees' Late Working Days Data.

```
DAY Stem-and-Leaf Plot

Frequency   Stem & Leaf

  7.00      0 . 2223333
   .00      0 .
  3.00      1 . 000

Stem width:   10.00
Each leaf:    1 case(s)
```

Fig. 5.15. Stem and Leaf Data of 10 Employees' Late Working Days Data.

Table 5.6. Entering Data of 10 Employees' Late Days Into SPSS.

	Day
1	2
2	2
3	2
4	3
5	3
6	3
7	3
8	10
9	10
10	10

Example 6:

In Table 5.8, monthly wage data of six employees from Enterprise A and five employees from Enterprise B are given in thousand TRY. When the histograms in Figs. 5.18 and 5.19 and the stem and leaf plots in Figs. 5.20 and 5.21 are examined, respectively, it is seen that the data in question imply a far from normal data.

However, since the sample size of the aforementioned data obtained by measurement is large enough, the **Central Limit Theorem** allows this non-normal distribution to be considered as a near-normal distribution, making it reasonable to use in parametric statistical applications.

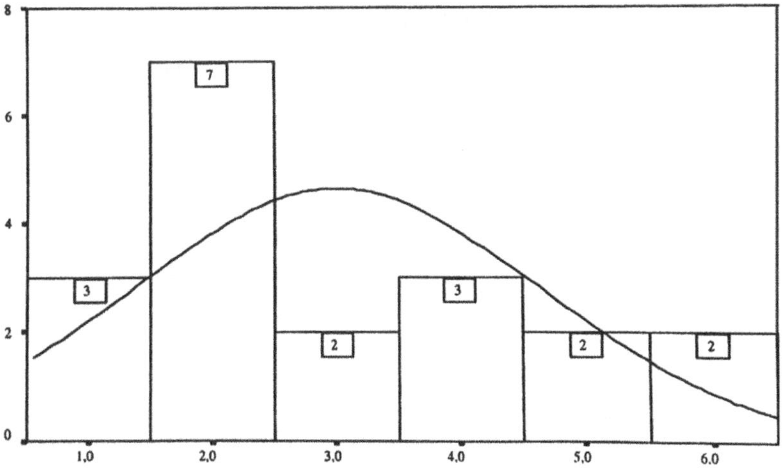

Fig. 5.16. Histogram of Excused Leave Data.

```
DAY Stem-and-Leaf Plot

 Frequency   Stem & Leaf

    3.00      1 . 000
    7.00      2 . 0000000
    2.00      3 . 00
    3.00      4 . 000
    2.00      5 . 00
    2.00      6 . 00

 Stem width:    1.00
 Each leaf:     1 case(s)
```

Fig. 5.17. Stem and Leaf Plot of Excused Leave Data.

Table 5.7. Entering the Data of 19 Employee's Excused Leave to SPSS.

	Day
1	2
2	4
3	2
4	2
5	6

(Continued)

Table 5.7. *(Continued)*

	Day
6	3
7	2
8	3
9	2
10	6
11	4
12	1
13	5
14	2
15	1
16	1
17	2
18	5
19	4

Table 5.8. Entering Monthly Wage Data Into SPSS.

	First	Second
1	83.6	90.2
2	68.4	100.7
3	103.4	118.3
4	83	101.6
5	85	87.1
6	80.4	

5.5 Symmetry and Skewness

Some histograms, stem and leaf plots, and frequency distributions can be classified as symmetrical or skewed. Graphs and frequency distributions are symmetrical if a line running vertically through the center of a histogram or horizontally through the center of a stem and leaf plot divides the graphs into two equal and similar parts.

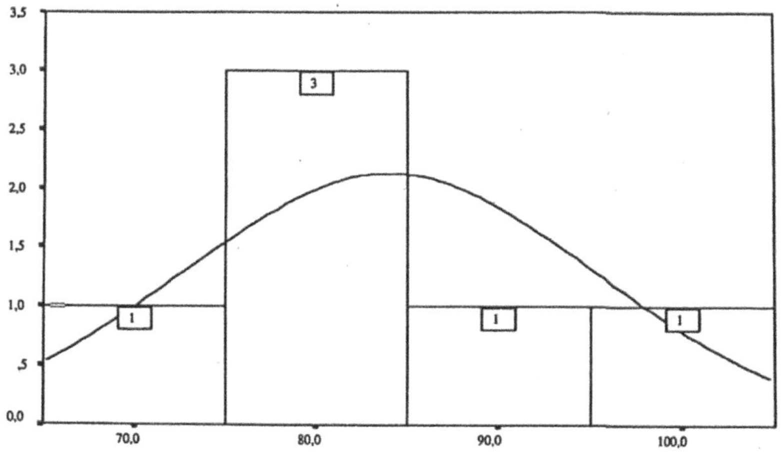

Fig. 5.18. Histogram of the Monthly Wage Data of the Employees in Enterprise A.

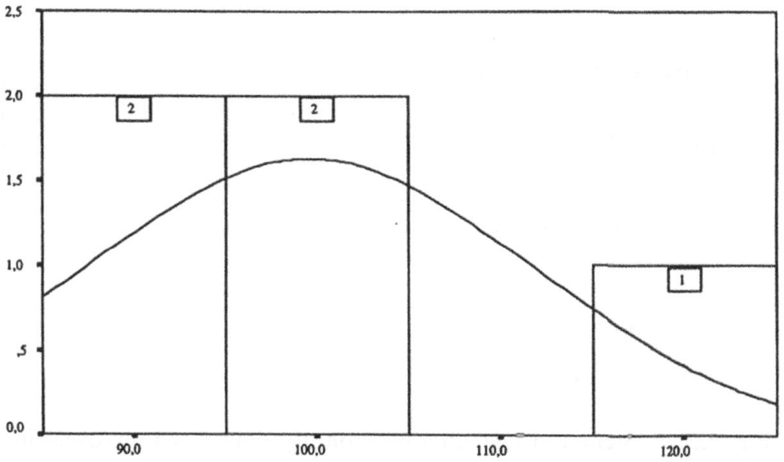

Fig. 5.19. Histogram of Monthly Wage Data of Employees in Enterprise B.

Skewness can be evaluated using the **Fisher Skewness Coefficient** and **Pearson Skewness Coefficient,** which will be explained later. Whether data are symmetrical or not is examined by the skewness coefficient.

```
FIRST Stem-and-Leaf Plot

 Frequency    Stem &  Leaf

     1.00 Extremes    (=<68)
     3.00        8 .  033
     1.00        8 .  5
     1.00 Extremes    (>=103)

 Stem width:     10.00
 Each leaf:       1 case(s)
```

Fig. 5.20. Stem and Leaf Plot of Monthly Wages of Employees in Enterprise A.

```
SECOND Stem-and-Leaf Plot

 Frequency    Stem &  Leaf

     1.00        8 .  7
     1.00        9 .  0
     2.00       10 .  01
     1.00       11 .  8

 Stem width:     10.00
 Each leaf:       1 case(s)
```

Fig. 5.21. Stem and Leaf Plot of Monthly Wages of Employees in Enterprise B.

Data from the **Wilcoxon Signed Rank Tests**, which will be examined in the next sections, are used as examples here. These data are found by taking the differences between the before and after values. The mentioned data and differences are given in Tables 5.9 and 5.10. The histograms of the aforementioned data are given in Figs. 5.22 and 5.24, and the stem and leaf plots are given in Figs. 5.23 and 5.25. Note that the Wilcoxon data are symmetrical, and the sign data are not symmetrical.

Table 5.9. Entering Wilcox Test Data Into SPSS.

	Before	After	Wilcox
1	115	115	0
2	81	81	0
3	110	110	0
4	136	130	6
5	111	111	0
6	91	96	−5
7	118	118	0
8	97	102	−5
9	93	93	0
10	96	96	0
11	89	84	5
12	86	92	−6
13	99	99	0
14	99	97	2
15	113	113	0
16	127	131	−4
17	106	· 11,000	−4
18	111	111	0
19	91	91	0
20	96	97	−1
21	105	112	−7
22	93	94	−1
23	113	113	0
24	83	83	0
25	114	114	0
26	117	110	7
27	86	82	4
28	106	106	0
29	105	105	0

Table 5.10. SPSS Entry of Sign Test Data.

	Before	After	Sign
1	2.00	1.00	−1.00
2	0.00	0.00	0.00
3	0.00	0.00	0.00
4	1.00	0.00	−1.00
5	3.00	3.00	0.00
6	1.00	0.00	−1.00
7	1.00	3.00	2.00
8	0.00	0.00	0.00
9	0.00	0.00	0.00
10	0.00	0.00	0.00
11	1.00	0.00	−1.00
12	1.00	1.00	0.00
13	2.00	1.00	−1.00
14	3.00	1.00	−2.00
15	0.00	0.00	0.00
16	0.00	0.00	0.00
17	0.00	3.00	3.00
18	2.00	3.00	1.00
19	2.00	3.00	1.00
20	3.00	2.00	−1.00
21	0.00	4.00	4.00
22	1.00	2.00	3.00
23	1.00	2.00	1.00
24	0.00	3.00	3.00
25	0.00	2.00	2.00
26	1.00	1.00	0.00
27	3.00	3.00	0.00
28	1.00	2.00	1.00
29	0.00	2.00	2.00

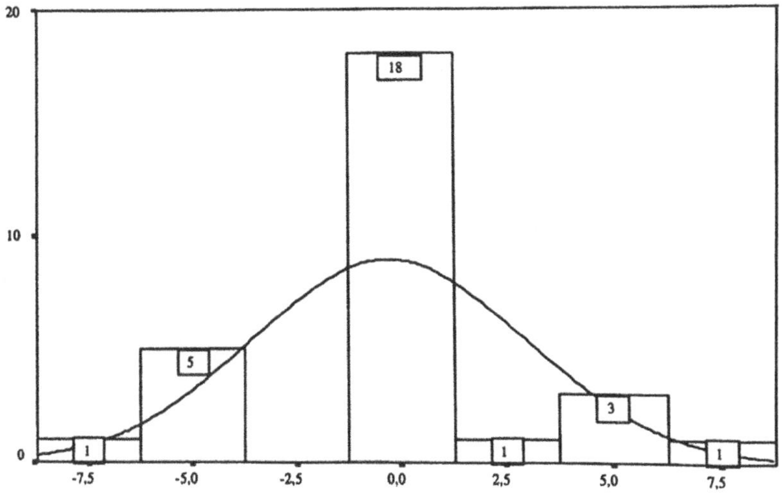

Fig. 5.22. Histogram of Wilcoxon Data.

```
WILCOX Stem-and-Leaf Plot
 Frequency    Stem & Leaf
     6,00 Extremes    (=<-4,0)
     2,00       -1 . 00
      ,00       -0 .
      ,00       -0 .
      ,00       -0 .
      ,00       -0 .
    16,00       -0 . 0000000000000000
     5,00 Extremes    (>=2,0)
  Stem width:      1,00
  Each leaf:       1 case(s)
```

Fig. 5.23. Stem and Leaf Plot of Wilcoxon Data.

5.6 Calculating Probability Using Normal Distribution

If the monthly wages of the workers in a working group are found to be normally distributed, with an average of 86 thousand TRY and an SD of 14 thousand TRY, is the monthly wage of a person with a monthly wage of 70 thousand TL a typical wage? First, it is necessary to find out how many SDs the said value is from the mean. Deviation from the mean in thousands of TRY,

$$86 - 70 = 16$$

and the deviation from the mean in terms of SD is $16/14 = 1.14$.

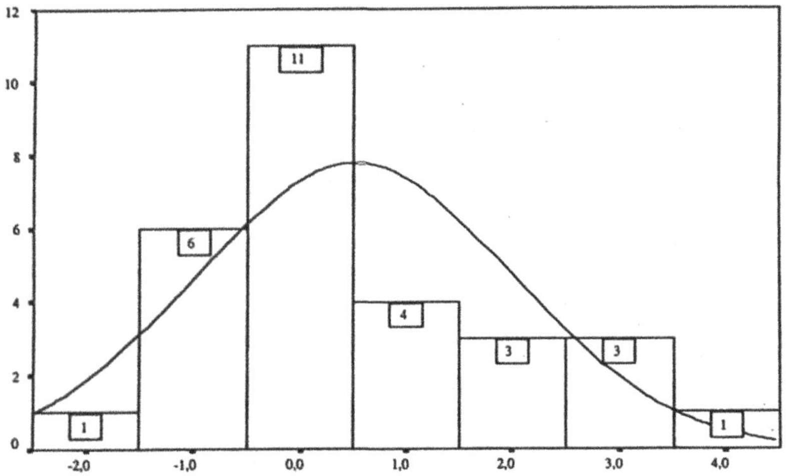

Fig. 5.24. Histogram of Sign Test Data.

```
SIGN Stem-and-Leaf Plot

Frequency   Stem & Leaf

1.00 Extremes   (=<-2.0)
6.00      -1 . 000000
.00       -0 .
.00       -0 .
11.00      0 . 00000000000
.00        0 .
4.00       1 . 0000
.00        1 .
3.00       2 . 000
4.00 Extremes   (>=3.0)

Stem width:    1.00
Each leaf:     1 case(s)
```

Fig. 5.25. Stem and Leaf Plot of Sign Test Data.

The monthly wage level in question is not very discrete from the mass average, as we only know about 1SS above the average, and we know that in the normal distribution, approximately 1/3 of individuals have atypical results.

"Standardizing" results by showing them in terms of SD serves two purposes. First, it helps to understand how typical the result is. Second, it saves the use of different units of measurement, as the results are expressed in SD. This standard value is denoted by "Z".

Using normal distribution tables, it can be found what percentage of the population is between the arithmetic mean and the SD determined above and below it.

In a study, let's assume that the average monthly market expenditure is 120 TRY, and the SD is 20 TRY. What is the percentage of people whose grocery spends is between 100 and 130 TRY? Deviation from the mean in TRY is as follows:

$$100 - 120 = -20 \quad 130 - 120 = 10 \text{ and}$$

If the deviation from the mean in terms of SD,

$$-20/20 = -0.110/20 = 0.5$$

Looking at the *Z*-values, the corresponding percentages are found 0.0398 and 0.1915, respectively. Then, these percentages are added together and the percentage of those with a market spending level between 100 and 130 TRY is found as follows:

$$0.0398 + 0.1915 = 0.2313 = \%23.13$$

The percentage of those with a market spending level of more than 130 TRY is found as follows: The percentage of those whose arithmetic average is between 120 TRY and 130 TRY is 0.1915. If the area to the right and left of the mean is subtracted from 0.50, the percentage of people with a grocery spending greater than "130 TRY" is 0.50–0.1915 = 0.3085. In this case, the percentage of people who spend more than "130 TRY" on the market is 30.85%.

Since many statistical processes require the use of data with a normal or near-normal distribution, it is important to evaluate the assumption of normality in the data set under consideration.

5.7 Normality Analysis in SPSS Software

In SPSS, whether the distribution is normal or close to normal through the "Explore" option can be determined in different ways:

- Calculation method
- Graphic method and
- Hypothesis testing methods

First, the normality of the data can be evaluated by calculating the **Fisher skewness and orthogonality coefficients** of the distribution and the values obtained by dividing them by their standard errors. Secondly, **"Histogram", "Stem and Leaf Plot", "Box Plot", "Normal Distribution Plot," and "Distance**

from Normality Plot" can be used. Third, **Shapiro–Wilks and K-S (Lilliefors) Normality Tests** can be used.

Except for the **"Explore"** option, the following tests can be used for normality analysis of the data:

- Chi-Square Goodness of Fit Test in One Group
- Kolmogorov–Smirnov Goodness of Fit Test in One Group
- Kolmogorov–Smirnov Test in Two Independent Groups and
- The Wald–Wolfowitz Test in Two Independent Groups

The "**Explore**" command of the SPSS statistical package program for normality analysis will be examined in detail on the following example case:

Let's consider a sample of randomly selected employees from a company, one of which is the experimental group and the other is the control group. While the experimental group was told how to reduce faulty production, no explanation was given to the control group. Table 5.11 shows the fictitious data about the sample in question.

After the experimental and control group values in Table 5.11 are entered into SPSS as a single variable under the name of "**error**", "**1**" code is given to the experimental group variable and "**2**" code is given to the control group variable, and they are entered from the "**Variable View**" in the lower left corner of the data entry screen, and a variable name named "**Factor**" is opened under "**Name**" in the second line on the screen. Then, under "**Values**", a variable named "**Factor**" is created by selecting "**Value Labels/Value(1)/Value Label(Experiment)/Add/ Value(2)/ValueLabel(Control)/Add/OK**" (Table 5.12).

Table 5.11. Defective Production Data for Experimental and Control Groups.

Group 1 Experimental	**Group 2 Control**
8	15
5	13
7	12
9	8
7	11
6	14
5	9
3	10
4	9
4	10

Table 5.12. Entry of Experimental and Control Group Data to SPSS.

	Defect	Factor
1	8	EXPERIMENTAL
2	5	EXPERIMENTAL
3	7	EXPERIMENTAL
4	9	EXPERIMENTAL
5	7	EXPERIMENTAL
6	6	EXPERIMENTAL
7	5	EXPERIMENTAL
8	3	EXPERIMENTAL
9	4	EXPERIMENTAL
10	4	EXPERIMENTAL
11	15	CONTROL
12	13	CONTROL
13	12	CONTROL
14	8	CONTROL
15	11	CONTROL
16	14	CONTROL
17	9	CONTROL
18	10	CONTROL
19	9	CONTROL
20	10	CONTROL

In the normality analysis, after the "**Analyze/Descriptive Statistics/Explore**" commands, the variable to be analyzed for normality is transferred to the "**Dependent List**" by the arrow in between. "**Display/Both**" is selected when both statistical analysis and graphics are required.

If the distribution of all measurements is to be evaluated, the "**Factor List**" is left blank. If the distribution of measurements in subgroups is to be evaluated separately, the variable that determines the subgroups should be selected in the "**Factor List**".

When it is necessary to investigate the homogeneity of the variances, it is necessary to define all the variables in the analysis under one variable. A factor variable is determined to separate the variables from each other. The variable that determines the subgroups should be selected as "**Factor List**". Later, "**Spread versus Level with Levene Test/Untransformed**" is selected. In this case, "**Levene's Test**" and Spread versus Level Plots, which determine the homogeneity of variances without applying transformation to the data, are obtained.

To get the output related to the analysis of normality and homogeneity of variances illustrated in Table 5.13 can be obtained by selecting **"Analyze/Descriptive Statistics/Explore/Dependent List (error)/Factor List (factor)/Both/Statistics/Descriptives/M-estimators/Outliers/Percentiles/Continue/Plots/Boxplots/Factor levels together/Stem-and-leaf/Histogram/Normality plots with tests/Spread versus Level with Levene Test/Untransformed/Continue/OK."**

When the above commands are used for the example of faulty production data, except for the "Stem and Leaf Plot" in Table 5.13, the "plots" command results in **Histogram, Box Plot, Normality Graph, Deviation Graph, and Anti-Spread Level Graph**. These graphs are given on next pages.

Explanations will be made for the analysis of normality using Table 5.13.

5.7.1 Taking into Account the Arithmetic Mean and Standard Deviation

If 95% of the data are in the range of 2 SDs greater and 2 SDs less than the arithmetic mean, it can be roughly stated that the data are distributed close to normal. In the standard normal distribution, the mean, median, and mode are equal.

5.7.2 Determining Skewness or Symmetry

In the case of **full symmetry** (Fig. 5.26), the arithmetic mean, mode, and median of the distribution are equal, and the skewness coefficient is zero. The skewness lies between −1 and +1. If the mean is greater than the median, the distribution of observations is **skewed to the right (positive)** (Fig. 5.27). If the mean is less than the median, the distribution of the observations is **skewed to the left (negative)** (Fig. 5.28).

In order to obtain the skewness and kurtosis statistics of the experimental and control groups, the "**Analyze/Descriptive Statistics/Explore/Dependent List**

Table 5.13. Different Test Results of Defective Production Data.

Case Processing Summary							
		Cases					
		Valid		**Missing**		**Total**	
FACTOR		*N*	**Percent**	*N*	**Percent**	*N*	**Percent**
DEFECT	Experimental	10	100%	0	0%	10	100%
	Control	10	100%	0	0%	10	100%

Descriptives

FACTOR				Statistic	Std. Error
DEFECT	Experimental	Mean		5.8	0.61101
		95% Confidence interval for mean	Lower Bound	4.4178	
			Upper Bound	7.1822	
		5% Trimmed mean		5.7778	
		Median		5.5	
		Variance		3.733	
		Std. deviation		1.93218	
		Minimum		3	
		Maximum		9	
		Range		6	
		Interquartile range		3.25	
		Skewness		0.236	0.687
		Kurtosis		−0.961	1.334
	Control	Mean		11.1	0.73711
		95% Confidence interval for mean	Lower Bound	9.4325	
			Upper Bound	12.7675	
		5% Trimmed mean		11.0556	
		Median		10.5	
		Variance		5.433	
		Std. deviation		2.33095	
		Minimum		8	
		Maximum		15	
		Range		7	
		Interquartile range		4.25	
		Skewness		0.442	0.687
		Kurtosis		−1.013	1.334

M-Estimators

FACTOR		Huber's M-Estimator[a]	Tukey's Biweight[b]	Hampel's M-Estimator[c]	Andrews' Wave[d]
DEFECT	Experimental	5.7125	5.7291	5.7488	5.7295
	Control	10.8262	10.8171	10.9294	10.8198

[a]The weighting constant is 1,339.
[b]The weighting constant is 4,685.
[c]The weighting constants are 1,700, 3,400, and 8,500.
[d]The weighting constant is 1,340*pi.

Percentiles

			Percentiles						
FACTOR			5	10	25	50	75	90	95
Weighted average (definition 1)	DEFECT	EXPERIMENTAL	3	3.1	4	5.5	7.25	8.9	,
		CONTROL	8	8.1	9	10.5	13.25	14.9	,
Tukey's Hinges	DEFECT	EXPERIMENTAL			4	5.5	7		
		CONTROL			9	10.5	13		

Extreme Values

Factor				Case Number	Value
DEFECT	Experimental	Highest	1	4	9
			2	1	8
			3	3	7
			4	5	7
			5	6	6
		Lowest	1	8	3
			2	10	4
			3	9	4
			4	7	5
			5	2	5

(Continued)

Extreme Values

Factor				Case Number	Value
	Control	Highest	1	11	15
			2	16	14
			3	12	13
			4	13	12
			5	15	11
		Lowest	1	14	8
			2	19	9
			3	17	9
			4	20	10
			5	18	10

Tests of Normality

		Kolmogorov-Smirnov[a]			Shapiro-Wilk		
FACTOR		**Statistic**	**df**	**Sig**	**Statistic**	**df**	**Sig.**
DEFECT	Experimental	0.161	10	0.200*	0.963	10	0.814
	Control	0.182	10	0.200*	0.947	10	0.63

*This is a lower bound of the true significance.

[a]Lilliefors Significance Correction.

Test of Homogeneity of Variance

		Levene Statistic	df1	df2	Sig.
DEFECT	Based on mean	0.46	1	18	0.506
	Based on median	0.32	1	18	0.578
	Based on median and with adjusted df	0.32	1	16.546	0.579
	Based on trimmed mean	0.427	1	18	0.522

DEFECT Stem-and-Leaf Plot for	
FACTOR = EXPERIMENTAL	
Frequency	Stem & Leaf
1	0, 3
4	0, 4455
3	0, 677
2	0, 89
Stem width:	10
Each leaf:	1 case(s)

DEFECT Stem and Leaf Plot for	
FACTOR = Control	
Frequency	Stem & Leaf
3	0, 899
6	1, 001234
1	1, 5
Stem width:	10
Each leaf:	1 case(s)

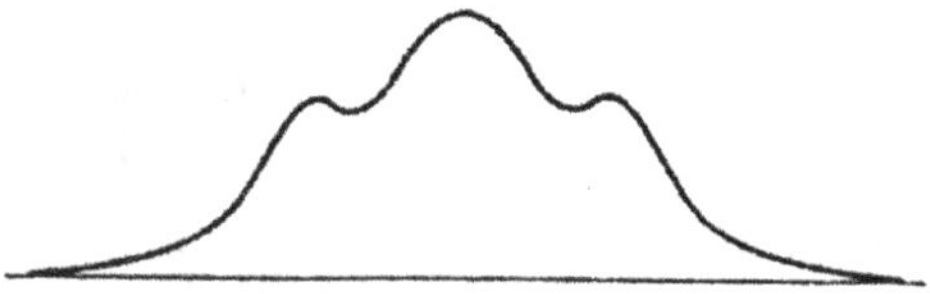

Fig. 5.26. Fully Symmetrical Distribution.

(error)/Factor List(factor)/Display (Statistics)/Statistics/Descriptives/Continue/ OK" commands are selected, and the descriptive statistics in Table 5.13 (1 and 2) are obtained.

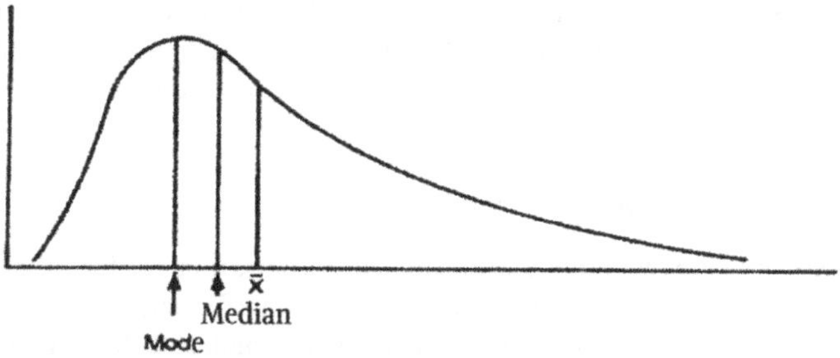

Fig. 5.27. Right Skewed Distribution.

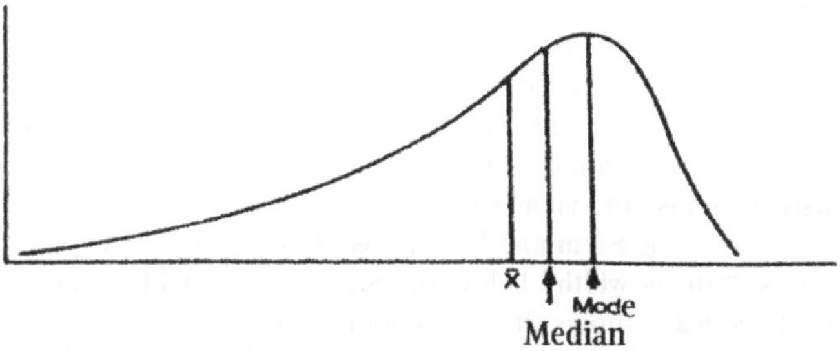

Fig. 5.28. Left Skewed Distribution.

Fisher's skewness coefficient can be calculated using SPSS. Dividing the skewness coefficient by the skewness standard error produces a result to be interpreted in terms of the normal distribution curve. This result is called **the skewness value**. Values obtained above 1.96 or below −1.96 as a result of the division process are significant at the 0.05 significance level. This is because approximately 95% of the values in a normal distribution lie between −1.96 and +1.96 standard deviations from the mean.

Considering the example of defective production data, the Fisher skewness coefficient for the experimental group data in Table 5.13(1) is 0.2357, which is close to zero. When the coefficient in question is divided by 0.6870, which is the standard error of the skewness, the skewness value (0.236/0.687 = 0.343) is very close to the normal distribution for the experimental group.

Similarly, when the skewness and kurtosis statistics of the control group are evaluated, the Fisher skewness coefficient obtained in Table 5.13(2) is reported.

It is 0.442, which is close to zero. When this coefficient is divided by 0.687, which is the standard error of the skewness, the skewness value of 0.643 indicates that the distribution with the control group is close to normal.

In the absence of a computer, **the Pearson skewness coefficient**, which is another skewness coefficient that can be easily calculated by hand, can be calculated as "**(Arithmetic Mean − Median)/Standard Deviation**". When the Pearson skewness coefficient is above 0.2 or below −0.2, there is statistically significant skewness. **The Fisher Skewness Coefficient**, which is included in the SPSS outputs, will be taken into account in the evaluations in this book.

5.7.3 Determining Kurtosis

The kurtosis indicates whether the normal distribution curve has a correct bell shape. In other words, it shows how steep or flat (flattened) the normal distribution curve is. **The kurtosis coefficient of a complete bell curve is zero**. If kurtosis coefficient is positive, the curve is steeper than normal. If it is negative, it is flatter than normal. Fisher's orthogonality coefficient can be calculated with the help of computer.

For example, Fisher kurtosis coefficients in the experimental group and control group are −0.961 and −1.013, respectively, as seen in Table 5.13. When we divide these values by the standard errors of the orthogonality, we get −0.7203 and −0.7593, respectively. Since the steepness values are within the range of ±1.96, it can be said that the distributions of the experimental and control groups are not significantly steep.

If the distribution is not symmetrical, there is no need to look at the kurtosis.

Table 5.13 shows the **Stem and Leaf Plots** obtained for the experimental and control groups. "**Steam width**" below the Stem and Leaf Plots shows the Stem width, and "**Each leaf**" shows the subjects in each leaf.

Stem and leaf plots for both groups show that the data are also distributed close to normal.

When the histograms of the experimental and control groups are examined, it can be said that the data in question show a distribution close to normal (Figs. 5.29 and 5.30).

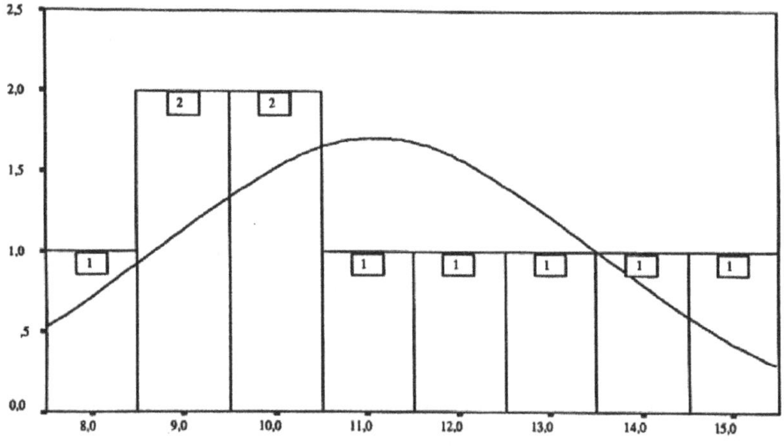

Fig. 5.29. Histogram of Experimental Group Defective Production Data.

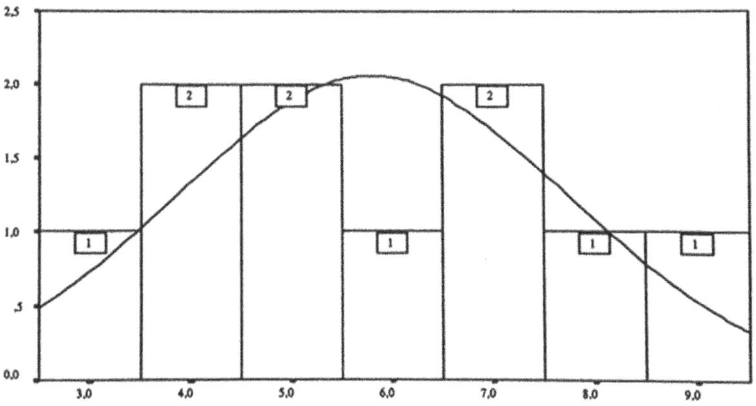

Fig. 5.30. Histogram of Control Group Defective Production Data.

Since the median lines of the box plots pass near the middle of the box, it can be accepted that the distributions of the experimental and control groups are close to normal (Fig. 5.31).

While performing the normality analysis, the **Normal Probability Plot**, in which the observed and expected values of the data in the distribution are displayed on a plot, can be used. If the sample studied was from a normally distributed stack, the values should be collected on or around a line. In the mentioned plot, one axis is observed values and the other axis is the expected normal axis according to the assumption of normal distribution. When the plots created for the experimental and control groups are examined, it is seen that the values are gathered around the line in both groups (Figs. 5.32 and 5.33).

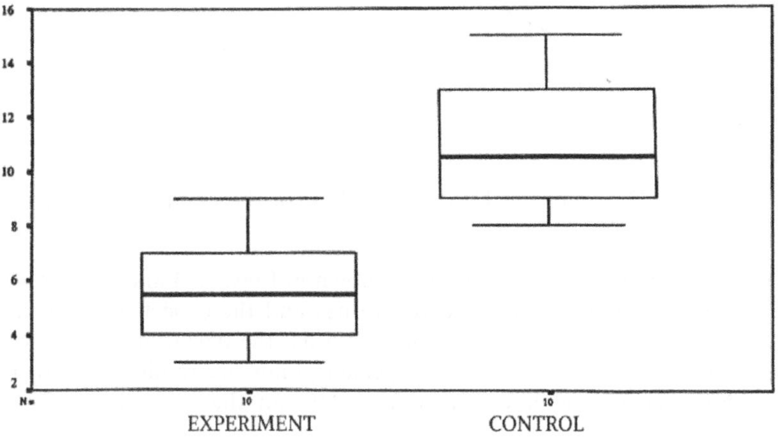

Fig. 5.31. Box Plots of Experimental and Control Group Faulty Production Data.

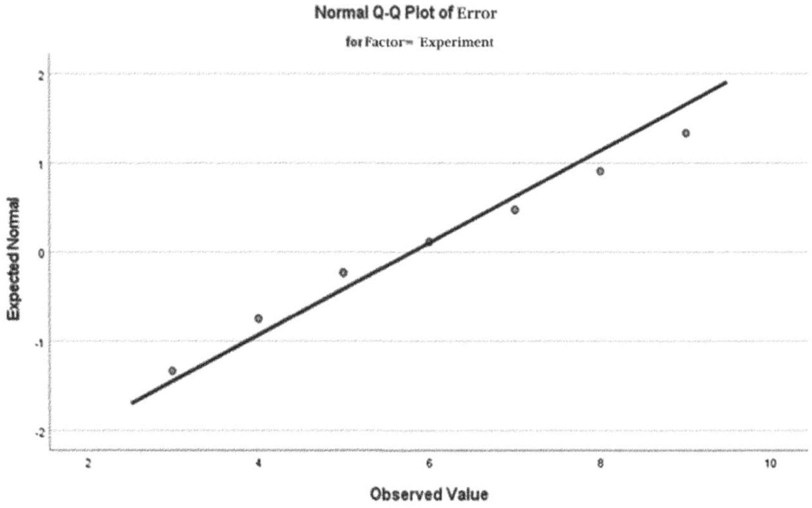

Fig. 5.32. Normal Distribution Plot of the Experimental Group.

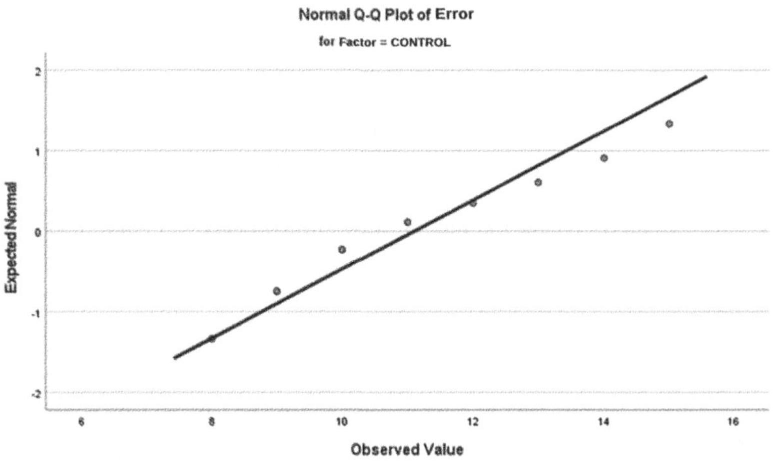

Fig. 5.33. Normal Distribution Plot of the Control Group.

In the **"detrended"** probability plot shown in Figs. 5.34 and 5.35, in which the differences between the observed values and the expected values in the case of a normal distribution, in other words, the deviations of the values from the zero line are shown, the expected points are randomly distributed around the horizontal line drawn from "0" on the vertical axis without forming a function.

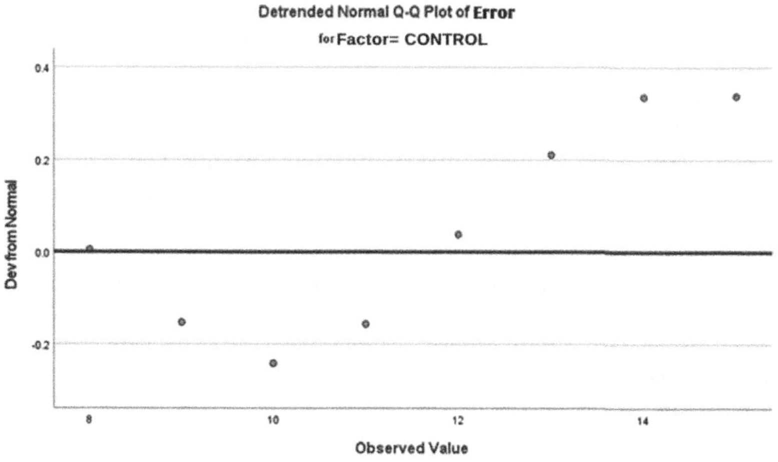

Fig. 5.34. Detrended Plot Showing the Deviations of the Experimental Group Data From Normal.

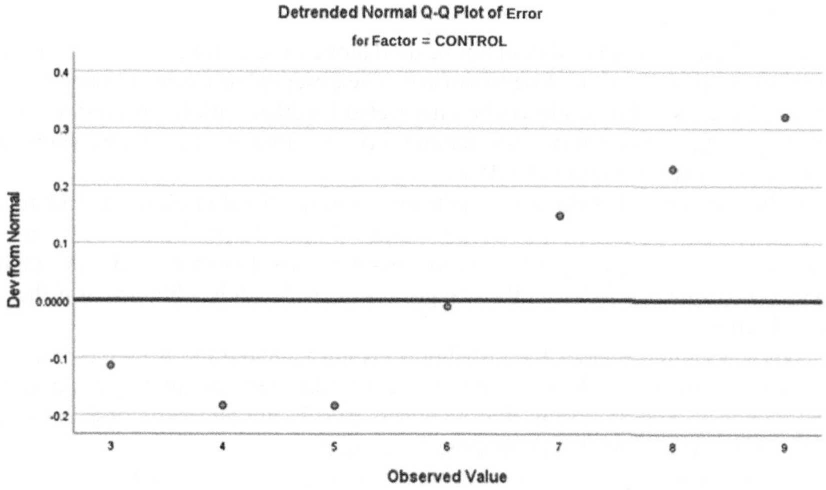

Fig. 5.35. Detrended Plot Showing the Deviations of the Control Group Data From Normal.

Although the normal probability plot gives a visual idea of normality, a statistical test is required for the hypothesis that the data come from a normal distribution. For this purpose, **Shapiro Wilks' and Lilliefors Tests** are used. The

Lilliefors test is based on a modified version of the Kolmogorov–Smirnov test and should be used when the mean and variance estimated from the data are unknown.

The Shapiro–Wilks Test can be used when the number of subjects is less than 29 and the **K-S (Lilliefors)** Test when the number of subjects is 29 or more. However, when there are more subjects, only the **Lilliefors Test** is used, as the Shapiro-Wilks test is likely to give erroneous results. The SPSS program does not calculate the Shapiro–Wilks statistics when the number of subjects is more than 50.

Shapiro–Wilks' p value was 0.816 for the experimental group, each consisting of 10 subjects, and 0.637 for the control group. At the 5% significance level, as the result of this test in both groups, the hypothesis that "**the data come from a normal distribution**" is accepted, and the data sets of the experimental and control groups are considered to be normal.

As the sample size increases, the null hypothesis is rejected in any goodness-of-fit test. Basically, it is very difficult to find a **standard normally** distributed data set. However, for most of the statistical tests, it is sufficient to have the data distributed close to the normal. For this reason, statistical analyzes should be performed not only by looking at the normality test results in large data sets but also by assuming that the data are distributed close to normal, especially if there are no serious deviations from the normal in graphs such as stem and leaf plots.

Hypothesis tests alone should not be used alone to determine whether the data are distributed normal or close to normal. The observed test value obtained as a result of the tests should always be interpreted together with the histogram and other graphics. Normality tests should not be used if the graphs show a non-normal distribution of the data.

Using measures that do not come from a normal distribution will calculate a smaller *p*-value or narrower confidence interval than it actually is. In this case, the probability of rejecting a true hypothesis increases. In other words, although there is no difference between the two groups, a result can be obtained as if there is a difference.

When deciding whether the distribution is normal/close to normal, especially when there are more than 30 subjects, graphical methods among evaluation methods may be more useful than skewness calculation and hypothesis tests in terms of detecting a distribution close to normal.

In cases where the data is not normal, two actions can be taken:

(1) Applying a transformation to the data to ensure that they fit a normal distribution.
(2) Applying a nonparametric test to existing data.

In order to apply parametric tests, the assumption of homogeneity of variances must be fulfilled as well as the normal distribution of the stack from which the data are drawn.

SPSS evaluates the homogeneity of variances by using Levene's Test.

In our example, the *p*-value of Levene's Test for homogeneity of variances is 0.506, and the "variances are equal" hypothesis is accepted at the 5% significance level. Thus, it is revealed that the variances of the experimental and control groups are homogeneous.

Below **the Spread versus Level Plot** is a correlation slope value. Since the power value is given as 1 at the bottom of the graph before the conversion is made, it is stated that there is no need for conversion. Such a plot is obtained when "**Untransformed**" is selected in the "**Explore/Plots**" menu (Fig. 5.36).

If the variances are not equal, **the Spread versus Level Plot** can be used to make appropriate transformations. There is usually a relationship between the **mean value (or level)** of a variable and its **associated change (or spread)**. One-tailed to examine this relationship is to draw a graph containing the spread and level values. If there is no relationship between them, the points gather around the horizontal line. If this is not the case, the observed relationship between the two variables can be used to select the appropriate transformation.

If the hypothesis that the variances are homogeneous is rejected, appropriate transformations are required on the data. However, before making these transformations, it is necessary to look at **the Spread versus Level Plot**.

To determine the appropriate power for the transformation of the data, a **Spread versus Level Plot**, which is a graph of the logarithm of the median versus the quartile width, is plotted for each group. The spread and level values for each group are put in the said graph.

Power conversion is often used to correct for variances. In power conversion, each value is increased to the specified power. For example, in a power of 2 conversion, all values are squared while in a 1/2 conversion, the square root of the values is taken. If the power is zero, the logarithm of the values is used.

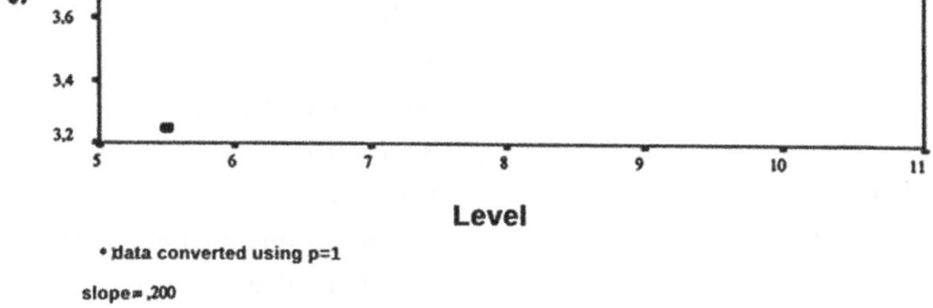

Fig. 5.36. Spread versus Level Plot (Defect Variable by Factor).

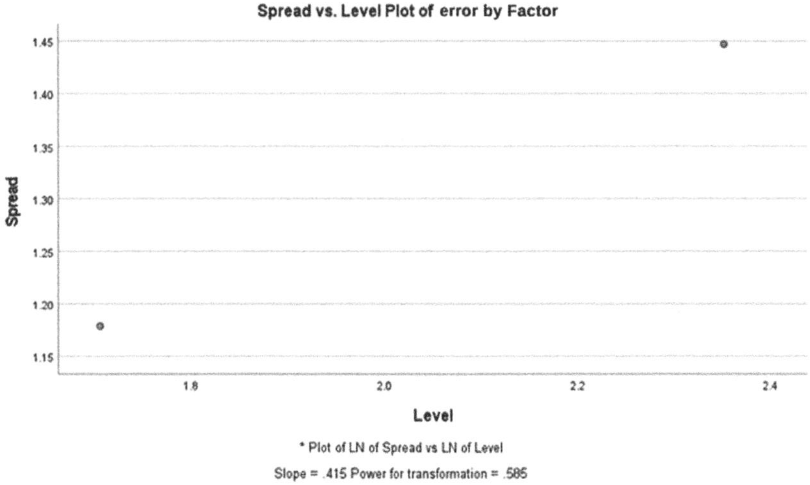

Fig. 5.37. Spread versus Level Plot (Defect Variable by Factor).

Although the variances are homogeneous in our example, the data in question will be transformed only for the sake of practice. When "**Power estimation**" is selected in the "**Explore/Plots**" menu, an Anti-Spread Level Chart with a **slope** of 0.415 and a power value of "**Power for Transformation**" 0.585 to transform the data are obtained (Fig. 5.37).

The power value to transform the data can be found by calculating (1 − slope). Although the aforementioned formula helps to find all kinds of power values, the power value which is close to 1/2 times is usually chosen as in Table 5.14 for simplicity and clarity.

Since the calculated power value in our example is 0.585, the necessary conversion can be made by selecting "**Transformed Power:/Square root,**" which is the

Table 5.14. Commonly Used Conversions.

Power	**Transformation**
3	Cube
2	Square
1	No transformation
1/2	Square root
0	Logarithm
−1/2	Inverted value of square root
−1	Inverted value

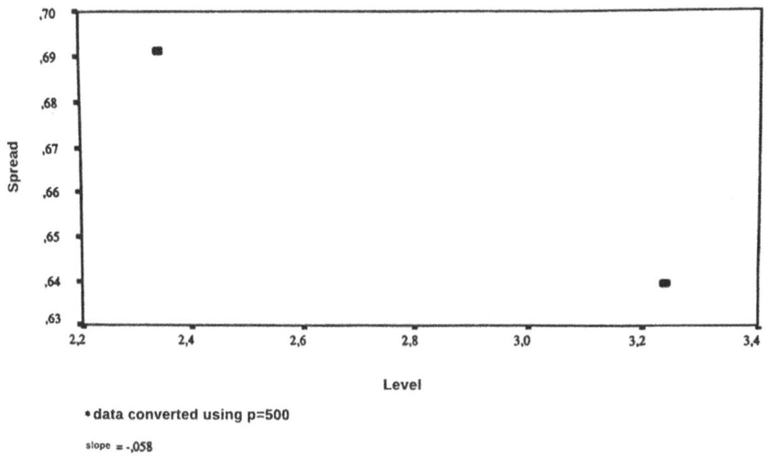

Fig. 5.38. Spread versus Level Plot (Defect Variable by Factor).

closest power value of 1/2 (square root) from the "**Explore/Plots**" menu. After the conversion, **the Spread versus Level Plot** should be taken from SPSS again (Fig. 5.38). From this plot, the success of the conversion can be evaluated.

5.8 Other Hypothesis Tests Related to Distributions

Besides the **Shapiro–Wilks and Lilliefors (K-S) Normality Tests** previously described and obtained using the "Explore" command, there are other tests that evaluate the distribution of the population.

To test whether the data on a group of subjects fit a certain theoretical distribution,

- **Kolmogorov–Smirnov Goodness of Fit Test in a Group and**
- **Chi-Square Goodness-of-Fit Test can be used in other group.**

SPSS uses the Kolmogorov–Smirnov Test in one group instead of the Chi-Square Goodness-of-Fit Test in one group to test whether the data fit binomial, Poisson, normal, and uniform theoretical distributions. In this regard, only the **Kolmogorov–Smirnov Test in One Group** will be discussed here in order to assess whether the data fit a theoretical distribution.

As the sample size increases, the null hypothesis can be rejected in any goodness-of-fit test. Basically, it is very difficult to find a **standard normally** distributed data set. **However, it is sufficient for the data to be distributed close to normal in order to apply most of the statistical tests.** For this reason, if there are no serious deviations from the normal in graphs such as histogram, stem and leaf plot, and normal distribution plot, as well as not only looking at the normality test results in large data sets, it is assumed that the data are distributed close to normal and statistical analyzes can be made accordingly.

5.8.1 Kolmogorov–Smirnov Goodness-of-Fit Test in One Group

It is used to test how well a randomly selected sample data fit a certain distribution such as uniform, normal, or Poisson.

The normal distribution is a symmetrical, bell-shaped distribution with one mode. The uniform distribution is a "uniform" distribution in which all possible outcomes are equally likely. The Poisson distribution is a skewed distribution used to explain the occurrence of rare events.

Especially in very small samples where Chi-Square cannot be applied, or when one of the expected frequencies in the chi-square goodness-of-fit test is less than 1, or when more than 20% of the cells have an expected frequency less than 5, the frequencies must be combined, "**The Kolmogorov–Smirnov Goodness-of-Fit Test in one Group**" can be used instead of the "**Chi-Square Goodness-of-Fit Test in one Group**".

The Kolmogorov–Smirnov Goodness of Fit Test in One Group can be used to test whether the "experimental" group data related to the defective production data used in previous analyzes are normally distributed. After entering the data for this, the output in Table 5.15 is obtained by using the commands "**Analyze/Nonparametric Tests/1-Sample K-S/Test Variable List(experiment)/Test Distribution(Normal)/OK**". The materiality level observed in the said table is given as 0.959. Thus, the null hypothesis that the data come from a normal distribution is accepted.

Table 5.15. Kolmogorov–Smirnov Goodness of Fit Test Results of Experimental Group Data.

One-Sample Kolmogorov–Smirnov Test		
		EXPERIMENTAL
N		10
Normal parameters[a,b]	Mean	5.8
	Std. Deviation	1.9322
Most extreme differences	Absolute	0.161
	Positive	0.161
	Negative	−0.133
Kolmogorov–Smirnov Z		0.508
Asymp. Sig. (2-tailed)		0.959

[a]Test distribution is Normal.
[b]Calculated from data.

5.8.2 Binomial Distribution

In some cases, the random variable can have two possible values. If an individual falls into only one of the two possible categories, it is called a "**binomial measurement**". Such situations are frequently encountered in different fields. For example, a patient may survive or die as a result of brain surgery, a person who has had a traffic accident has a broken collarbone or not, an enterprise produces or does not produce substance X, etc. The distribution of variables specified by such counting is called the binomial distribution.

The event examined in the binomial distribution has two independent possible outcomes: "**p: probability of occurrence**", "**q = 1 - p: probability of non-occurrence**". When **p = q**, the distribution is symmetrical while the binomial distribution approaches the Poisson distribution as the probability of occurrence decreases and p approaches zero.

The following formula is used to calculate the probability with the binomial distribution:

$$P(r) = \frac{n!}{(n\text{-}r)!.r!} p_r q_{n-r} , r = 0, 1, \ldots\ldots\ldots, n$$

n: Total number of events.
r: The number of occurrences of the desirable event
n-r: The number of occurrences of the undesirable event.
p: The probability of occurrence of the desirable event.
q: The probability of the undesirable event occurring.
!: Factorial.

The probability of being born male is 0.5. The probability of having no sons in families with four children is as follows:

$$P = \frac{4!}{(4\text{-}0)!.0} (0.5)^0 (0.5)^4 = 0{,}0625$$

The probability of having a son in this family is 6.25%.

5.8.3 Binomial Test

The binomial test is used to test the null hypothesis that the data "**comes from the binomial distribution determined to be likely the first in two categories**".

The binomial distribution is the sampling distribution of the rates observed in random samples from a two-category population. In this test, it is investigated whether the rates or frequencies observed in the sample are taken from a population with a certain p-value.

In the binomial test, the null hypothesis that "**the probability of p being a particular outcome is equal to a desired number**" is tested. For example, testing whether a coin tossed a certain number of times in a row is fraudulent, according to heads and tails, is an example of a binomial test. Let's assume that the coin in question is tossed 20 times in a row, with 1 = heads, 0 = tails, resulting in:

1 1 0 0 1 1 1 1 1 1 0 1 1 1 1 0 1 1 0 1 1

Here, the hypothesis is that the probability of a heads or tails occurring is equal to 1/2. After entering the aforementioned data in SPSS, the output in Table 5.16 is obtained by selecting "**Analyze/Nonparametric Tests/Binomial/Test Variable List(coin)/Test proportion(0.50)/OK**". For the first value (0), the test rate of cases was taken as 0.50 (1/2). The observed ratio is 0.25.

When the significance level is 0.05, the null hypothesis is rejected. Thus, it is concluded that p is not equal to 1/2, so the coin may be fraudulent.

5.8.4 Poisson Distribution

The Poisson distribution, like the binomial distribution, is the distribution of discrete variables. There are two important differences between binomial and Poisson distributions. First, p, which is the probability of the event under consideration, is large in the binomial distribution and very small in the Poisson distribution. Second, n is small in the binomial distribution while n is very large in the Poisson distribution.

The following formula can be applied to the Poisson distribution, which is used to find the probability of less frequent events:

$$P(r) = \frac{x^t}{r!}e^{-x}$$

x = np: Arithmetic mean.
r: Number of occurrences of the desired event.
e^{-x}: Obtained by calculating these values (e = 2.7182).

Table 5.16. Binomial Test Results of Coin Data.

	Category	N	Observed Prop.	Test Prop.	Exact Sig. (2-tailed)
COIN Group 1	Heads	15	0.75	0.5	0.041
Group 2	Tails	5	0.25		
Total		20	1		

Let's assume that a group of 1,000 people is followed in terms of smoking. What is the probability of not being a smoker, given that previous research has identified the smoking status for this study group as one in 1,000 people? Here, the probability of smokers is $p = 0.001$, $n = 1000$ and $X = np = 1.0$.

$$P = e_{-10} = 0.368$$

Thus, the probability of never smoking in this group was found to be 36.8%.

The Kolmogorov–Smirnov Goodness-of-Fit Test in one Group can also be used to test whether a randomly selected sample fits the Poisson distribution or the uniform distribution. For this, "**Analyze/Non-parametric Tests/1-Sample K-S/ Test Variable List(experiment)/Test Distribution (Poisson or uniform)/OK**" commands are used after the data are entered.

If it is desired to determine whether the data are distributed uniformly, "**- Test Distribution (uniform)**" is selected.

Chapter 6

Confidence Interval Estimates

Objectives

- To determine the confidence interval (CI) for population proportions.
- To determine the CI for population means.

6.1 Introduction

Researchers want to make generalizations by using the collected data about a sample selected from a population. Two main approaches, **statistical tests and statistical estimation** (point estimation and CI), are used for the statistical decision.

Point estimation and CI, "How big is the difference between groups?" seeks an answer to the question. This is analogous to statistical significance in the case of whether the hypothesis is nonzero in statistical tests.

While making any statistical evaluation, there is no difference between hypothesis testing and the use of CIs in terms of statistical significance. In this regard, the two can be used interchangeably.

CIs can provide more information, as is the case for specifying economic materiality. For this reason, in recent years, there has been a tendency in many studies to specify the CI in addition to hypothesis testing.

When the population parameters are given as an estimated figure, it is called a "**point estimate**". The arithmetic mean of a sample is a point estimate. **CI** or interval is the **interval of estimated values**. CI is the range of values, containing the unknown population value within a certain probability.

6.2 CI for Population Proportions

CIs for population proportions are based on the following assumptions about their data:

- **Random Sampling:** Although random sampling is preferred, the CI for population proportions can be obtained even if the sample is not random. However, one should not take sides in the preparation of the sample.

Statistical Analysis Techniques, Volume 1, 121–146

doi:10.1108/978-1-80592-341-120261007

- **Independent Observations:** This assumption should not be violated. If the observations are not independent, the CI for the population proportions cannot be calculated.
- **Sufficiently Large Sample:** A sample of about 10 subjects is sufficient. If p' is very close to zero or 1, a larger sample is required. The closer the sample rate, p', is to zero or 1, the larger the sample is required.

In a study, it was found that 94% of 54 businesses also trade stocks and bonds along with their main activities. Let's calculate the CI using the data in question. The sample rate in this sample is 0.94. Since the sample size is 54, the sample rate *p*' is considered approximately normal according to the central limit theorem.

When the data in this sample are examined, it is seen that the independence assumption is met. Knowing that a business is trading stocks and bonds outside of its main activity does not give any information about whether another business is doing the same. Given 0.94, the third assumption is satisfied since the sample of 54 subjects is large enough.

The sample of businesses studied was not randomly selected from all trading companies as well as stock and bond trading companies. However, random sampling is not an absolute necessity. As the second and third assumptions are satisfied, the CI for the population proportions can be obtained.

To calculate the 90% CI for the companies mentioned above, $\alpha = 0.10$ is used. Since $\alpha/2 = 0.05$, $z_{.05} = 1.645$ is found when looking for z_{05} in the Standard Normal Distribution Z Table. The estimated standard deviation of p is:

$$S_{proportion} = \sqrt{\frac{p'(1-p')}{n}} = \sqrt{\frac{(0.94)(1-0.94)}{54}}$$

$$= 0.032$$

Using this data, the confidence interval is calculated as :

$$(\text{p}' - (Z_{\alpha/2})(S_{difference});\ \text{p}' + (Z_{\alpha/2})(S_{difference}))$$

$$(0.94 - (1.645)(0.032);\ 0.94 + (1.645)(0.032))$$

$$(0.94 - 0.05;\ 0.94 + 0.05)$$

$$(0.89;\ 0.99)$$

From this, the CI is found as 90% (0.89; 0.99) for population proportion *p*.

We are 90% sure that the proportion of companies that trade stocks and bonds outside of their core business in the population is between 0.89 and 0.99. We can never know whether this interval estimate (0.89; 0.99) actually includes the population proportion "*p*". Let's assume that if we're unlucky we get a sample with a 90% CI that doesn't include *p*. Since such a situation occurs only 10% of the time, the population proportion of the interval (0.89; 0.99) includes *p*.

We are 90% sure. However, we can be wrong about this.

As long as the evaluation is made by taking samples from the population, there is always such a risk. Since only the sample is studied, the evaluations about the population may be wrong. By calculating the 90% CI, we use a method that gives an accurate interval estimate 90% of the time.

Here, let's calculate the 95% and 99% CIs for the population proportion of companies that buy and sell stocks and bonds outside of their core business. At the 95% CI, $\alpha = 0.05$, where $\alpha/2$ is 0.025 and z.025 is 1.96. Thanks to the formula used earlier, the CI becomes:

$$(0.94 - (1.96)(0.032) \; ; \; 0.94 + (1.96)(0.032))$$

$$(0.94 - 0.06); \; (0.94 + 0.06)$$

$$(0.88; \; 1.00)$$

From here, CI is found as 95% (0.88; 1.00) for the population proportion p.

At the 99% CI, $\alpha = 0.01$, $\alpha/2$ is 0.005 and z.005 is 2.576. Applying the formula used earlier, the CI becomes:

$$(0.94 - (2.576)(0.032); \; 0.94 + (2.576)(0.032))$$

$$(0.94 - 0.08) \; ; \; (0.94 + 0.08)$$

$$(0.86; \; 1.02)$$

Since the proportions cannot be greater than 1, we can replace the extreme value 1.02 with 1. Thus, the CI is 99% (0.86; 1) population proportion p. We are 95% sure since that the interval (0.86; 1) contains p 99%, the population proportion of the interval (0.88; 1) will contain p. In other words, we are 95% sure that the proportion of companies that trade stocks and bonds outside of their core business is between 0.88 and 1 in the population. On the other hand, we are 99% sure that the proportion of companies that trade stocks and bonds outside of their core business in the population is between 0.86 and 1.

When calculating the CI for the population proportion, it is possible to obtain a negative or greater than 1 endpoint. Since the proportions must be between 0 and 1, the negative endpoint should be replaced by 0 while an endpoint greater than 1 should also be replaced by 1.

6.3 CI for Differences in Population Proportions in Independent Samples

In some statistical studies, two proportions are compared. If an organization has one workgroup trained to increase productivity and the other workgroup to another type of training, we may want to compare the proportion of productive workers in the two groups. Similarly, the proportion of people who have worked and succeeded in a particular field can be compared to the proportion of people who have worked and succeeded in another field.

The CI for the difference in population proportions is based on the following assumptions about the data:

- **Random Sampling:** Although random sampling is preferred, the CI for the difference between population proportions can be obtained even if the sample is not random. However, one should not take sides in determining the sample.
- **Independent Observations:** Observations in one sample should be independent from observations in the other sample. If this assumption is violated, the formula given here cannot be used to calculate the CI of $(p_1 - p_2)$.
- **Independence of Observations Within the Sample:** Observations within each sample should be independent. CI of population proportions difference $(p_1 - p_2)$ cannot be made when this assumption is violated.
- **Sufficiently Large Sample:** A sample of about 10 subjects is sufficient. If the difference in sample rates $(p_1 - p_2')$ is very close to 0 or 1, a larger sample is required. The closer $(p_1 - p_2')$ to 0 or 1, the larger sample is required.

Let's assume that the population proportions are compared in the evaluation of the data on the effect of the companies operating in the same sector on the average profitability of the investments made by foreign resources. In such a study, 24 companies in the same sector financed their investments with foreign resources while another 24 companies opted for auto financing instead. While the average profitability of the group investing with foreign resources is 50%, the average profitability of the companies investing with auto financing is 21%. The proportions in the samples are quite different from each other, and it is implied that the profitability of the companies investing with foreign funding will be high, and the reason for this is financial leverage. We would like to make evaluations about theoretical populations by using the sample proportions in question.

Regarding this sample data, except the first assumption, all the others seem to be satisfied. Observations in both samples are independent from each other. Because the profitability of companies in one group does not give any information about the profitability of those in the other group. At the same time, the subjects in both samples are independent from each other. Because the profitability of the company in a sample does not give information about the profitability of the other company in the same sample. Finally, given the 0.50 and 0.21 sample rates, a sample size of 24 in each group is sufficient.

To obtain the CI of the difference between the proportions of the two populations, it is necessary to create samples from the first and second population. **The number of subjects in the samples in question need not be equal to each other. However, having an equal number of subjects in the two groups reduces the risk of Type II error (likelihood of rejecting the actually false null hypothesis).**

Using the central limit theorem, it can be said that sample differences $(p_1 - p_2')$ are approximately normally distributed. The standard error used in the calculations can be determined as:

$$S_{difference} = \sqrt{\frac{p_1'(1-p_1')}{n_1} + \frac{p_2'(1-p_2')}{n_2}}$$

If the samples are independent and of sufficient size, the CI formula becomes:

$$\left[(p_1' - p_2') - (Z_{a/2})(S_{difference}), (p_1' - p_2') + (Z_{a/2})(S_{difference})\right]$$

Let's calculate the 95% CI using the profitability data:

$$= \sqrt{\frac{(0.50)(1-0.50)}{24} + \frac{(0.24)(1-0.24)}{24}}(S_{difference})$$

$$= \sqrt{0.0104 + 0.0069}$$

$$= \sqrt{0.0173} = 0.13$$

Using the CI formula, the 95% CI is calculated as follows:

$$(0.29 - (1.96)(0.13)\ ;\ 0.29 + (1.96)(0.13))$$

$$(0.29 - 0.25\ ;\ 0.29 + 0.25)$$

$$(0.04;\ 0.54)$$

Accordingly, we are 95% sure that the difference in population proportions ($p_2 - p_2$) is between 0.04 and 0.54. Thus, we are 95% sure that the difference is positive. This means we are 95% sure that p_1 is greater than p_2. If p_1 was less than p_2, the difference $p_1 - p_2$ would be negative. The CI in question can be interpreted as follows:

We are 95% sure that p_1 is greater than p_2 and that the difference between these population proportions is between 0.04 and 0.54. Thus, companies that are outsourced are more likely to be more profitable than similar companies that do not outsource. Companies that outsource may be slightly less profitable ($p_1 - p_2$ can be as low as 0.04); or even more likely to be more profitable (p_1 to p_2 can be as large as 0.54); or they may be more profitable with a probability somewhere in between ($p_1 - p_2$ can be worth somewhere between 0.04 and 0.54).

How should the small, medium, or large difference be determined between the population proportions? When the difference between the rates is quite small, a difference of 0.4 or greater between two proportions is considered a large difference, while a difference of 0.2–0.3 is generally considered moderate, and a difference of 0.1 or less is considered small.

When obtaining the 99% CI for $p_1 - p_2$, z005 = 2.576 is used since $\alpha/2 = 0.01/2 = 0.005$.

$$(0.29 - (2.576)(0.13)\ ;\ (0.29 + (2.576)(0.13))$$

$$(0.29 - 0.33;\ 0.29 + 0.33)$$

$$(-0.04;\ 0.62)$$

We are 99% sure that the difference between $(p_1 - p_2)$ is between -0.04 and 0.62. Since the lower limit value is negative and the upper limit value is positive, the CI includes zero. Thus, we cannot say that we are 99% sure that there is a difference between p_1 and p_2. When zero is contained, the condition $(p_1 - p_2) = 0$ cannot be neglected. It can be said that there is a difference between the rates in the lower CI (95%). The result reached in this data set depends on the confidence level used.

If the two endpoints of the population proportion difference $(p_1 - p_2)$ CI are positive, we are fairly certain that p_1 is greater than p_2. If both endpoints are negative, we are pretty sure that p_1 is less than p_2. If the low end is negative and the high end is positive, we are not sure that p_1 is not equal to p_2 since the CI contains zero. If the CI for $(p_1 - p_2)$ contains zero, we cannot state that the population proportions are different at that confidence level.

Since population proportions range from 0 to 1, the largest possible difference is $1 - 0 = 1$. The smallest possible difference is $0 - 1 = -1$. CIs for differences can sometimes have endpoint values less than -1 and greater than 1. These should be replaced with -1 and $+1$ respectively.

6.4 CI for Population Mean

The CI for the population mean is based on the following assumptions:

- **Random Sampling:** This assumption is not mandatory unless there is sampling bias. However, obtaining random sampling provides the opportunity to generalize the results obtained from the sample to the population.
- **Independent Observations:** If this assumption is violated, the CI for the population mean cannot be calculated.
- **Selection of the Sample from the Normal Population:** If the population is not standard normal, a CI can still be obtained for the population mean. Thanks to the central limit theorem, a sufficient sample size compensates for the non-normal population situation. The further away from normality, the larger the sample size. If there are too many anomalies, the population mean CI cannot be calculated.

In a research about the packing times of the workers working in the packing unit in a factory, the average packing times (min) of the 22 workers in the packing unit were explained as in Table 6.1 and entered into SPSS as given in Table 6.2.

Let's assume that we want to find the average of the packaging time of the same product from the population of employees in the packaging unit, which is similar in this study. The sample's mean packing time of 9.7 populations generates a point estimate for the mean packing time. But the interval estimation of the population mean packing time is better than the point estimation.

Let's evaluate the above assumptions using packing time data. The data in question are not a random data set, as there is no list of all employees in the

Table 6.1. Average Packing Times of Employees in the Packing Unit.

9.3	8.9	9.6
10.3	10.3	10.4
10.3	10.2	8.7
9.5	10.8	9.8
7.7	8.4	8.7
9.6	11.4	11.1
10.2	8.5	9.5
10.9		
Mean ± SS 9.7 ± 1.0		

Table 6.2. Entering Average Packing Time Data Into SPSS.

	Time
1	9.3
2	10.3
3	10.3
4	10.4
5	8.9
6	10.3
7	10.2
8	8.7
9	9.6
10	9.5
11	10.8
12	9.8
13	7.7
14	8.4
15	8.7
16	9.6
17	11.4
18	11.1
19	10.2
20	8.5
21	9.5
22	10.9

```
TIME Stem-and-Leaf Plot
 Frequency   Stem & Leaf

    1,00      7 . 7
    5,00      8 . 45779
    6,00      9 . 355668
    8,00     10 . 22333489
    2,00     11 . 14

 Stem width:     1,00
 Each leaf:      1 case(s)
```

Fig. 6.1. Stem and Leaf Plot Related to Packing Time Data.

packaging unit. However, this is not important. The observations are independent, as the average packing time of one worker gives no information about the packing time of another worker. Does this dataset come from a normal population? Considering the stem and leaf plot related to the packaging time given in Fig. 6.1, it is seen that this is compatible with the normal or near-normal population. Thus, the data show that the CI can be calculated.

After the packaging time data in Table 6.1 is entered into SPSS as in Table 6.2, a CI of 99.9% of the packaging time population mean level can be obtained. For this, the output in Table 6.3 is obtained by using **"Analyze/DescriptiveStatistics/Explore/Dependentlist(time)/Display/Statistics/Descriptives/ConfidenceIntervalforMean(99.9)/Continue/OK"** in SPSS.

From this, we can state that we are 99.9% sure that the average packing time population average is between 8.9 and 10.5. Indeed, we can never know that the mean time of the population is between 8.9 and 10.5. However, we are 99.9% sure that this is so.

Once the CI is obtained, a choice must be made between sensitivity and confidence. **The higher the confidence level, the wider the CI**. Because the high confidence level of 99.9% was chosen, the 99.9% CI chosen for the packing time data is also quite wide. The CI based on the lower confidence level is narrower. This preference can also be observed in the data of the fields of activity of the above companies.

The 99% CI for p is wider than 95%, which is the 90% CI. Because the wide CI contains more values, we are more certain that it contains the population parameter.

There is a relationship between "**t-Test in one Group**" and "**Population Mean Confidence Interval in one Group**". At a certain level of significance, if the null hypothesis of the t-Test is rejected, the CI for the population mean does not include the μ_0 determined by the researcher. On the other hand, if the null hypothesis is accepted as a result of the t-Test at a certain level of significance, the CI for the population mean includes μ_0 determined by the researcher.

You can access the video "Confidence Interval for the Population Mean" by scanning the QR code.

Table 6.3. 99.9% Confidence Interval of Packing Time Data.

Descriptives				
			Statistic	**Std. Error**
Time	Mean		9.73	0.206
	99.9% confidence interval for mean	Lower bound	8.95	
		Upper bound	10.52	
	5% trimmed mean		9.75	
	Median		9.7	
	Variance		0.933	
	Std. Deviation		0.966	
	Minimum		8	
	Maximum		11	
	Range		4	
	Interquartile range		1	
	Skewness		−0.258	0.491
	Kurtosis		−0.545	0.953

Table 6.4. 95% Confidence Interval of Packing Time Data.

Descriptives				
			Statistic	**Std. Error**
Time	Mean		9.73	0.206
	95% confidence interval for mean	Lower bound	9.3	
		Upper bound	10.16	
	5% trimmed mean		9.75	
	Median		9.7	
	Variance		0.933	
	Std. deviation		0.966	
	Minimum		8	
	Maximum		11	
	Range		4	
	Interquartile range		1	
	Skewness		−0.258	0.491
	Kurtosis		−0.545	0.953

For the more precise interval estimation regarding the population mean of packing times, let's assume we chose a lower confidence level. If the confidence level is 95%, the SPSS output will be as in Table 6.4.

Thus, for the packing time data, the 95% CI (9.3; 10.2) is obtained. The 95% CI is much more precise than the 99.9% CI. In this case, we can state that we are 95% sure that μ lies between 9.3 and 10.2.

Two other factors affecting the precision of the CI are the dispersion of the data and the sample size. The more extensive the data and the smaller the sample size, the lower the precision of the CI.

6.5 CI for Difference Between Population Means

Comparing means is one of the main reasons for the use of statistical evaluations in many fields. If done properly, it is very useful in determining the profitability, employment, and production of businesses. Here,

- "Confidence interval of difference between population means in independent groups with equal variance."
- "Confidence interval of difference between population means in independent groups with different variances."

- "Confidence interval of the difference between two means in paired samples" was examined.

There is a relationship between "**t-Test of Difference between Population Means**" and "**Confidence Interval of Difference between Population Means**". At a certain level of significance, if the null hypothesis is rejected according to the *t*-Test, the CI for the population mean is H_0: μ_1. Since $\mu_2 = 0$, it does not contain "0". On the other hand, if the null hypothesis at a certain significance level is accepted as a result of the *t*-Test, the CI for the population mean includes "0".

6.5.1 CI for the Difference in Population Means with Equal Variances in Independent Groups

Let's assume that there are two different samples from two populations with normal distribution and equal variance, whose mean is μ_1 and μ_2. Here, the variance of the first stage is assumed to be equal to the variance of the second stage. To compare population means, we may want to obtain the CI for the difference $\mu_1 - \mu_2$ of the population means. A sample of size n_1 with a mean of X_1 and a standard deviation of s_1 is taken from the first population. Similarly, a sample of size n_2 with a mean of X_2 and a standard deviation of s_2 is taken from the second population. Sample sizes n_1 and n_2 need not be equal. However, having an equal number of units in the two groups reduces the risk of **Type II** error (the probability of rejecting the actually false null hypothesis).

If the confidence level is chosen to be 98%, 98% of all possible samples form 98% CIs containing $\mu_1 - \mu_2$. Thus, we can state that we are 98% sure that this range will contain μ_1-μ_2.

In the equal variance approach, population variances are assumed to be equal. How can this assumption be checked? As a rough measurement, the following rule can be applied:

$$0.5 \leq \frac{s_1^2}{s_2^2} \leq 2$$

Therefore, assume that the population variances are equal. If the sample variance ratio (s_{21}/s_{22}) is less than 0.5 or greater than 2, do not assume that the population variances are equal.

SPSS evaluates the homogeneity of variances using the Levene test. If the *p* value of **Levene's test** for homogeneity of variances is greater than the determined significance level, the "variances are equal" hypothesis is accepted. Thus, it is revealed that the variances of the experimental and control groups are homogeneous. In this case, the equal variance approach should be applied instead of the differential variance approach.

The equivariance CI approach is based on the following assumptions:

- **Random Sampling:** Random sampling is not necessary unless bias is taken. However, obtaining a random sample provides the opportunity to generalize the results obtained from the sample to the population.
- **Independent Samples:** Equal variance CIs for μ_1 - μ_2 cannot be obtained unless the samples are independent.

- **Independent Observations Within Each Sample:** CIs for μ_1 - μ_2 cannot be calculated if this assumption is violated.
- **Obtaining Samples from Normal Populations:** If the population is not normal, the CI for μ_1 - μ_2 can be calculated if sample sizes are available to compensate for slight skewness. Equal variance CIs should not be calculated using highly skewed data.

In order to determine which of the A and B model machines used in tea processing is more efficient, the data of a study containing the daily production figures of 11 machines from A model machines and seven machines from B model machines are given in Table 6.5.

While the average production amount of A model machines is 524.0 kg, the average production amount of B model machines is 701.1 kg. Is it possible to obtain an equal variance CI for the difference between the means of population production quantities?

Here, the first population consists of A model machines in the first sample, and the second population consists of B model machines in the second sample.

Before examining the data, it should be checked whether the above-mentioned assumptions are met. The selected samples are not random. However, this is not mandatory. Because the samples are independent of each other, the production amount values in one sample do not give any information about the production amount values in the other sample. In addition, the observations in the samples are also independent of each other.

Table 6.5. Daily Production Quantities of A and B Model Machines.

Model A		**Model B**	
Machine No.	**Quantity of Sale (kg)**	**Machine No.**	**Quantity of Sale (kg)**
1	484	12	934
2	559	13	809
3	431	14	791
4	418	15	703
5	447	16	584
6	554	17	490
7	874	18	597
8	605	Mean ± SS	701.1 ± 154.4
9	399		
10	562		
11	431		
Mean ± SS 524.0 ± 135.2			

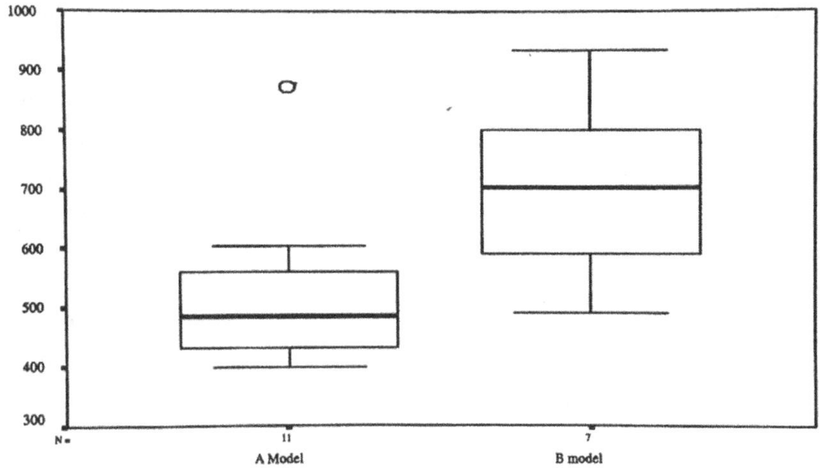

Fig. 6.2. Box Plot of Daily Production Amount of A and B Model Machines.

The box plots for the production quantity values in the samples are given in Fig. 6.2, and it shows a little positive skewness since the median for the A model machine is close to the lower quartile, and for the B model machine, it shows slightly negative skewness since the median is closer to the upper quartile in the box plot given for the B model machine. However, it can be said that both groups showed a distribution close to normal. The model A machine sample, consisting of 11 machines, is large enough to compensate for the current skewness here.

To check whether there is an equal variance situation, s_{21}/s_{22} = (135.2)2/(154.4)2 = 0.8 is obtained by using the standard deviations of the data in Table 6.5. Since $0.5 \leq 0.8 \leq 2$, it can be assumed that the population variances are equal. The said evaluation can also be done by using SPSS. For this, the **Levene's Test** value, which shows whether the variances in Table 6.7 are equal or not, can be checked. Since the p-value of the test in question was 0.531 > (α = 0.10 or 0.05 or 0.01) significance level, it was decided that the variances were equal.

Thus, the equal variance CI for $\mu_1 - \mu_2$ can be calculated using the relevant commands in the "SPSS for Windows" statistical computer program. First, the data in Table 6.5 are entered into the SPSS program as in Table 6.6. Then, to obtain a 99% CI, "**Analyze/Compare Means/Independent-Samples T Test/Test Variable (productionamount)/Grouping Variable(group)/Define Groups/Group 1 (1)/Group 2(2)/Continue/Options/Confidence Interval(99)/Continue/OK**" commands are selected, and the output in Table 6.7 is obtained.

We are 99% sure that μ_1 to μ_2 is between −379.2 and 25. Since the lower limit value is negative and the upper limit value is positive, 0 is included in the CI.

Table 6.6. Entering Daily Production Amount Data of A and B Model Machines to SPSS.

	Production Amount	**Group**
1	484	Model A
2	559	Model A
3	431	Model A
4	418	Model A
5	447	Model A
6	554	Model A
7	874	Model A
8	605	Model A
9	399	Model A
10	562	Model A
11	431	Model A
12	934	Model A
13	809	Model A
14	791	Model A
15	703	Model A
16	584	Model A
17	490	Model A
18	597	Model A

At the 99% CI, we cannot exclude the possibility that $\mu_1 - \mu_2$ equal to 0. Based on this CI, we cannot say that the model A machine population and the model B machine population have different production volume averages. If a lower confidence level is chosen, it may be possible to say that this difference exists.

6.5.2 CI for the Difference in Population Means with Unequal Variances in Independent Groups

The data can provide all the necessary assumptions for the equal variance process, with the exception of the equal variance assumption. In such a data set, the CI for $\mu_1 - \mu_2$ can be obtained using the differential variance process.

Interpretation of this is like the previous ones. For example, if the confidence level is 90%, 90% of the possible samples form CIs that will contain $\mu_1 - \mu_2$. 10% of probable samples form a 90% CI that does not include $\mu_1 - \mu_2$. In this case, we are 90% sure that the range will include $\mu_1 - \mu_2$.

The differential variance CI approach is based on the following assumptions:

Table 6.7 Confidence Interval of Daily Production Quantity Data of Models A and B Machines.

Group Statistics

	GROUP	*N*	Mean	Std. Deviation	Std. Error Mean
Production Amount	Model A	11	524	135.7638	40.9343
	Model B	7	701.1429	154.4252	58.3672

Independent Samples Test

		Levene's test for Equality of variances		*t*-Test for Equality of Means						
									99% Confidence Interval of the difference	
		F	Sig.	*t*	df	Sig. (2-tailed)	Mean difference	Std. Error difference	Lower	Upper
Production Amount	Equal variances assumed	0.41	0.531	−2.561	16	0.021	−177.1429	69.1625	−379.151	24.866
	Equal variances not assumed			−2.485	11.661	0.029	−177.1429	71.2906	−396.06	41.774

- **Random Sampling:** Random sampling is not necessary unless it is biased. However, obtaining random sampling provides the opportunity to generalize the results obtained from the sample to the population.
- **Independent Samples:** CIs with different variances cannot be obtained for $\mu_1 - \mu_2$ unless the samples are independent.
- **Independent Observations Within Each Sample:** CIs for $\mu_1 - \mu_2$ cannot be calculated if this assumption is violated.
- **Obtaining Samples from Normal Populations:** If the population is not normal, but there are sample sizes to compensate for this slight skewness, the CI for $\mu_1 - \mu_2$ can be calculated. CIs with different variances should not be calculated using highly skewed data.

The differential variance CI process does not make the assumption that the population variances are unequal. In other words, it does not assume that the variances are equal. Simply put, it does not require population variances to be equal. In this case, it is not wrong to obtain a CI with different variances when the population variances are equal. However, in a situation where the population variances are not equal, it would be wrong to obtain an equal variance CI. If for some reason you believe that the population variances are unequal, do not use the equal variance CI.

The periods when 29 high school graduates and 20 primary school graduates working in a factory were absent from their workbenches for a day due to various reasons are given in Table 6.8. While the average time of absence from work was 30.9 minutes for workers who graduated from primary school, it was determined as 5.6 minutes for workers who graduated from high school. Is it possible to calculate the CI of the difference between the mean time of absence from work in the population of high school graduate workers and the mean time of absence from work in the population of workers graduated from primary school? Here the populations are like the workers in the samples.

As always, the samples were not randomly selected, which is not important. The workers in the two samples are different, and the Time of absence from work in one group does not give an idea about the Time of absence from work in the other group. The periods of absence from work in each group are independent of each other as they are taken from different workers. Histograms related to absenteeism are given in Figs. 6.3 and 6.4 and show non-normal populations. However, the sample sizes are sufficient to compensate for this.

In this regard, **Levene's Test value**, which shows whether the variances in Table 6.10 are different, can be looked at to determine which kind of CI to use. Since the p-value of the test in question is 0.006 $<$ ($\alpha = 0.10$ or 0.05 or 0.01) significance level, it is decided that the variances are different. In another way, it can be determined that the equal variance approach cannot be applied because the proportion of two sample variances (s_1/s_2 = (3.6)2/(6.9)2 = 0.3) is less than 0.5. In this case, the differential variance CI approach is appropriate.

In order to obtain 95% CI with different variance for $\mu_1 - \mu_2$, the data in Table 6.8 are entered into SPSS as in Table 6.9. Then, to obtain a 95% CI with different variances, "**Analyze/Compare Means/Independent-Samples T Test/Test Variable (time)/Grouping Variable(group)/Define Groups/Group 1(1)/Group 2(2)/Continue/Options/Confidence Interval(95)/Continue/OK**" commands are selected to obtain the output in Table 6.10.

Table 6.8. Absence of High School and Primary School Graduates From Their Daily Duties.

Skilled Workers		**Unskilled Workers**	
Worker No	**Absence From Work (min)**	**Worker No**	**Absence From Work (min)**
1	8.6	30	31
2	2.9	31	36
3	8.1	32	31.2
4	11.4	33	24.2
5	9.9	34	36
6	10.4	35	36.8
7	2.6	36	25.7
8	10.2	37	42.8
9	3.7	38	22
10	3.8	39	32.1
11	8	40	28
12	7.8	41	30
13	1	42	42.6
14	7.3	43	23.1
15	2.5	44	30.4
16	7.7	45	23.7
17	5	46	33.8
18	8.9	47	25.2
19	1.1	48	41.9
20	2.5	49	20.6
21	2.6	Mean ± ss 30.9 ± 6.9	
22	3.7		
23	1		
24	8.3		
25	0.4		
26	2.8		
27	6.8		
28	12.9		
29	1.4		
Mean ± SS 5.6 ± 3.6			

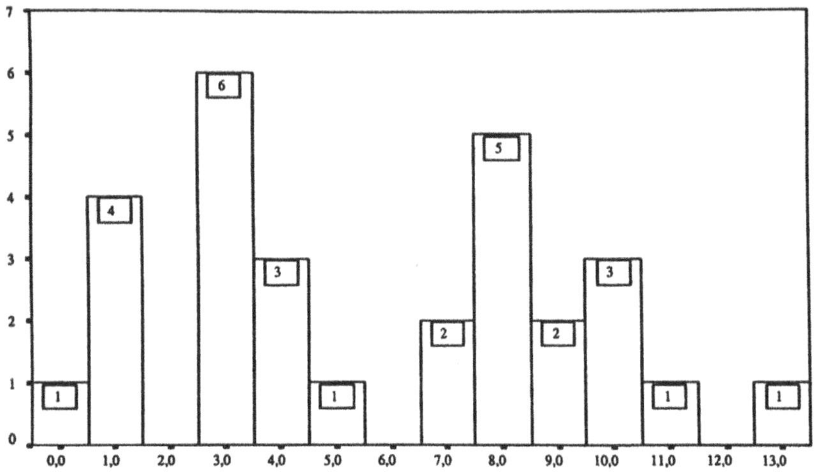

Fig. 6.3. Histogram of Absence Periods for the High School Graduate Group.

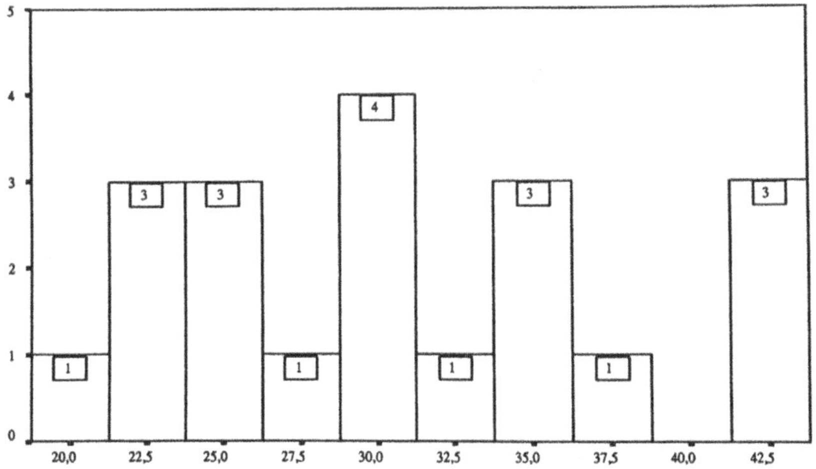

Fig. 6.4. Histogram of Absence Periods for Primary School Graduates Group.

Table 6.9. Entering the Periods of Absence of High School and Primary School Graduates Into SPSS.

	Time	Group
1	8.6	HIGH SCHOOL
2	2.9	HIGH SCHOOL
3	8.1	HIGH SCHOOL
4	11.4	HIGH SCHOOL
5	9.9	HIGH SCHOOL
6	10.4	HIGH SCHOOL
7	2.6	HIGH SCHOOL
8	10.2	HIGH SCHOOL
9	3.7	HIGH SCHOOL
10	3.8	HIGH SCHOOL
11	8	HICH SCHOOL
12	7.8	HIGH SCHOOL
13	1	HIGH SCHOOL
14	7.3	HIGH SCHOOL
15	2.5	HIGH SCHOOL
16	7.7	HIGH SCHOOL
17	5	HIGH SCHOOL
18	8.9	HIGH SCHOOL
19	1.1	HIGH SCHOOL
20	2.5	HIGH SCHOOL
21	2.6	HIGH SCHOOL
22	3.7	HIGH SCHOOL
23	1	HIGH SCHOOL
24	8.3	HIGH SCHOOL
25	0.4	HIGH SCHOOL
26	2.8	HIGH SCHOOL
27	6.8	HIGH SCHOOL
28	12.9	HIGH SCHOOL
29	1.4	HIGH SCHOOL
30	31	PRIMARY SCHOOL
31	36	PRIMARY SCHOOL
32	11.2	PRIMARY SCHOOL
33	24.2	PRIMARY SCHOOL

(Continued)

Table 6.9. *(Continued)*

	Time	Group
34	36	PRIMARY SCHOOL
35	36.8	PRIMARY SCHOOL
36	25.7	PRIMARY SCHOOL
37	42.8	PRIMARY SCHOOL
38	22	PRIMARY SCHOOL
39	32.1	PRIMARY SCHOOL
40	28	PRIMARY SCHOOL
41	30	PRIMARY SCHOOL
42	42.6	PRIMARY SCHOOL
43	23.1	PRIMARY SCHOOL
44	30.4	PRIMARY SCHOOL
45	23.7	PRIMARY SCHOOL
46	33.8	PRIMARY SCHOOL
47	25.2	PRIMARY SCHOOL
48	41.9	PRIMARY SCHOOL
49	20.6	PRIMARY SCHOOL

Since both ends of the CI are negative, we are 95% sure that $\mu_1 - \mu_2$ is negative. Thus, we are 95% sure that the population mean of absenteeism of high school graduates is $\mu 1$ smaller than the average of $\mu 2$ of the time of absence of workers with primary education.

Since the mean time of absence from work of high school graduates in the population is smaller than that of workers who are primary school graduates, there is a difference between the population means.

We're 95% sure it's between −28.7 and −21.8. Thus, the mean time of absenteeism of the high school graduate population is considerably smaller than the mean time for loafing of the population who graduated from primary school.

When both extremes of the CI $\mu_1 - \mu_2$ are negative, such as (−28.7; −21.8), we are fairly confident that μ_1 is smaller than μ_2. If both extremes are positive, such as (8.9; 10.5), we are fairly certain that μ_1 is greater than μ_2. If the lower bound is negative and the upper bound is positive (−3.79; 2.25), we cannot be sure that μ_1 is not equal to μ_2 since it is included in the "0" CI. Because the null hypothesis is established as "H_0: $\mu_1 - \mu_2 = 0$", if "0" is included in the CI, H_0 is accepted and μ_1 can be equal to $\mu 2$.

Table 6.10. Confidence Interval of the Data on Absence of Workers with High School and Primary School Graduates.

Group Statistics

Group		*N*	Mean	Std. Deviation	Std. Error Mean
Time	Skilled unskilled	29	5.631	3.6488	0.6776
		20	30.855	6.9134	1.5459

Independent Samples Test

		Levene's test for Equality of variances		*t*-Test for Equality of Means					95% Confidence Interval of the difference	
		F	Sig.	*t*	df	Sig. (2-tailed)	Mean difference	Std. Error difference	Lower	Upper
Time	Equal variances assumed	8.329	0.006	−16.623	47	0	−25.224	1.5174	−28.277	−22.171
	Equal variances not assumed			−14.944	26.342	0	−25.224	1.6879	−28.691	−21.757

6.5.3 CI for the Difference in Population Means in Matched Samples

Not all comparisons between population means are made on independent samples. "Before-after" designs are also used, in which pretreatment and post-treatment comparisons are made in health research and pre-education and posteducation comparisons in business research. In this case, the data obtained are dependent.

Two co-samples are converted into a difference sample to obtain a matched CI for $\mu_1 - \mu_2$. If the observations for the first sample are denoted by X_{11} and the observations for the second sample by X_{21}, the CI can be calculated by considering the difference for each partner.

The CI is interpreted as before. If the 95% confidence level is chosen, 95% of the possible samples give CIs containing $\mu_1 - \mu_2$. 5% of samples give CIs that do not include $\mu_1 - \mu_2$. For this reason, 95% of the calculated CIs include $\mu_1 - \mu_2$.

CIs for paired samples are based on the following assumptions:

- **Random Selection of Differences:** Differences do not need to be randomly selected, as long as the sample selection is not biased. However, obtaining a random sample provides the opportunity to generalize the results obtained from the sample to the population.
- **Paired Samples:** If the samples are not matched, the matched CI for μ_1 to μ_2 cannot be obtained.
- **Independent Differences**: Knowing one difference value should not give an idea about the other difference value. If the differences are not independent, a matched CI for $\mu_1 - \mu_2$ cannot be obtained.
- **Selecting Differences from the Normal Population:** Ideally, differences should come from the normal population. If the population of differences is not normal and the number of differences is large enough to remove skewness, a matched CI for $\mu_1 - \mu_2$ can be obtained.

A matched CI should not be calculated using a data set that consists of several values and is very skewed.

In one study, the effect of technical training given to workers in a factory on the time that workers to manufacture a part was evaluated. The production time of the relevant part of 14 workers before giving training to the workers and the time of manufacture of the same part by the same workers after two weeks of training are given in Table 6.11.

Two samples were matched. Because both quantities are taken from the same worker. Can one obtain a CI for the difference between the population mean fabrication time before technical training and the population mean fabrication time after technical training? The populations here are theoretical populations and have a distribution similar to the manufacturing times in the samples.

In order to obtain the differences between before and after in Table 6.12 from SPSS, "**Transform/Compute/Target variable(differences)/Beforetraining [click minus (−) on the calculator] Aftertraining/OK**" commands are used.

Table 6.11. Production Times Before and After Technical Training (min).

Worker No	Before Technical Training	After Technical Training	Differences (Before-After)
1	158	150	8
2	162	122	40
3	138	125	13
4	191	164	27
5	148	138	10
6	172	134	38
7	156	114	42
8	197	199	−2
9	162	122	40
10	234	222	12
11	172	141	31
12	127	136	−9
13	183	132	51
14	195	193	2
Ort + ss	171.1 + 27.6	149.4 + 33.0	21.6 + 19.0

Table 6.12. Entering Production Times Before and After Training Into SPSS.

	Before Training	After Training	Differences
1	158	150	8
2	162	122	40
3	138	125	13
4	191	164	27
5	148	138	10
6	172	134	38
7	156	114	42
8	197	199	−2
9	162	122	40
10	234	222	12
11	172	141	31
12	127	136	−9
13	183	132	51
14	195	193	2

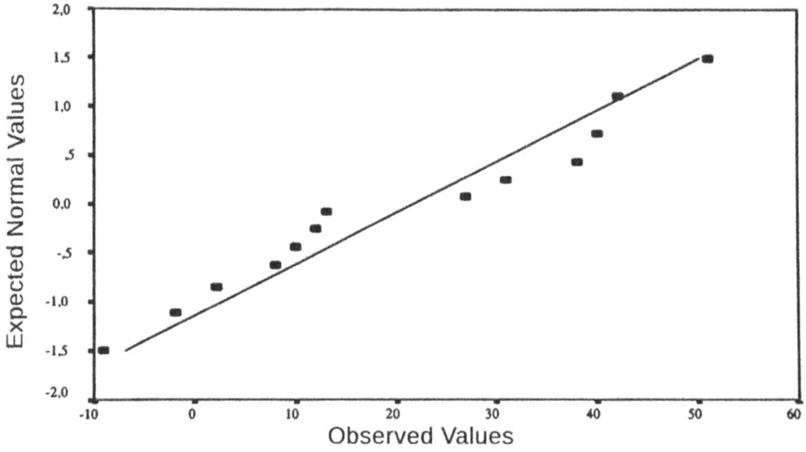

Fig. 6.5. Normal Distribution Plot of Observed and Expected Values for Differences.

The differences, although not random, appear to be independent of each other. Because the difference in one worker gives no idea for the difference in the other worker. Regarding the differences, the "normal distribution plot", which is a graphic representation of the observed and expected values of each data in the distribution, is given in Fig. 6.5. To obtain this chart, the commands "**Analyze/Descriptive Statistics/Explore/Dependent List (Differences)/Display/Plots/Plots/Normality plots with tests/Continue/OK**" are used. Since all the manufacturing time differences are not collected around a straight line, a normal distribution cannot be mentioned. However, the sample selected is large enough to compensate for the slight abnormality.

Thus, since the data are suitable for calculating the CI in paired samples, the CI can be calculated for $\mu_1 - \mu_2$. The data in Table 6.11 are entered into SPSS as seen in Table 6.12. Then, to obtain the 90% confidence interval in paired samples, the following SPSS commands are used: **"Analyze/Compare Means/Paired-Samples T Test/Current Selections/Variable 1 (before training)/Variable 2 (after training)/Paired Variables/Options/Confidence Interval (90)/Continue/OK"**, and the output shown in Table 6.13 is obtained.

Since both extremes of the (12.6; 30.7) CI are positive, we are 90% sure that the population mean fabrication time before technical training is greater than the population mean fabrication time after technical training. This CI can be interpreted as:

We are 90% sure that the population mean of manufacturing time before technical education is greater than the population mean of manufacturing time after technical education, and the difference between population averages is

Table 6.13. *t*-Test Results and Confidence Interval of Manufacturing Times Before and After Technical Training.

Paired Samples Statistics

		Mean	*N*	Std. Deviation	Std. Error Mean
Pair 1	Before training	171.0714	14	27.5638	7.3667
	After training	149.4286	14	32.9515	8.8067

Paired Samples Correlations

		N	Correlation	Sig.
Pair 1	Before training After training	14	0.817	0

Paired Samples Test

		Paired Differences							
					90% Confidence Interval of the Difference				
		Mean	Std. Deviation	Std. Error Mean	Lower	Upper	*t*	df	Sig. (2-tailed)
Pair 1	Before training After training	21.6429	19.0288	5.0856	12.6365	30.6492	4.256	13	0.001

between 12.6 and 30.7. The difference can be as small as 12.6, medium up to 30.7 or in between.

How should one decide whether the difference between the population averages is small, medium, and large? This distinction does not require economic knowledge of the variable being studied. The size of the difference is determined by the size of the data. The fabrication times taken from the impact study of technical training ranged from 122 to 234 minutes, with most of them less than 170 minutes. In such a data set, a population mean difference of 12.6 would be considered small and a difference of 30.6 would be considered a medium difference while a difference of 60 would be considered large.

If the data were distributed between 0 and 10, a difference of 12.6 would be a huge difference. If the data were distributed between 1,000 and 3,000, the difference of 12.6 would be very small. The values in the data should be taken into account when deciding how large the population mean difference is. Evaluations about the magnitude of the difference may vary from person to person. What may be small for one person can be medium for another. Such disagreements are generally unimportant as long as the interpretations in question are not very different from each other.

There is no difference between the CI method and the hypothesis testing method in terms of the result obtained from testing the hypotheses. In both cases, the same result is obtained as to whether there is a difference between the two population means. In this respect, one of these techniques is preferred in some studies while in others, CI for the evaluation of functional significance and hypothesis testing are used together for the evaluation of statistical significance.

Before starting the analysis of the data, the box plots of the data can be evaluated by using the "**Explore**" process in SPSS to detect any outliers or unsuitable data for analysis.

Chapter 7

Hypothesis Testing With One Group

Objectives

- To distinguish between parametric and nonparametric tests.
- To apply hypothesis tests in a group.
- To interpret SPSS outputs in testing.
- To relate the results of the analysis to the research question.

7.1 Introduction

There are parametric and nonparametric hypothesis tests that test hypotheses about population parameters in a group. These include techniques that assess differences in paired samples. Before examining these tests, the distinction between parametric and nonparametric tests should be evaluated.

7.2 Parametric and Nonparametric Tests

When using a **parametric** significance test, at least one population parameter is estimated from the sample statistics. However, some assumptions need to be made in order to make such an estimate. The most important of these is that the variable measured in the selected sample is **normally distributed** within the population to which the findings are planned to be generalized. Another assumption that needs to be made about the population is **the homogeneity of variances.** The sample should be randomly selected from the population, and the selection of one subject should not affect the selection of other subjects.

In **nonparametric** hypothesis testing, no assumption is made about the distribution of the variable in the population. While parametric tests were previously used only for nominal and interval data, they have now become widespread to use parametric tests in the evaluation of ordinal data if the data show a distribution close to normal.

Parametric tests are more powerful and flexible than nonparametric tests. Parametric tests help to examine the effect of many independent variables on the dependent variable and evaluate their interactions with each other.

Statistical Analysis Techniques, Volume 1, 147–174

Published under exclusive licence by Emerald Publishing Limited
doi:10.1108/978-1-80592-341-120261008

Nonparametric techniques are easier to calculate by hand; however, the increasing use of computers has eliminated this advantage. It is appropriate to use nonparametric techniques when a small sample size is used or the data deviate significantly from normality.

7.3 Wald–Wolfowitz Runs Test in One Group

The Wald–Wolfowitz Sequences Runs Test, which can be applied to a group, is a test of randomness. Given a series of observations, the test examines whether an observation value influences the value of the observation that follows it. No influence means that the succession is random. This can also give an idea about independence.

In other words, if there is no influence, it means that the series is independent and random. **In this test, the null hypothesis "The data set is random" is also tested for binary variables.**

7.3.1 Randomness Test for Continuous Variables

Sequences are the order in which observations are taken; the order of values is important when recording the age or gender of customers in a bank queue. The test essentially examines whether there is anything unusual about the occurrence of events. For example, if we assume that any cut-off point (or calculated arithmetic mean) for the age of customers in a bank queue, which is a continuous variable, is 50, there will be formed five sequences as stated below:

46 58 35 22 55 68 70 14 30 31 90 60 58 52

The total number of arrays is an indicator of randomness. Too few arrays or too many arrays imply dependence between observations. The Wald–Wolfowitz runs test transforms the total number of sequences into a Z statistic with an approximately normal distribution.

For the array test to be applied, the variable must be binary (dichotomous). When the arithmetic mean is given as the cut-off point for the continuous variable age in Table 3.8, there are 69 cases below the mean and 44 cases above the mean. In order to test the randomness hypothesis, the output in Table 7.1 is obtained by using the **"Analyze/Non-parametric Tests/Legacy Dialog/Runs/Run Test Variable List(age)/Cut point(Mean)/OK"** commands to apply the sequence test to the variable in question.

Since the observed significance level is very small (0.00005), the null hypothesis of randomness is rejected. In this case, it can be stated that the data were not obtained randomly. However, for practical purposes, the data can be accepted as randomized data, and statistical analyses can be performed using the data in question.

Table 7.1. Array Test Results of Age Data.

Runs Test	
	Age
Test value[a]	47.6283
Cases < Test value	69
Cases >= Test value	44
Total cases	113
Number of runs	2
z	−10.484
Asymp. Sig. (2-tailed)	0

[a]Mean.

7.3.2 Randomness Test for Discrete Variables

As an example of a discrete variable, when a coin is tossed 15 times, heads (1) and tails (2) are determined.

The sequence is a row of similar observations, and the results obtained when a coin is tossed 15 times are as follows:

HHH T HHHH TTTTTTT

There are four sequences in this series. These are HHH, T, HHHH, and TTTTTTT. The number of sequences is a measure of randomness. Too few or too many sequences imply dependence between observations. There is no other requirement for the Wald-Wolfowitz test to be applied to a group, except that the variable to be tested must be a dichotomous outcome.

After entering the data on coin toss into SPSS as shown in Table 7.2, the computer output in Table 7.3 is obtained by using the commands: **"Analyze/Nonparametric Tests/Legacy Dialog/Runs/Run Test Variable List(money)/Cut Point/Custom(2)/OK"**. A cut point is set to determine the number of runs. The normal setting for this test is the median.

Since the observed significance level $p = 0.033$ is smaller than the specified α (0.05), the "randomness" hypothesis is rejected. In this case, the arrival of H (or T) in this data set affects what comes next.

The cut-off point can be set by the researcher, as in the discrete variable above (custom "2"), or **it can be chosen as the arithmetic mean, as well as the median and the mode, as in the continuous variable.**

Table 7.2. Entering the Coin Toss Data Into SPSS.

Money	
1	H
2	H
3	H
4	T
5	H
6	H
7	H
8	H
9	T
10	T
11	T
12	T
13	T
14	T
15	T

Table 7.3. Array Test Result of Coin Toss Data.

Run Test 2	
	Money
Test values	2
Total cases	15
Number of runs	4
z	−2.136
Asymp. Sig. (2-tailed)	0.033
User-specified	

7.4 Kolmogorov–Smirnov Goodness-of-Fit Test in One Group

Kolmogorov–Smirnov Goodness-of-Fit Test in a Group is used to determine how well a random sample fits a given distribution (uniform, normal, or

Poisson). By using this test, one can determine whether a series is normally distributed.

"Kolmogorov-Smirnov (K-S) Goodness-of-Fit Test in One Group" can be used instead of **"Chi-Square Goodness-of-Fit Test in One Group",** especially in very small samples where the chi-square test cannot be applied, or in cases where, to apply the chi-square, one of the expected frequencies in the chi-square goodness-of-fit test is less than 1 or more than 20% of the cells have an expected frequency less than 5 and the frequencies must be combined.

When "$p < 0.05$" is found in relation to normality tests, especially when the number of units is high, the data are not normally distributed, and sometimes a wrong conclusion may be reached. In this respect, graphical methods may be preferred to hypothesis testing or used together for confirmation when deciding whether a distribution is normal, especially when the data are large.

As expected, when the age variable data consisting of 113 subjects as described in the previous sections are used, it is seen in the output given in Table 7.4, obtained by using the **"Analyze/Nonparametric Tests/1-Sample K-S/ Test Variable (age)/Test Distribution/Normal/OK"** commands, that the data are not distributed "standard normal" [$P(0.007) < 0.05$]. However, contrary to the Kolmogorov–Smirnov test, it is possible to see from the **"Stem and Leaf Plot"** in Fig. 7.1 that the data are distributed close to normal.

On the other hand, when the small data set given in Table 7.5, consisting of 10 subjects, is used, it can be stated that the data in question has a normal distribution since "$p = (0.959) > 0.05$" as seen in Table 7.6. However, the stem and leaf plot of these data in Fig. 7.2 actually shows a slight skewness compared to the age data.

Table 7.4. Kolmogorov–Smirnov Test Results of Age Data.

One-Sample Kolmogorov–Smirnov Test		
		Age
N		113
Normal parameters[a,b]	Mean	47.6283
	Std, deviation	10.1473
Most extreme	Absolute	0.158
Differences	Positive	0.158
	Negative	−0.074
Kolmogorov–Smirnov *Z*		1.679
Asymp, sig. (2-tailed)		0.007

[a]Test distribution is Normal.
[b]Calculated from data.

```
AGE Stem-and-Leaf

Frequency  Stem & Leaf
    1,00     2.9
    6,00     3 . 002344
   12,00     3 . 566778899999
   31,00     4. 0000112222222222222333333444444
   30,00     4. 555555666667777777888888889999
   11,00     5. 00012333444
    7,00     5 . 6667789
    6,00     6. 000123
    1,00     6. 6
    8,00 Extremes    (>=69)

Stem width:   10,00
Each leaf:     1 case(s)
```

Fig. 7.1. Stem and Leaf Plot of Age Data.

Table 7.5. Seniority Data of 10-Year Employees Entered Into SPSS.

	Seniority
1	8
2	5
3	7
4	9
5	7
6	6
7	5
8	3
9	4
10	4

7.5 Binomial Test

A **binomial test** is used to test the null hypothesis that the data "come from a binomial distribution with a probability of being in the first two categories."

The binomial distribution is the sampling distribution of observed proportions in random samples drawn from a population with two categories. This test investigates whether the proportions or frequencies observed in the sample are taken from a population with a certain p-value.

The binomial test measures the **"hypothesis that the probability of a given outcome is equal to a desired number"**. For example, if a coin is tossed a certain number of times in a row, it is tested whether the coin is fraudulent or not,

Table 7.6. Kolmogorov–Smirnov Test Results of Seniority Data of 10-Year Employees.

One-Sample Kolmogorov–Smirnov Test		
		Seniority
N		10
Normal parameters[a,b]	Mean	5.8
	Std. Deviation	1.9322
Most extreme	Absolute	0.161
Differences	Positive	0.161
	Negative	−0.133
Kolmogorov–Smirnov *Z*		0.508
Asymp. Sig. (2-tailed)		0.959

[a]Test distribution is Normal.
[b]Normal Calculated from data.

```
SENIORITY Stem-and-Leaf Plot

Frequency  Stem & Leaf
  1,00      0. 3
  4,00      0. 4455
  3,00      0. 677
  2,00      0. 89

Stem width:   10,00
Each leaf:    1 case(s)
```

Fig. 7.2. Stem and Leaf Plot of Seniority Data of 10-Year Employees.

depending on whether it lands heads or tails. Let's assume that the coin in question is tossed 20 times in a row and the following result is obtained : 1 = heads and 0 = tails.

1 0 0 1 1 1 1 1 1 0 1 1 1 1 0 1 1 0 1 1

The hypothesis here is that "the probability of heads or tails is equal to 1/2". After entering the data into SPSS as shown in Table 7.7, the command **"Analyze/ Nonparametric Tests/Legacy Dialogs/Binomial/Test Variable List(money)/Test**

proportion(0,50)/OK" is selected to obtain the output shown in Table 7.8. For the first value (0), the test proportion of cases is taken as 0.50(1/2). The observed proportion is 0.25.

You may access the "Binomial Test" video by scanning the QR code:

Table 7.7. Entering the Coin Toss Experiment Data Into SPSS.

	Money
1	1
2	0
3	0
4	1
5	1
6	1
7	1
8	1
9	1
10	0
11	1
12	1
13	1
14	1

Table 7.7. *(Continued)*

	Money
15	0
16	1
17	1
18	0
19	1
20	1

Table 7.8. Binomial Test Results of Coin Toss Data.

Binomial Test						
		Category	***N***	**Observed Pron.**	**Test Prop.**	**Exact Sig. (2-tailed)**
MONEY	Group 1	1	15	0.75	0.5	0.041
	Group 2	0	5	0.25		
	Total		20	1		

When the significance level is 0.05, the null hypothesis is rejected. Thus, it is concluded that p is not equal to 1/2; hence, the money may be rigged.

7.6 Chi-Square Test in One Group

Once the data is classified, the **Chi-Square Test in a Group (Hypothesis Test of Proportions of Two or More Populations)** can be applied to test whether the frequency distribution is evenly or equally likely to be distributed across categories. This test is also used to determine whether two or more percentages falling into categories are identical.

"Chi-Square Test in a Group" or **"Chi-Square Test of Hypothesized Proportions"** is always a two-tailed test, and a one-tailed alternative hypothesis cannot be used. To apply the chi-square test in a group, the following assumptions must be met:

- **Random Sampling:** If the sample is unbiased, random sampling is not necessary.

- **Frequency Data:** The data should be frequency data.
- **Independent Observations:** A Chi-Square Test cannot be applied to a group unless the independence criterion is met.
- **Completely Independent Categories Containing All Observations:** If the categories overlap or do not contain all data, the Chi-Square Test in a Group cannot be applied. No observation should be included in more than one category. The categories "female" and "male" are completely independent categories because a subject cannot be both male and female. However, the categories of "being a senior manager", "being a family head", and "being a father" are not completely independent from each other because a man can have more than one status.
- **Expected Frequencies of Sufficient Size:** The Chi-Square Test in a Group works best when **the expected frequencies** are relatively large. For this purpose, the following rough rule can be applied: *No expected frequency should be less than 1. Also, no more than 2% of the expected frequencies should be less than 5. If this is not possible, categories can sometimes be combined to increase the expected frequencies. No assumptions are made about* ***the observed frequencies.***

In order to determine how the occupational accidents occurring in the K enterprise, which works 7 days a week, are distributed over the days of the week, the days of the week on which 100 accidents occurred were obtained from the records of the enterprise. Let's apply the **"Chi-Square Test in a Group"** using these data.

These data were entered into SPSS using the commands **"Variable View/Name (accident)/Label (Distribution of occupational accidents by days of the week)/ Values/Value Labels/Value (1,...,7)/Value Label(Sunday,...,Saturday)/OK"** as shown in Table 7.9. When the data is optionally displayed as text or numbers, **"View/Value Labels"** commands are used.

In order to apply the Chi-Square Test in a Group, the data must be categorized. In this respect, the data in Table 7.9 were first classified.

The distribution of the number of occupational accidents according to days can be classified as shown in Table 7.10 after sorting by using the **"Data/Sort Cases/Sortby (accident) / Sort Order/Ascending/OK"** commands. If frequencies are entered into SPSS, the variable in question must be weighted using the **"Data/ Weight cases"** commands.

Before applying the Chi-Square Test in a Group, let us consider the above assumptions with respect to the accident data. Random sampling was not used, but this is not necessary as long as the selection is not biased. Independence is valid for the data set in question because the day of one accident does not give an idea about the other. The days of the week are independent of each other and cover all accidents.

Before evaluating the expected frequencies of the data, let us formulate the hypotheses. Here, the null hypothesis can be established as follows since it is investigated whether **"the accident rates for each day of the week are equal (100/7 = 14.29)"**; in other words, whether **"the expected frequencies are equal"**:

Table 7.9. Entering the Data on the Days of Occupational Accidents Into SPSS.

	Accident
1	SUNDAY
2	TUESDAY
3	TUESDAY
4	MONDAY
5	WEDNESDAY
6	THURSDAY
7	TUESDAY
8	FRIDAY
9	SATURDAY
10	FRIDAY
11	SATURDAY
12	THURSDAY
13	WEDNESDAY
14	TUESDAY
15	WEDNESDAY
16	MONDAY
17	SUNDAY
18	SUNDAY
19	MONDAY
20	TUESDAY
21	WEDNESDAY
22	THURSDAY

H_0: $p_1 = p_2 = p_3 = p_4 = p_5 = p_6 = p_7 = 14.29$.

or

H_0: There is no statistically significant difference between the days of the week in terms of the number of accidents.

or

H_0: The number of accidents is evenly distributed across the days of the week.

Table 7.10. Distribution of Work Accidents by Days of the Week.

Days	Frequency
SUNDAY	10
MONDAY	13
TUESDAY	21
WEDNESDAY	13
THURSDAY	12
FRIDAY	17
SATURDAY	14
TOTAL	100

The alternative hypothesis can be formulated as follows:

H_1: At least one of the hypothesized population proportions is false.

or

H_1: In terms of the number of accidents, there is a statistically significant difference between the days of the week.

or

H_1: The number of accidents is not evenly distributed across the days of the week.

Since p_i is the percentage of the population for category i, p_{io} is the **hypothesized** percentage of the population for category i, and n is the total number of observations, the expected value of category i, EI, can be calculated as follows:

$$E_i = n \times p_{i0}$$

Hence, since the expected frequencies of the accident data are all equal, the expected frequencies are found as follows:

$$100 \times 0.1429 = 14.29$$

Here, since the expected frequencies are also large enough, all assumptions are met and the **"Chi-Square Goodness of Fit Test in a Group"** can be applied. The expected frequencies can also be read directly from the SPSS output in Table 7.11 without the need for manual calculation.

Table 7.11. Chi-Square Test Results of the Distribution of Work Accidents by Days of the Week.

	ACCIDENT		
	Observed N	**Expected N**	**Residual**
SUNDAY	10	14.3	−4.3
MONDAY	13	14.3	−1.3
TUESDAY	21	14.3	6.7
WEDNESDAY	13	14.3	−1.3
THURSDAY	12	14.3	−2.3
FRIDAY	17	14.3	2.7
SATURDAY	14	14.3	−0.3
Total	100		

Test Statistics

	ACCIDENT
Chi-Square[a]	5.56
df	6
Asymp. Sig.	0.474

[a]0 cells (0.0%) have expected frequencies less than 5. The minimum expected cell frequency is 14.3.

In order to perform the Chi-Square Test in a Group using the data in question, the output in Table 7.11 is obtained by using the **"Analyze/Nonparametric Tests/Legacy Dialogs/Chi-Square/Chi-Square Test Variable List:(accident)/OK"** commands in SPSS.

The Chi-Square Test in a Group, which tests the null hypothesis that "Each day of the week has the same risk of accidents" or "Accidents are evenly distributed across the days of the week," requires the above-mentioned assumptions to be met.

Since the $p = 0.474$ value obtained as a result of the test is greater than the specified α (0.05), the null hypothesis is accepted. Thus, in this example, occupational accidents are evenly distributed across the days of the week, and the conclusion is **"There is no statistically significant difference between the days of the week in terms of occupational accidents."**

7.7 Hypothesis Test for Population Proportion

According to a survey conducted among 32 people working at XY LTD., 34% of the workers in the food department of the company are satisfied with their work environment. Let us assume that a manager believes that the population proportion of satisfaction with this work environment is much higher, say 60%. Does the data show that the workers' satisfaction with their work environment is not equal to 60%?

Initially, without any statistical evaluation, it can be said that the sample rate of 34% is far from the manager's claim of 60%. However, without a statistical test, it would be useless and a waste of time for researchers to discuss these issues.

Hypothesis testing on the population proportion is based on the following assumptions about the data, as in the calculation of the confidence interval for the population proportion.

- **Random Sampling:** Although random sampling is preferred, a Z Test in a group can also be obtained when the sample is not random. However, the preparation of the sample should not be biased.
- **Independent Observations:** This assumption should not be violated. If observations are not independent, the Z Test for the proportion of the population cannot be calculated.
- **Sufficiently Large Sample:** The closer p_0 or $1 - p_0$ is to 0, the larger the sample required. Conversely, the closer these proportions are to 1, the larger the sample required. As a rough rule of thumb, np_0 and $n\,(1 - p_0)$ should not be smaller than 5.

Except for random sampling, the other assumptions are provided by the data on satisfaction with the environment. Observations are independent, since knowing one worker who is satisfied with the work environment gives no information about whether another worker is satisfied with the work environment. Both np_0 and $n(1 - p_0)$ are greater than 5. Thus, in our example, $np_0 = 32(0.60) = 19.2$, and since $n(1 - p_0) = 32(0.40) = 12.8$, the selected sample is of sufficient size.

In order to conduct a statistical test, the hypothesis to be tested is first determined. The hypothesis to be tested is called **the null hypothesis,** denoted as H_0. In the example of satisfaction with the work environment, the null hypothesis can be expressed as **"The proportion of the population who are satisfied with their work environment is 0.60."** The null hypothesis can be written as follows:

$$H_0: p = 0.60$$

Once the initial hypothesis has been determined, the alternative hypothesis, H_A (or H_1), should be stated. In the example of satisfaction with the work environment, the alternative hypothesis can be stated as follows:

$$H_A: p \neq 0.60$$

The alternative hypothesis stated above is two-tailed, and the one-tailed hypotheses is H_A: $p > 0.60$.

or

H_A: $p < 0.60$ can be stated. However, in this example, a two-tailed hypothesis is considered.

When the null hypothesis is rejected, the alternative hypothesis that the population proportion of those who are satisfied with their work environment is not 0.60 is accepted.

The null hypothesis about the population proportion states that the population proportion is equal to p_0 a certain number. p_0 is determined by the researcher. For the data on satisfaction with the work environment, $p_0 = 0.60$.

To test this null hypothesis, **Z Test in a Group** is used. This test is based on the following one-group Z statistic.

$$z = \frac{p' - p_0}{S_{proportion}}$$

Here, p' is the sample proportion, p_0 is the population proportion, and $s_{proportion}$ can be calculated as follows:

$$S_{proportion} = \frac{\sqrt{p'(1-p')}}{n}$$

As mentioned before, n indicates the sample size. Let's make calculations related to the hypothesis at the 0.01 significance level:

$$S_{proportion} = \frac{\sqrt{(0.34)-(1-0.34)}}{32} = \frac{\sqrt{(0.34)(0.66)}}{32} = 0.084$$

When these values are placed into the Z statistical formula, the following result is obtained:

$$z = \frac{0.34 - 0.64}{0.084} = \frac{-0.26}{0.084} = 3.10$$

Since it is a two-tailed hypothesis, after finding 3.10 in the z column, the probability in the two-tailed probability column corresponding to $z = 3.10$ in the row is determined. This value is the p-value of 0.0019.

How to interpret the p-value? First, 0.0019 is less than the significance level of 0.01, so the null hypothesis is rejected. Using the significance level of 0.01, the data shows a situation contrary to the manager's claim that the population proportion of satisfaction with the work environment is 60%. Second, if the null hypothesis is rejected, the probability of obtaining a Z statistic in a group with an outlier of at least -3.10 is 0.0019. In other words, if the null hypothesis is true, only 0.19% of the possible samples yield a Z statistic with a group with an outlier of at least -3.10.

When a decision is made on the basis of hypothesis testing, we can never know whether the decision is correct or not. Two mistakes can be made here:

- We can reject a null hypothesis that is true.

or

- We can accept a null hypothesis that is not true.

The first error is called a **Type I error,** and the second error is called a **Type II error.** The best thing to do is to reduce the chance of one of these errors occurring. If the null hypothesis is true, the significance level is the probability of rejecting the null hypothesis. Since we set the significance level ourselves, we control the chance of making a **Type I error**. One way to control for a **Type II** error is to choose an appropriate sample size.

If the sample size is fixed, reducing the probability of a **Type I error** increases the probability of a **Type II error.** Conversely, decreasing the probability of a **Type II error** increases the probability of a **Type I error**.

With a constant sample size, the only way to reduce the chance of a **Type I error** is to reject the null hypothesis less frequently. This increases the chance of a **Type II error** occurring. Similarly, when the sample size is fixed, the only way to reduce the chance of a **Type II error** is to reject the null hypothesis more often. This increases the chance of a **Type I error** occurring.

The only way to reduce the probability of one type of error occurring while increasing the probability of another is to increase the sample size. No sample size less than the entire population will reduce these probabilities to 0.

The "confidence interval" of the population proportion p and the **"Z Test in a Group"** are related. If the null hypothesis is accepted at a specified significance level, the confidence interval for p includes p_0. If the null hypothesis is rejected at a specified significance level, the calculated confidence interval for p does not include p_0. Since H_0: $p = 0.60$ is rejected at the 0.01 significance level, the 99% confidence interval for p on the satisfaction with the work environment data does not include 0.60.

Having decided that p is not equal to p_0, we may want to estimate p. The 99% confidence interval for p is (0.12, 0.56) and does not include 0.60. Thus, we are 99% sure that the population proportion of satisfaction with the work environment is between 0.12 and 0.56.

7.8 Hypothesis Test for Population Mean

The **t-Test in One Group** regarding the population mean is based on the following assumptions:

- **Random Sampling:** This assumption is not mandatory as long as the sample is not biased. However, it is possible to generalize the results obtained from the sample for the population by obtaining a random sample.
- **Independent Observations:** If this assumption is violated, a t-Test in One Group cannot be performed for the population mean.
- **Sample Selection from a Normal Population:** If the population is not perfectly normal, a t-Test in One Group can still be obtained for the population mean. The sample size should be selected in sufficient size to compensate for the non-normal population. The sample size increases as you move away from normality. If the data is too far from normality, a t-Test in One Group cannot be applied.
- In a study on the economic life of type A furnaces produced in the MN enterprise, the economic life values (in years) are given in Table 7.12 and were determined from 12 furnaces. The mean of these economic life values is 11.9 years, and the standard deviation is 3.6 years. The competitors of the enterprise claim that the population average economic life of the ovens is 8.4 years. Do the data show any contradictions to the hypothesis that the population average economic life is 8.4 years? Here, the population is similar to the ovens in the sample.

Table 7.12. Average Economic Life of Furnaces Produced in MN Enterprise.

Number of Furnaces	Average Economic Life (year)
1	6.7
2	8
3	13.4
4	12.4
5	14.9
6	6.3
7	16.5
8	13.5
9	12.4
10	16.9
11	9.1
12	13
Average ± SS	11.9 ± 3.6

Is the ***t*-Test in one Group** appropriate for testing the null hypothesis that the population mean of economic life is 8.4? Not necessarily, as long as the data is not biased, although it is not random. Since the economic life of one furnace does not give an idea about the economic life of another furnace, the independence assumption seems to be satisfied. As can be seen in the Stem and Leaf Plot in Fig. 7.3, the population is slightly skewed. However, the sample size is large enough to compensate for this slight skewness. For these reasons, ***t*-Test in one Group** is appropriate for the data in question.

We might want to test the null hypothesis that the population mean μ in the economic life sample is equal to $\mu_0 = 8.4$ as determined by the researcher.

H_0: $\mu = 8.4$ or H_0: $\mu = \mu_0$ .The alternative hypothesis is as follows:
H_A: $\mu \neq 8.4$ or H_A: $\mu \neq \mu_0$

Since there is no reason to exclude "$\mu < 8.4$ or $\mu > 8.4$" from the study, these cases are not neglected by establishing a two-tailed hypothesis here.

In order to test the null hypothesis using **the *t*-Test in One Group**, after entering the data in the SPSS program as shown in Table 7.13, the output in Table 7.14 is obtained when the **"Analyze/Compare Means/One-Sample *t*-Test/ TestVariable(economiclife)/Test Value(S.4)/OK"** commands are selected, respectively.

To test the null hypothesis, a significance level of 0.05 was used. The *p*- value obtained for these data is 0.006. Thus, since $p < 0.05$, the null hypothesis is rejected. Since the *p*-value is less than 0.01, the null hypothesis is also rejected at the 0.01 significance level. If the null hypothesis is true, less than 1% of the possible samples would generate a t-Statistic in One Group with an outlier of at least 3.38.

There is a relationship between the **"*t*-Test in One Group"** and the **"Confidence Interval of the Population Mean in One Group"**. If the null hypothesis is rejected at a given significance level, the confidence interval for the population mean does not contain μ_0 as determined by the researcher. On the other hand, if the null hypothesis is accepted at a certain significance level, the confidence interval for the population mean contains μ_0 as determined by the researcher.

Since we reject the null hypothesis at the 0.05% significance level , we specifically request the calculation of the 95% confidence interval of the population

```
ECONOMICLIFE Stem-and-Leaf-Plot

Frequency Stem & Leaf

  4.00    0. 6689
  6.00    1 . 223334
  2.00    1 . 66

Stem width:   10.00
Each leaf:    1 case(s)
```

Fig. 7.3. Stem and Leaf Plot of Economic Life Data.

Table 7.13. SPSS Entry of Economic Life Spans.

	Economiclife
1	6.7
2	8
3	13.4
4	12.4
5	14.9
6	6.3
7	16.5
8	13.5
9	12.4
10	16.9
11	9.1
12	13

Table 7.14. Results of *t*-Test of Economic Life Spans in One Group.

One-Sample Statistics				
	N	**Mean**	**Std. Deviation**	**Std. Error Mean**
ECONOMICLIFE	12	11.925	3.6071	1.0413

One-Sample Test						
	Test Value – 8.4					
					95% Confidence Interval of the Difference	
	t	**df**	**Sig. (2-tailed)**	**Mean Difference**	**Lower**	**Upper**
ECONOMICLIFE	3.385	11	0.006	3.525	1.2332	5.8168

mean. For this purpose, **"Analyze/DescriptiveStatistics/Explore/DependentList (economiclife)/Display(Statistics)/Statistics/Descriptives/Confidence Interval for Mean(95)/Continue/OK"** is used in SPSS to obtain the SPSS output in Table 7.15.

The 95% confidence interval (9.6; 14.2) does not include the hypothesized population mean of 8.4. Thus, the hypothesis H_0 is rejected. We are 95% sure that the population mean economic life of the furnaces produced in the MN enterprise is between 9.6 and 14.2.

Table 7.15. Confidence Interval of Economic Life Data.

Case Processing Summary

	Cases					
	Valid		Missing		Total	
	N	Percent	*N*	Percent	*N*	Percent
ECONOMICLIFE	12	100.00%	0	0.00%	12	100.00%

Descriptives

			Statistic	Std. Error
ECONOMICLIFE	Mean		11.925	1.0413
	95% Confidence Interval for Mean	Lower Bound	9.6332	
		Upper Bound	14.2168	
	5% Trimmed Mean		11.9611	
	Median		12.7	
	Variance		13.011	
	Std. Deviation		3.6071	
	Minimum		6.3	
	Maximum		16.9	
	Range		10.6	
	Interquartile Range		6.275	
	Skewness		−0.348	0.637
	Kurtosis		−1.065	1.232

7.9 Testing the Population Median in a Group

Since the data set is not normally/non-normally distributed, two parametric tests can be used to test **the Population Median in a Group** for highly skewed data instead of **the *t*-Test in a Group**. **"Wilcoxon Signed Rank Test in One Group"** can be applied if the data are very far from normal and symmetrical. The **"Sign-Test"** is applied if the data are too far from both normal and symmetrical.

7.9.1 Wilcoxon Signed-Rank Test in One Group

In cases where the data are far from normal but symmetrical or close to symmetrical, the nonparametric **"Wilcoxon Signed Rank Test"** is used as an alternative to the parametric **"*t*-Test in One Group".** On the other hand, when the data are far from normal and symmetrical, the nonparametric **"Sign-Test"** is used as an alternative to the **"*t*-Test in One Group".**

While the parametric ***t*-Test in One Group** uses the arithmetic mean in the evaluation, these two alternative nonparametric tests use the median in the evaluation. Since the applications of these two tests in a group are not very common, they are not provided in SPSS, and the manual calculation forms are analyzed.

When there is a sample of size n, the null hypothesis that the median is equal to a number such as m_0 is tested. Here, m_0 is a number determined by the researcher.

H_0: Population median $= m_0$

The two-tailed null hypothesis is as follows:

H_A: Population median $\neq m_0$

In order to apply the Wilcoxon Signed-Rank Test in a group, the following assumptions must be met:

- **Random Sampling:** This is not necessary as long as the sample selection is not biased.
- **Independence:** If observations are not independent, the Wilcoxon Signed-Rank Test cannot be applied.
- **Symmetry of the Population with respect to the Median:** Ideally, a vertical line through the median of the population should divide the graph showing the distribution of the population into two equal parts. In other words, let us assume that the population median is m_0. One would expect half of the observations in the sample to lie above m_0 and the other half below. If the population is approximately symmetric, the Wilcoxon Signed-Rank Test in One Group can still be applied. If the population is far from symmetrical, this test should not be applied.

- Although the symmetry assumption is less important than the normality assumption, it is often neglected in research. The data to which this test is applied are skewed data. If the data are highly skewed, this test should not be applied.

7.9.2 Sample Problem

In the interview conducted with 10 employees before the in-service training, the number of points that the employees complained about regarding the lack of information is given in Table 7.16.

The education manager believes that the population median for the number of complaints about lack of knowledge is 6. Do the data show any indication that the population median is not 6? Here, $m_0 = 6$ and the null hypothesis can be formed as follows:

H_0: Population median = 6

The alternative hypothesis is as follows:

H_A: Population median $\neq$ 6

Since the ***t*-Test in One Group** is more powerful than the Wilcoxon Signed-Rank Test, it should first be investigated whether it is possible to apply it. For this purpose, the Stem and Leaf Plot in Fig. 7.4 can be examined.

Table 7.16. Number of Points of Complaint by Employees Regarding Insufficient Information.

Employee No	Number of Points Complained About
1	4
2	1
3	2
4	1
5	0
6	5
7	4
8	7
9	6
10	3

```
COMPLAINT Stem-and-Leaf Plot

 Frequency    Stem & Leaf

    3,00      0. 011
    2,00      0. 23
    3,00      0. 445
    2,00      0. 67

 Stem width:    10,00
 Each leaf:      1 case(s)
```

Fig. 7.4. Stem and Leaf Plot of Information Deficiency Data.

As can be seen from Fig. 7.4, the Wilcoxon Signed-Rank Test can be applied since the information deficiency data is a data set that is far from normality but close to symmetry with respect to the median, making it unsuitable for the application of the *t*-Test in One Group. For the information deficiency data, to calculate W, first 6 is subtracted from each observation to obtain the following differences:

4–6 = −2	1–6 = −5	2–6 = −4
1–6 = −5	0–6 = −6	5–6 = −1
4–6 = −2	7–6 = 1	6–6 = 0
3–6 = −3		

The nine new nonzero observations can be arranged in increasing absolute value as follows:

−1   1   −2   −2   −3   −4   −5   −5   −6

The ranks given to the new observations, taking into account the absolute value, are as follows:

New observations:	−1	1	−2	−2	−3	−4	−5	−5	−6
Rows:	1.5	1.5	3.5	3.5	5	6	7.5	7.5	9

If there is more than one difference with the same value, the average of their corresponding ordinal numbers becomes the ordinal number of the observations in question. The values −1 and 1 are given the ordinal number 1.5. This is because 1 + 2 = 3/2 = 1.5. The other two numbers with the same value are −2 and −2, and the sequence number is 3 + 4 = 7/2 = 3.5. When the sign of the differences is placed in front of the sequence numbers, the marked sequence is obtained as follows:

−1.5	1.5	−3.5	−3.5	−5	−6	−7.5	−7.5	−9

The row numbers of the rows with plus and minus signs are summed, whichever is less. Since there is one row with a positive sign in our example, the sum of the rows with a positive sign is $W = 1.5$. The number of nonzero differences is $n = 9$, and the table value obtained at the 0.05 significance level is 6. Since the calculated value (1.5) is smaller than the table value (6), the H_0 hypothesis is rejected. Thus, the median of the population is different from what the education manager believes.

7.9.3 Sign Test in One Group

If the data are too far from normality and symmetry, the Sign Test needs to be applied. The only assumption required by the Sign Test is the independence of observations.

In a study, the number of excused leaves taken by employees in a public organization in a month was evaluated. Table 7.17 shows the excused leaves taken by 16 employees in a month.

A manager believes that the population median of excused leave taken is 50 hours/month and wants to test the following hypothesis using the Sign Test:

H_0: Population median = 50

The counter hypothesis is as follows:

H_A: Population median ≠ 50

The assumptions required to apply **the Sign Test in a Group** are the same as for **the Wilcoxon Test in a Group.** The difference here is that the data are far from symmetry. Note in Fig. 7.5 that the data are far from normal and far from symmetry. The independence assumption is valid here because one employee's monthly use of excused leave does not give any information about the other employee's monthly use of excused leave. As the data are far from normal, highly

Table 7.17. Excused Leaves Taken by Employees in a Month.

Employee No	Excused Leaves Taken (hour/month)
1	1.5
2	7.5
3	14
4	8
5	22.5
6	8
7	30
8	48
9	80
10	7.5
11	50
12	4
13	20
14	22.5
15	100
16	15

```
EXCUSEDLEAVE Stem-and-Leaf Plot

Frequency    Stem & Leaf

  6,00       0 . 147788
  2,00       1.  45
  3,00       2.  022
  1,00       3.  0
  1,00       4.  8
  1,00       5.  0
   ,00       6.
   ,00       7.
  1,00       8.  0
  1,00 Extremes    (>=100)

Stem width:    10,00
Each leaf:     1 case(s)
```

Fig. 7.5. Stem and Leaf Plot of Data on Excused Leave.

skewed, and not symmetrical, the more powerful tests **"*t*-Test in One Group"** and **"Wilcoxon Signed Rank Test One Group"** cannot be applied. In this case, **"Sign Test in One Group"** can be applied.

By subtracting 50 from each value in Table 7.17, the new observation values are found as follows:

−48.5	−42.5	−36.0	−42.0	−27.5	−42.0
−20.0	−2.0	30.0	−42.5	0.0	−46.0
−30.0	−27.5	50.0	−35.0		

Since there are few positive observations, nonzero positive differences are counted. Here, $s = 2$. Since the number of subjects in our example is $n = 16$ and $s = 2$, the table value shows $p = 0.002$ at the 0.05 significance level. Since $p < 0.05$, the H_0 hypothesis is rejected. Therefore, it can be stated that the population median of monthly excused leave is different from 50 hours.

7.10 Chi-Square Goodness-of-Fit Test in a Group

The Chi-Square Goodness-of-Fit Test in a Group can be used to test whether the sample comes from a population with a particular theoretical distribution.

The Chi-Square Goodness-of-Fit Test can be used to test whether the frequency distributions in a group conform to binomial, Poisson, normal, uniform, and other theoretical distributions; Hardy-Weinberg and Mendelian probabilities; or any postexperimental probability distributions.

However, SPSS uses the Chi-Square Test in one Group to test whether the data are evenly distributed into categories. **Chi-Square Goodness-of-Fit Test in One Group**, which tests whether frequency distributions fit a theoretical distribution, is not used in SPSS but is replaced by the **Kolmogorov–Smirnov Test in One Group.**

7.11 *p*-Value Stated in the Research Results

After analyzing the data with statistical tests, a *p*-value is obtained. The *p*-value is the probability of obtaining the research results by chance when the null hypothesis is true. When the *p*-value is less than the specified α, the null hypothesis is rejected in favor of the alternative hypothesis.

"Non-significant" results when the *p*-value is greater than α do not imply that there is no relationship in the population. It only means that the observed association in the sample is smaller than the association that could occur by chance alone. For example, in one study, it was found that students who stayed at home attended classes twice as much as those who stayed in dormitories. However, $p = 0.09$ was found. Although this implies that there is no relationship between those who stay at home and those who stay in dormitories in the population, there is a 9% chance of finding such a relationship due to random sampling error.

If the significance level is set at 0.05, it is concluded that the relationship in the sample is "not statistically significant". However, if the researcher sets the significance level at 0.10, "The results indicate a significant relationship ($p < 0.10$)." A better choice is that "Although the results imply a relationship, it is not statistically significant ($p = 0.09$)".

In research, after the results are stated, notations such as $p < 0.05$ are encountered. This is an expression of the probability of the observed difference occurring due to chance. It also means that the probability of seeing an atypical result is less than 0.05. In other words, out of 100 people, fewer than five people, or 5%, may have an atypical outcome.

In the majority of studies, the significance level α is taken as 0.05. This means that there is a one in 20 chance that the researcher concludes that there is a difference when there is not. It also means that one in 20 of the published studies with a "significant difference" is "wrong".

***p*-values are sometimes misinterpreted. The most common of these is "the probability that the null hypothesis is true". Since population parameters are fixed numbers, the null hypothesis about the population parameter is either true or false. If true, the probability that the null hypothesis is true is 1. If false, the probability that the null hypothesis is true is 0.**

The confidence interval provides more information than the *p*-value. This is because a confidence interval equals a significance test for all values of the parameter, not just one value.

7.12 Functional Significance in Contrast to Statistical Significance

A rejection of the null hypothesis indicates that the hypothesis test is statistically significant. However, statistical significance is often confused with practical significance. No matter how small the *p*-value, a statistically significant test does not guarantee that the results have any practical significance. For example, let us assume that $p = 0.0002$ means that the population mean of error-making by employees who did not receive in-service training is greater than the population mean of error-making by employees who received in-service training.

As a result of the hypothesis test, after it is determined that the population mean of making mistakes of those who did not receive in-service training is greater than that of those who received in-service training, the confidence interval can be used to determine the importance of the training. If the 99% confidence interval of the difference between the population means of making mistakes of the employees is between 1 mistake and 3 mistakes, there is no functional importance of this training when the situation of eliminating mistakes of in-service training is taken into consideration.

If these results are published as "in-service training significantly reduces the average error-making rate of employees", readers will be misled into thinking that in-service training has a large effect on the average error-elimination rate.

For this reason, researchers should avoid statements such as **"The difference between the means is significant"** or **"The mean is significantly different from 0"**. Instead, the results should be stated as follows:

> It is concluded that the population mean of error making of employees who received in-service training is not equal to the population mean of error making of employees who did not receive in-service training.

or

> The null hypothesis that the population mean difference is zero is rejected.

7.13 Summarizing Statistical Results for Publication Purposes

Many researchers have difficulties when summarizing statistical results in scientific publications. This is not surprising because most statistical textbooks do not specify appropriate ways to explain statistical results. In this section, some guidelines for explaining statistical results will be presented, taking into account common errors encountered when summarizing statistical results.

The following points can be used to summarize statistical results correctly:

- The statistical process used should be specified. If more than one method is used, make it clear which method was used to obtain which result.
- If groups are compared, state clearly what is being compared (means, percentages, medians, etc.).
- Where possible, state the p-value calculated. The use of computers has made it very easy to find p-values.
- When an assessment of economic significance is to be made, appropriate statistics such as confidence intervals, squared correlation coefficients, etc. should be used.
- If the results are not found to be significant, provide an explanation of the strength of your statistical method where possible.
- There are two reasons for not rejecting the null hypothesis:
- The null hypothesis is actually true or close to true.
- The null hypothesis is false, but the study failed to infer this.

The inclusion of power calculations in the study is important for readers to examine whether the study had a chance to reject the false null hypothesis.

Chapter 8

Hypothesis Tests Applied in Two Groups

Objectives

- To evaluate the parametric tests applied in two groups.
- To evaluate nonparametric tests applied in two groups.

8.1 Wald–Wolfowitz Runs Test in Independent Two Groups

The Wald–Wolfowitz Sequences Test in Two Groups can be used to test the hypothesis that "two samples come from populations with the same distribution." To perform this test, the values of the two samples are combined and ordered. Too few rows imply that the two populations have different distributions. The hypotheses for this test can be formulated as follows:

H_0: The two samples were taken from populations with the same distribution.
H_A: Two samples were taken from populations with different distributions.

In order to apply this test, the following assumptions must be met:

- **Random Sampling:** As long as there is no bias in sample selection, random sampling is not necessary. However, obtaining a random sample provides the opportunity to generalize the results obtained from the sample to the population.
- **Two Independent Samples:** This test is not applied unless the samples are independent.
- **Independent Observations within Each Sample:** This test cannot be applied if this assumption is violated.

The data in Table 8.1 can be used to apply the **Wald–Wolfowitz Sequences Test for Two Independent Groups**.

After entering the data set in Table 8.2 into SPSS as in Table 8.2, **"Analyze/Nonparametric Tests/2 Independent Samples/Test variable List(profitability)/Grouping Variable(Group)/Define Groups/Group 1(1)/Group 2(2)/Continue/Wald–**

Statistical Analysis Techniques, Volume 1, 175–231

Published under exclusive licence by Emerald Publishing Limited
doi:10.1108/978-1-80592-341-120261009

Table 8.1 Profitability of Two Groups of Investments (TRY).

Group 1	Group 2
58	87
92	199
47	124
126	83
53	115
85	68
	156

Table 8.2. Entering Investment Profitability Data Into SPSS.

	Profitability	Group
1	58	GROUP1
2	92	GROUP1
3	47	GROUP1
4	126	GROUP1
5	53	GROUP1
6	85	GROUP1
7	87	GROUP2
8	199	GROUP2
9	124	GROUP2
10	83	GROUP2
11	115	GROUP2
12	68	GROUP2
13	156	GROUP2

Wolfowitz runs/OK" commands are selected, and the SPSS output in Table 8.3 is obtained.

When Table 8.3 is analyzed, since $p = 0.733$ is obtained, the null hypothesis H_0 is accepted at a significance level of 0.05. In other words, the null hypothesis that **"the two samples come from populations with the same distribution"** is accepted.

Table 8.3 Wald-Wolfowitz Runs Test Results for Return on Investments Data.

Frequencies		
GROUP		**N**
PROFITABILITY	Group 1	6
	Group 2	7
	Total	13

Test Statistics[b,c]			
	Number of runs	**z**	**Exact sig. (1-tailed)**
PROFITABILITY exact number of runs	8[a]	0.606	0.733

[a]No inter-group ties encountered.
[b]Wald–Wolfowitz Test.
[c]Grouping Variable: GROUP.

8.2 Kolmogorov–Smirnov Test in Independent Two Groups

Kolmogorov–Smirnov Test for Two Independent Groups is another technique used to test the null hypothesis that "two samples come from populations with the same distribution." The hypotheses related to this test can be formed as follows:

H_0: The two samples were taken from populations with the same distribution.
H_A: The two samples were taken from populations with different distributions.

In order to apply this test, the following assumptions must be met:

- **Random Sampling:** As long as there is no bias in sample selection, random sampling is not necessary. However, obtaining a random sample provides the opportunity to generalize the results obtained from the sample to the population.
- **Two Independent Samples:** This test is not applied unless the samples are independent.
- **Independent Observations within Each Sample:** If this assumption is violated, this test cannot be applied.

In order to apply Kolmogorov–Smirnov Test for Two Independent Groups, the data in Table 8.1 given in the **Wald–Wolfowitz Runs Test** in **Two Groups** application can be used.

After entering the data set in Table 8.1 into SPSS as given in Table 8.2, **"Analyze/Nonparametric Tests/2 IndependentSamples/Test variable List(profitability)/Grouping Variable(Group)/Define Groups/Group 1(1)/Group2(2)/Continue/Kolmogorov-Smirnov Z/OK"** commands are selected, and the SPSS output in Table 8.4 is obtained.

When Table 8.4 is analyzed, since $p = 0.395$ is obtained, the null hypothesis H_0 is accepted at 0.05 significance level. In other words, the null hypothesis that **"the two samples come from populations with the same distribution"** is accepted.

Table 8.4. Kolmogorov–Smirnov 2-Sample Test Results for Profitability Data.

Frequencies

GROUP		**N**
PROFITABILITY	Group 1	6
	Group 2	7
	Total	13

Test Statistics[a]

		PROFITABILITY
Most Extreme	Absolute	0.5
Differences	Positive	0
+	Negative	−0.5
Kolmogorov–Smirnov Z		0.899
Asymp. Sig. (2-tailed)		0.395

[a]Grouping Variable: GROUP.

8.3 Median Test in Independent Two Groups

The median of a normal distribution is the same as its mean. Thus, if the sample data come from a normal distribution, testing whether the medians are equal is the same as testing whether the means are equal. However, **if the groups do not come from a normal distribution, t-distribution should not be used to test for**

equality of two means in small samples. Also, if the population distributions are skewed, medians are better measures of central tendency. At this stage, it is more appropriate to test the equality of the two medians instead of testing the two means.

Median Test for Two Independent Groups is used to test the hypothesis that two groups come from populations with the same median. **For the median test to be applied**, the data must be measured with at least an ordinal scale.

The following assumptions must be met for the test to be applied:

- **Random Sampling:** As always stated, random sampling is not very necessary unless bias is taken.
- **Independent Samples:** The result of the Median in Two Groups Test cannot be obtained unless the samples are independent.
- **Independent Observations Within Each Sample:** If this assumption is violated, the Two-Group Median Test cannot be applied.

In order to apply **the Median Test for Two Independent Groups** in SPSS, the two groups are combined and the median for the total distribution is calculated. The profitability data of the two investment groups in Table 8.1 can be used as an example.

Let us evaluate the profitability data for the application of the **Median Test in Two Groups.** Since the profitability level in one group does not give an idea about the profitability level of the other group, the observations can be said to be independent. The profitability levels of investments within each group are independent of each other.

In the Median Test for Two Independent Groups, two groups are combined to find the common median by entering Group 1 and Group 2 data in SPPS under the variable "**profitability**" as shown in Table 8.2.

In the profitability example, where it is investigated whether the two samples come from populations with the same median, the null hypothesis can be formed as follows:

H_0: The medians of the profitability levels of investments in Group 1 and Group 2 are the same.

or

H_0: Difference in population medians = 0.

The null hypothesis is formulated as follows:

H_A: The medians of the profitability levels of investments in Group 1 and Group 2 are different.

or

H_A: Difference in population medians $\neq 0$

Table 8.5. Median Test Results of Profitability Data.

Frequencies

		GROUP	
		Group 1	**Group 2**
PROFITABILITY	> Median	2	4
	<= Median	4	3

Test Statistics[a]

	PROFITABILITY
N	13
Median	87
Exact Sig.	0.592

[a]Grouping Variable: GROUP.

To test the null hypothesis, the output in Table 8.5 is obtained by using the **"Analyze/NonparametricTests/Independent Samples/Test VariableList(profitability)/GroupingVariable:(Group)/Define Range/Minimum(1)/Maximum(2)/Continue/Test-Type(Median)/OK"** commands in SPSS.

According to the common median, a **Four-fold Chi-Square** table is created according to whether the corresponding levels of both groups are above or below. The general representation of this table is given in Table 8.6.

When the output in Table 8.5 is analyzed, a classification as in Table 8.6 is observed while obtaining the solution. Observed at 0.05 significance level p = 0.592, the median of the groups is statistically the same. In other words, there is no statistically significant difference between the medians of the profitability levels of Group 1 and Group 2 investments.

8.4 Hypothesis Tests for the Difference Between Two Population Proportions in Independent Samples

For the difference between two proportions in independent observations, two different hypothesis tests can be used that give the same result in different ways:

- Z-Test for Two Groups.
- **Chi-Square Test to Compare the Proportions of Two Independent Populations.**

Let us know evaluate these two hypothesis tests.

Table 8.6. Group Values Above and Below Common Median.

Median Test Results of Profitability Data		
	Groups	
Above and Below Common Median	**Group1**	**Group 2**
Above Common Median	A	B
Below Common Median	C	D

8.4.1 Z-Test in Two Groups

In many studies, two proportions may be compared. For example, the success rate of personnel who have undergone a certain in-service training can be compared with the success rate of personnel who have undergone a different training. In such a case, the null hypothesis can be formed as follows:

H_0: There is no statistically significant difference between the two population proportions.

or

$$H_0 : p_1 = p_2$$

The alternative hypothesis can be stated as follows:

H_A: There is a statistically significant difference between the two population proportions.

or

$$H_A : p_1 \neq p_2$$

The alternative hypothesis stated above is two-tailed and in **Z-Test for Two Groups**, one-tailed hypotheses can be stated as H_A: $P_1 > P_2$ or H_A: $P_1 < P_2$.

To test this null hypothesis, **the Z-Test of the Difference between Two Independent Population Proportions (Z-Test for Two Groups)** is used, which is based on the following formula.

$$z = \frac{p_1' - p_2'}{s_{difference}}$$

p_1' and p_2' are the sample percentages, and $s_{\text{difference}}$ can be calculated as follows:

$$s_{difference} = \frac{\sqrt{p'1(1\text{-}p'1)}}{n_1} + \frac{\sqrt{p'2(1\text{-}p'2)}}{n_2}$$

Here, n_1 and n_2 are the sample sizes.

Z-Test for Two Groups, which is a hypothesis test of the difference between two population proportions, is based on the following assumptions about the data.

- **Random Sampling:** Although random sampling is preferred, the hypothesis test of the difference between population proportions can be obtained when the sample is not random. However, there should be no bias in the preparation of the sample data.
- **Independent Observations:** Observations in one sample should be independent of observations in the other sample. If this assumption is violated, *Z*-Test cannot be calculated for two groups.
- **Independence of Observations within a Sample:** Observations within each sample must be independent. *Z*-Test for Two Groups cannot be performed if this assumption is violated.
- **Sufficient Sample Size:** A sample of 10 subjects is sufficient unless p_1'or p_2' is very close to 0 or 1. The closer p_1' or p_2 is to 0 or 1, the larger the sample needed.

8.4.1.1 Sample Application

Enterprises A and B, which produce consumer goods, have equal market shares. The managers of enterprise A believe that the enterprises are at the forefront in terms of having regular customers. In order to test this, 223 customers of Enterprise A and 262 customers of Enterprise B were selected for the survey. As a result, 56% (125 people) of the customers of Enterprise A and 75% (197 people) of the customers of Enterprise B are regular customers. Accordingly, what can be said about the beliefs of the managers 'of Enterprise A? Can a **Z-Test for Two Groups** be used to test whether the percentages of these two businesses are equal?

Unless there is a relationship between the businesses, the fact that the customers of one business are regular customers is independent of the fact that the customers of the other business are regular customers. Also, since the regular customers in the two groups are independent of each other, the independence assumption is fulfilled. The sample is of sufficient size and nonrandomness is not a major problem. For this reason, the Two Group *Z*-Test can be used.

Using the 0.10 significance level, this test value can be calculated as follows:

$$S_{difference} = \frac{\sqrt{(0.56)(1-0.56)}}{233} + \frac{\sqrt{(0.75)(1-0.75)}}{262}$$

$$S_{difference} = \frac{\sqrt{(0.56)(0.44)}}{233} + \frac{\sqrt{(0.75)(0.25)}}{262}$$

$$= \sqrt{0.0018} = 0.042$$

$$z = \frac{0.56\text{-}0.75}{0.042} = \frac{\text{-}0.19}{0.042} = \text{-}4.52$$

The p-value corresponding to $Z = 4.52$ is 0.0001. Since this value is less than the significance level of 0.10, the null hypothesis is rejected. In fact, since the p-value is very small, it allows the null hypothesis to be rejected at other reasonable significance levels.

If the percentages of the two populations were equal, the probability of obtaining the Z-statistic in the two groups would be less than 0.0001, with an extreme value of at least -4.52. In other words, if the two population percentages are equal, it is very unlikely to obtain results like the one obtained here. If the null hypothesis is true, only the probable samples 0.01% gives Z-statistics in two groups with an extreme value of at least -4.52. Since the data provide evidence against the null hypothesis, it allows its rejection.

There is a relationship between **Z-Test for Two Groups** (Chi-Square Test for Comparison of Two Independent Percentiles) and the confidence interval of p_1 and p_2. If we reject the null hypothesis, at the specified alpha level, the 100% (1-α) confidence interval of p_1 and p_2 does not contain 0. If we accept the null hypothesis, at the specified alpha level, the 100% (1-α) confidence interval of p_1 and p_2 contains 0. The confidence interval result is always consistent with the corresponding **z-test for Two Groups** result. When we reject the null hypothesis, since p_1 and p_2 is not equal to 0, we obtain an interval that estimates p_1 and $p_{2.}$

Since at the 0.10 significance level we reject the null hypothesis, the confidence interval p_1 and p_2 based on these data does not contain 0. Calculating the 90% confidence interval for p_1 and p_2 using the formulation given in the confidence interval section, we obtain the interval (-0.26; -0.12). Since both boundary values of the confidence interval are negative, we are 90% sure that p_1 is smaller than $p_{2.}$

8.4.2 Chi-Square Test to Compare Independent Two Population Proportions

In order to solve the sample problem to which the **Z-Test for Two Groups** is applied with the Chi-Square Test and using SPSS, it is necessary to reconstruct it as frequency data as in Table 8.7. In this case, **"Chi-Square Test for Comparing the Proportions of Two Independent Populations"** will be applied. For this test, let's create the Chi-Square table in Table 8.7, which consists of the frequencies of regular and nonregular customers.

Thus, a data set was created in which the Chi-Square Test design could be used. **Chi-Square Test is always a two-tailed test and one-tailed alternative hypothesis cannot be used. On the other hand, the "Z-Test for Two Groups" used in the solution of the same problem can be a two-tailed test as well as a one-tailed test.**

Since the attendance data are redesigned as frequency data for the Chi-Square Test, the following assumptions about the data must be met in order to apply the **"Chi-Square Test to Compare the Proportions of Two Independent Populations"**:

Table 8.7. Customers of Enterprises and Attendance Data.

	Number of Customers	Attendance		Percentages
		Regular Customers	Irregular Customers	
Enterprise A	223	125	98	0.56(p1)
Enterprise B	262	197	65	0.75(p2)
Total	485	322	163	0.66(p)

- **Random Sampling:** If the sample is not biased, random sampling is not very important.
- **Frequency Data:** Data should be in the form of frequency data. In other words, the subjects in each analyzed situation should be countable. If the data are not normally distributed and parametric test assumptions are violated, categorization may be appropriate.
- **Independent Observations:** The Chi-Square Test cannot be applied to compare two independent proportions unless the independence criterion is met.
- **Completely Independent Row and Column Categories Containing All Observations:** If the categories overlap or do not contain all data, the Chi-Square Test for Comparing Two Independent Proportions cannot be applied. No observation should be included in more than one category.
- **Expected Frequencies of Sufficient Size:** In 2 × 2 Chi-Square tables, no expected frequency should be less than 5. On the other hand, if one of the expected frequencies is less than 5 in a 2 × 2 Chi-Square table, there are other solutions that can be applied. **First,** a larger data set can be used to increase the expected frequencies. **Second**, the "Chi-Square Statistic with Continuity Correction" or "Chi-Square Statistic with Yates Correction", which is often used in the same sense, can be used in a 2 × 2 arrangement. **Third, Fisher's Exact Chi-Square Test** can also be applied if one of the expected frequencies in the 2 × 2 Chi-Square Table is less than 5. The order of preference among the alternatives in practice follows the order of presentation here.

8.4.2.1 SPSS Application Example

Let us consider the above assumptions for the continuity data. No random sampling was done. However, this is not necessary as long as there is no bias. The assumption of independence is valid and the answers of customers of enterprise A do not give an idea about the answers of customers of Enterprise B. The categories of regulars and nonregular and the categories of Business A and Business B are completely independent of each other and contain all observations. Moreover, since the minimum expected frequency is 74.946 from the SPSS output of Table 8.9, **"Chi-Square Test"** can be applied.

The null hypothesis can be formulated as follows:

H_0: The proportion of regular customers of Enterprise A is the same as the proportion of regular customers of Enterprise B.

or

$$H_0 : p_1 = p_2$$

The alternative hypothesis can be formulated as follows:

H_A: The proportion of regular customers of Enterprise A is different from the proportion of regular customers of Enterprise B.

or

$$H_A : p_1 \neq p_2$$

After entering the data into SPSS as shown in Table 8.8, the frequency variable is weighted using the **"Data/Weight Cases/Weight cases by (frequency)OK"** commands.

(Here, 1 is Enterprise A, 2 is Enterprise B; 1 is regular customer, 2 is nonregular customer).

Then, **"Analyze/DescriptiveStatistics/Crosstabs/Row(business)/Column(continuity)/Statistics/Chisquare/Continue/Cells/Counts/Observed/Percentages/Total/Continue/OK"** commands are selected, and the SPSS output in Table 8.9 is obtained. Note that the *p*-value obtained is the same as that obtained with the "Two Group *Z*-Test". Here too, the population proportions were found to be different.

Table 8.8. Entering Data of Customers of Enterprises and Continuity Into SPSS.

	Enterprise	Continuity	Frequency
1	1	1	125
2	1	2	98
3	2	1	197
4	2	2	65

Table 8.9. Chi-Square Test Results of Customers and Continuity Status Data.

ENTERPRISE *REGULARITY Crosstabulation

		CONTINUITY		
		1	**2**	**Total**
ENTERPRISE	1,00 count	125	98	223
	% Of total	25.80%	20.20%	46.00%
	2,00 count	197	65	262
	% Of total	40.60%	13.40%	54.00%
Total	Count	322	163	485
	% Of total	66.40%	33.60%	100.00%

Chi-Square Tests

	Value	**df**	**Asymp. Sig. (2-sided)**	**Exact Sig (2-sided)**	**Exact Sig. (1-sided)**
Pearson Chi-Square[a]	19.772[b]	1	0		
Continuity correction	18.924	1	0		
Likelihood ratio	19.824	1	0		
Fisher's exact test					
Linear-by-linear association	19.731	1	0	0	0
N of valid cases	485				

[a]Computed only for a 2 × 2 table.
[b]0 cells (,0%) have expected count less than 5. The minimum expected count is 74,95.

8.5 Fourfold Chi-Square Test for the Relationship Between Two Variables

Chi-Square is the most commonly used nonparametric test. It is used when the data are categorical. **Chi-Square Test is always a two-tailed test and one-tailed alternative hypothesis cannot be used.**

In order to apply the **"Four-Eyed Chi-Square Correlation Test"**, the following assumptions about the data must be met:

- **Random Sampling:** As long as there is no bias in sample selection, random sampling is not necessary. However, obtaining a random sample allows the results obtained from the sample to be generalized to the population.
- **Frequency Data:** Data should be in the form of frequency data. In other words, the subjects in each analyzed situation should be countable. If the data are not normally distributed and parametric test assumptions are violated, categorization may be appropriate. Creating economically valid categories allows for better interpretation.
- **Independent Observations:** Unless the independence criterion is met, the Four-eyed Chi-Square Correlation Test cannot be applied.
- **Completely Independent Row and Column Categories Containing All Observations:** If the categories overlap or do not contain all data, the Four-eyed Chi-Square Test of Association cannot be applied. No observation should be included in more than one category.
- **Expected Frequencies of Sufficient Size:** The Chi-Square distribution is a continuous distribution. However, if the expected frequency of any cell in a 2 × 2 Chi-Square table is less than 5, the Chi-Square distribution of that analysis becomes very far from the norm. In 2 × 2 Chi-Square tables, no expected frequency should be less than 5 for the Chi-Square Association Test to be applicable. If this is not possible, then this Quadratic Chi-Square Association Test cannot be applied.
- However, there are other solutions that can be applied in such a situation. First, a larger data set can be used to increase the expected frequencies. Second, one can use **the Chi-Square Statistic with Continuity Correction** or **the Yates Correction Chi-Square Statistic,** which is often used in the same sense. Third, in a 2 × 2 Chi-Square table, **the Fisher's Exact Chi-Square Test** can also be applied if one of the expected frequencies is less than 5. The order of preference among the alternatives in practice follows the order given here.

8.5.1 SPSS Application Example

It may be desirable to investigate whether women or men are more successful as managers. In initial tests, after selecting people with similar characteristics for the sample, it was determined whether managers were successful or not depending on gender. These data are collected in the Chi-Square table in Table 8.10. Here, out of the group of 69, 45 male and 24 female managers were considered successful.

Table 8.10. Dataset for Four-fold Chi-Square Analysis.

Gender		
Successful in Management	**Male**	**Female**
No	15	16
Yes	45	24

Let us consider the above assumptions for the achievement data. Random sampling was not used, but this is not essential as long as the sample selection is not biased. The independence assumption is met. Because the success of one manager does not give an idea about the success of another manager. The gender categories are completely independent of each other and cover all success cases. In addition, since the minimum expected frequency is 12.4 in the computer-generated Table 8.12, the **"Four-fold Chi-Square Correlation "** can be applied.

In this example, the null hypothesis can be expressed as there is no relationship between managerial success and gender.

H_0: There is no statistically significant relationship between managerial success and gender

or

H_0: There is no statistically significant relationship between row and column variables

or

H_0: Row and column variables are independent.

The counter hypothesis related to the data in question can be formed as follows:

H_1: There is a statistically significant relationship between managerial success and gender

or

H_1: There is a statistically significant relationship between row and column variables

or

H_1: Row and column variables are dependent.

After entering the data into SPSS as shown in Table 8.11, the data can be displayed as numbers or expressions using **the "View/Value Labels"** commands (Here, 1 No, 2 Yes for success; 1 Male, 2 Female for gender).

Frequency variable "Data/Weight Cases/Weight cases by(frequency)/OK" are weighted using the commands.

Then, after selecting **"Analyze/Descriptive Statistics/Crosstabs/Row(successful)/Column(gender)/Statistics/Chisquare/Nominal(since it is nominal data)/Contingency**

Table 8.11. Entering Success Data Into SPSS.

	Successful	Gender	Frequency
1	NO	MALE	15
2	NO	FEMALE	16
3	YES	MALE	45
4	YES	FEMALE	24

coefficient/Phi/Lambda/Uncertaintycoefficient/Continue/Cells/Counts/Observed/ Expected/Percentages/Row/Column/Total/Continue/OK" commands, the SPSS output in Table 8.12 is obtained.

8.5.2 Evaluation of SPSS Output

Table 8.12 is similar to Table 8.10, with each cell showing observed frequencies, expected frequencies, percentages by rows, columns, and totals respectively.

The table shows Chi-Square values, degrees of freedom, and significance (probability levels). Which of these should be used? Although we want one Chi-Square value, there are four different Chi-Square values and their significance levels. Let us evaluate them.

The **Pearson value** is the result obtained when the calculations are done by hand. In this respect, since the observed significance level of the test is $p = 0.112$, the null hypothesis **"there is no significant relationship between gender and managerial success"** is accepted. Thus, it is concluded that there is no difference between men and women in terms of managerial success.

If the null hypothesis of **"no relationship"** is not rejected in the Chi-Square analysis, the assessment is complete at that point. If the null hypothesis is rejected, further analysis is required to establish the nature of the relationship. To perform such analysis, row percentages or column percentages are evaluated.

In the success example, since the null hypothesis was not rejected, the row or column percentages were not evaluated because the relationship was not detected. However, in the example for the **Multivariate Chi-Square Test** given in Chapter 9, percentages were analyzed.

The continuity correction is also known as the **Yates correction**. In a 2×2 design, when there is an expected frequency of less than 5 in one of the cells, the "Chi-Square statistic with continuity correction" or **"Chi-Square statistic with Yates correction",** which is often used in the same sense, can be used if the survey cannot be renewed by increasing the sample size.

In the output, the Pearson Chi-Square p-value is 0.112 while the p-value of the continuity corrected Chi-Square statistic is 0.171. Thus, applying the correction reduces the power of the analysis. In our example, the Pearson result is used

Table 8.12. Chi-Square Test Results of Success Data.

SUCCESS* GENDER Crosstabulation

			GENDER		
			Male	**Female**	**Total**
SUCCESS	No	Count	45	24	69
		% Within success	65.2%	34.8%	100.0%
		% Within gender	75.0%	60.0%	69.0%
		% Of total	45.0%	24.0%	69.0%
	Yes	Count	15	16	31
		% Within success	48.4%	51.6%	100.0%
		% Within gender	25.0%	40.0%	31.0%
		% Of total	15.0%	16.0%	31.0%
Total		Count	60	40	100
		% Within success	60.0%	40.0%	100.0%
		% Within gender	100.0%	100.0%	100.0%
		% Of total	60.0%	40.0%	100.0%

Chi-Square Tests

	Value	**df**	**Asymptotic significance (2-sided)**	**Exact sig. (2-sided)**	**Exact sig. (1-sided)**
Pearson Chi-Square[a]	2.525	1	0.112		
Continuity correction[b]	1.872	1	0.171		
Likelihood ratio	2.499	1	0.114		
Fisher's Exact test				0.127	0.086
No. of valid cases	100				

[a]0 cells (0.0%) have expected count less than 5. The minimum expected count is 12.40.
[b]Computed only for a 2 × 2 table.

Directional Measures

			Value	Asymptotic standard Error[c]	Approximate T[d]	Approximate Significance
Nominal by Nominal	Lambda	Symmetric	0.014	0.078	0.18	0.857
		Success dependent	0	0	.[e]	.[e]
		Gender dependent	0.025	0.137	0.18	0.857
	Goodman and Kruskal tau	Success dependent	0.025	0.032		0.114[f]
		Gender dependent	0.025	0.032		0.114[f]
	Uncertainty Coefficient	Symmetric	0.019	0.024	0.79	0.114[g]
		Success dependent	0.02	0.025	0.79	0.114[g]
		Gender dependent	0.019	0.023	0.79	0.114[g]

[c]Not assuming the null hypothesis.
[d]Using the asymptotic standard error assuming the null hypothesis.
[e]Cannot be computed because the asymptotic standard error equals zero.
[f]Based on Chi-Square approximation.
[g]Likelihood ratio Chi-Square probability.

Symmetric Measures

		Value	Approximate Significance
Nominal by Nominal	Phi	−0.159	0.112
	Cramer's V	0.159	0.112
	Contingency Coefficient	0.157	0.112
N of valid cases		100	

[h]Not assuming the null hypothesis.
[i]Using the asymptotic standard error assuming the null hypothesis.

because the minimum expected frequency is 12.4. If this value were less than 5, the continuity corrected value would be used.

The likelihood ratio Chi-Square statistic is based on maximum likelihood theory. It is mostly used when fitting models such as structural equation models. When the sample is large, the "likelihood ratio" It is very similar to Pearson statistics. This is also seen in our example.

Although SPSS automatically gives **Mantel Haenszel test for linear association-Fisher's Exact Test Linear-by-Linear Association** when asked for a Chi-Square, it is not suitable for nominal data. This is because this test is based on the relationship between two variables measured by Pearson's correlation coefficient.

The table also includes other statistics appropriate for nominal data. Phi is an estimation method for calculating the correlation coefficient when both variables are dichotomous. It is used to measure the relationship between two variables. **The Phi coefficient is only appropriate when the Chi-Square is significant.**

In our example, Phi should not be used because there is no significant relationship between gender and managerial success as measured by the Chi-Square. When it is appropriate to use it, it is interpreted as a measure of strength of association. In other words, the relationship between these two variables is 0.1589. It helps to interpret the strength of the relationship. It is most appropriate for 2 × 2 tables, where the Phi value varies between 0 and 1.

It is less useful in larger tables as it takes values greater than 1. It is compatible with the Chi-Square statistic and is less sensitive to sample size. It can be used in comparisons between studies.

The contingency coefficient is also used to measure the relationship between variables with two nominal levels. It is a nonparametric technique and not an estimation of the parametric correlation coefficient. It can be used at any table size. However, the coefficient is affected by the number of cells. Its maximum value is 0.707 in 2 × 2 tables and 0.87 in 4 × 4 tables. If it is to be used in comparisons between studies, care should be taken to ensure equal numbers of rows and columns.

Lambda measures the reduction in the estimation error rate as a result of obtaining additional information. In other words, it is the percentage reduction in the prediction error rate of the dependent variable due to the independent variable information. The dependent variable is predicted. For example, in this example, since the success status is known, the gender of the individuals can be predicted. In this case, gender becomes the dependent variable, while achievement becomes the independent variable.

Three different lambdas can be calculated from a given Chi-Square table. The first one uses the column variable as the estimator. In the second, the row variable is used as the estimator. In some cases, if the dependent and independent variables are not explicitly expressed, a symmetric lambda is calculated.

As seen in the SPSS output, a symmetric lambda can be calculated if there is no situation where one variable is dependent (no variable information) and the other variable is independent (variable information). Next, the lambda values calculated when achievement is the dependent variable (knowledge of gender) and when gender is the dependent variable (knowledge of achievement) are given.

As can be seen in the SPSS output, in addition to the symmetric lambda, two nonsymmetric, one-tailed lambdas are given. In our example, when achievement was the dependent variable, the independent variable gender did not contribute to the reduction of the prediction error. Because in this case, the lambda was 0.00000.

On the other hand, if we want to predict the gender of the respondents when the achievement status is known, the error rate is reduced by 2.5%. Because when gender is dependent, lambda is 0.025 in the light of achievement information. Thus, the lambda values change according to the status of the variable chosen as dependent. However, they are not symmetric. Therefore, the first two examples are one-tailed lambda values.

When we do not consider one variable as dependent and the other as independent, in other words, if there is a reciprocal relationship between the variables, symmetric lambda can be calculated. However, when there is a bidirectional relationship, it is necessary to look at the symmetric lambda. In this case, lambda is 0.01408.

Lambda varies between 0 and 1. A value of 0 indicates that having information about the independent variable does not help in reducing the prediction error of the dependent variable. In other words, it means that the independent variable cannot help in predicting the dependent variable. 1 is perfect and indicates that the correct prediction is made. In other words, it means that the independent variable perfectly predicts each category of the dependent variable. Perfection only occurs if the cell in each row has a value greater than zero. If two variables are independent, lambda is 0. However, lambda 0 does not imply statistical independence.

Asymp. Std. Error (ASEI) is the asymptotic standard error and can be used to construct confidence intervals.

Goodman and Kruskal Tau measures the asymmetric relationship in nominal measures. Sometimes, lambda can be 0 even if there is a link between variables. In this case, it is necessary to use the Goodman & Kruskal Tau measure. In our example, whether the dependent variable is achievement or gender, the prediction error is 2.5%.

The uncertainty coefficient measures how much of the uncertainty in the dependent variable is reduced by the knowledge of the independent variable. The coefficient ranges from 0 to 1, with 0 representing complete uncertainty and 1 representing complete certainty.

8.6 Hypothesis Tests for the Difference Between Matched Two Population Proportions

To test the difference between two paired population proportions, it is necessary to use **McNemar Test.** In other words, **McNemar test, which is used to measure the significance of changes, is suitable for "before and after" research designs where each unit is used as its own control.** This test is used to test the effect of an event or practice on individuals.

In the before and after design, the answers obtained by placing the information before in the row and after in the column should be shown as in Table 8.13 in order to apply the McNemar test.

Here, B and C are the cases where the responses do not change, and A and D are the cases where they do. The McNemar test uses a binomial distribution process when there are less than 25 subjects and Chi-Square distribution process when there are 25 or more subjects.

8.6.1 SPSS Application Example

Let us assume that a researcher asks high school students who are going to take university exams whether they consider accountancy as a profession. At the beginning of the research, before the students were informed about accountancy,

Table 8.13. General Table in the Application of the McNemar Test.

	Answers Received After		**Total**
Answers received first	**Yes**	**No**	
Yes	A	B	A + B C + D
No	C	D	
Total	A + C	B + D	A + B + C + D

they were asked whether they considered accountancy as a profession, and 175 of the 200 students answered "**no**" while 25 answered "**yes**".

Then, after the same group of students were informed about the accountancy profession, they were asked again whether they were considering the accountancy profession. After the information was given, 50 male students answered "**yes**" while 150 male students answered "**no**".

As seen in Table 8.14, 30 students who initially said "**no**" now answered "**yes**" while 5 students who initially said "**yes**" later answered "**no**". The other males did not change their opinions. In both cases, 145 male students said "**no**" while the number of those who said "**yes**" in both cases was 20.

In order for the McNemar test to be applied, both "before" and "after" variables must be dichotomous variables with binary outcomes.

In order to apply the **"McNemar test"**, the following assumptions about the data must be met:

Random Sampling: Random sampling is not necessary, as long as the sample selection is not biased. However, obtaining random sampling provides the opportunity to generalize the results obtained from the sample to the population.

Dependent Samples: As long as there is no bias in sample selection, random sampling is not necessary. However, obtaining a random sample provides the possibility of generalizing the results obtained from the sample to the population.

Independence of Subjects in Each Sample: All observations in the first sample should be independent while all observations in the second sample should be independent.

Frequency: The data should be in the form of frequency data. In other words, the subjects in each analyzed situation should be countable.

Hypotheses can be formulated when p_1 is defined as the proportion of the population of students who consider accountancy as a profession before being given information about accountancy and p_2 is defined as the proportion of the population of students who consider accountancy as a profession after being given information about accountancy.

Table 8.14. Students Considering Accountancy as a Profession.

Answers Received Before Information is Provided		**Answers Received After Information is Provided**	
	Yes	**No**	**Total**
No	20	5	25
Yes	30	145	175
Total	50	150	200

The null hypothesis can be formulated as follows:

H_0: There is no statistically significant difference between the population proportion of students who considered accounting as a profession before being given information about accounting and the population proportion of students who considered accounting as a profession after being given information about accounting.

or

$$H_0 : p_1 = p_2$$

or

H_0: Half of the change is in one direction and the other half in the other direction. The change is the same in both directions.

The counter hypothesis can be formulated as follows:

H_A: There is a statistically significant difference between the proportion of the population of students who considered accounting as a profession before being given information about accounting and the proportion of the population of students who considered accounting as a profession after being given information about accounting.

or

$$H_A : p_1 \neq p_2$$

or

H_A: The change in both directions is different.

After entering the accounting data into SPSS as shown in Table 8.15, the data can be displayed as numbers or expressions using the **"View/Value Labels" commands. The frequency variable is weighted using the "Data/Weight Cases/ Weight cases by(frequency)/OK"** commands.

Table 8.15. Entering Accounting Data Into SPSS.

	Before	After	Frequency
1	1.00	1.00	20.00
2	1.00	2.00	5.00
3	2.00	1.00	30.00
4	2.00	2.00	145.00

Then, after selecting the **"Analyze/Nonparametric Tests/2 Related Samples/Variable 1 (Before)/Variable 2 (After)/Test Pair(s) 'Before2After'/Test Type/McNemar/OK"** commands, the SPSS output in Table 8.16 is obtained.

By scanning the QR code, you can access the video "Applying the McNemar Test."

Table 8.16. McNemar Test Results for Accountancy Data.

BEFORE and AFTER		
	AFTER	
BEFORE	**1**	**2**
1	20	5
2	30	145

Test Statistics[b]	
	BEFORE and AFTER
N	200
Chi-Square[a]	16.457
Asymp. Sig.	0

a. McNemar Test.
b. Continuity Corrected.

According to the McNemar test result, $p = 0.00005$ is obtained, and H_0 hypothesis is rejected at 0.05 significance level. Accordingly, there is a statistically significant difference between the population proportion of students who consider accounting as a profession before being given information about accounting and the population proportion of students who consider accounting as a profession after being given information about accounting.

In other words, male students started to think positively about the accounting profession at a significant level after being given information about the accounting profession. The proportion of those who consider accountancy as a profession increased after the information was given.

8.7 Hypothesis Tests for the Difference Between Population Means

Many studies are designed to test the difference between two groups. If done properly, comparing means is very useful in determining the effects of training or productive work.

Means can be compared by testing the null hypothesis in the following form:

$$H_0 : \mu_1 - \mu_2 = d_0$$

Here, d_0 is a number determined by the researcher, like p_0 and μ_0. However, since d_0 is usually taken as 0, the null hypothesis can be written as follows:

$$H_0 : \mu_1 - \mu_2 = 0$$

or

$$H_0 : \mu_1 = \mu_2$$

Here, μ_1 is the mean of the first population and μ_2 is the mean of the second population. The alternative hypothesis can be stated as follows when $d_0 \neq 0$:

$$H_A : \mu_1 \neq \mu_2$$

The one-tailed hypotheses H_A: $\mu_1 < \mu_2$ and H_A: $\mu_1 > \mu_2$ are rarely used. The *t*-Test requires a proportional or interval measurement format. However, as mentioned earlier, the ordinal data set can be treated as an interval measurement and used in the *t*-Test analysis.

The t-Test is commonly used to compare two groups. However, when comparing two groups with proportional or interval data, there is no difference between using the t-Test or one-tailed analysis of variance. The results are mathematically the same. The t-statistic from the *t*-Test is equal to the square root of the F-statistic from the one-tailed analysis of variance. In this case, the relationship expressed in symbols can be shown as follows:

$$T = \sqrt{F} \text{ and } F = t^2$$

Although the ***t*-Test** is easier when done by hand because it requires fewer mathematical operations than the one-tailed analysis of variance, in evaluations using computers, some researchers use analysis of variance for comparisons of two groups. Both ways are correct, and the choice between the techniques is entirely up to the researcher.

Three different methods for testing the null hypothesis used in comparing two groups will be discussed. Although all three methods use a *t*-Test, t-statistics are calculated in different ways. These include,

- Equal-Variance *t*-Test in Two Independent Groups.
- While **Differential-Variance t-Test in Two Independent Groups** requires independent samples.
- **T-Test in Paired Samples**, on the other hand, requires dependent samples.
- In addition, when the data in independent groups are far from normality, **Manu-Whitney Test** is used instead of **t-Test** in independent groups. Similarly, instead of *t*-Test in Paired Samples, **Wilcoxon Signed Rank Test** is used if the data are symmetrical, and **Sign Test in Two Paired Groups** is used if the data are not symmetrical.

The wrong choice of *t*-Test or the wrong choice of nonparametric tests to be applied when the data are far from normality can lead to serious errors. In this respect, one must be careful in choosing the appropriate test.

8.7.1 Equal-Variance t-*Test in Independent Two Groups*

Let us assume that there are two different samples from two populations with mean μ_1 and μ_2, which are normally distributed and have equal variance. The variance of the first population is assumed to be equal to the variance of the second population.

To compare population means, we perform a hypothesis test for the difference in population means μ_1 and μ_2. From the first population, a sample of size n_1 is taken with mean X_1 and standard deviation s_1. Similarly, a sample of size n_2, with mean X_2 and standard deviation s_2, is taken from the second population.

Sample sizes n_1 and n_2 need not be equal. However, an equal number of subjects in the two groups reduce the risk of **Type II error** (the possibility of rejecting the null hypothesis when it is actually false). Homogeneity of variances also reduces the risk of **Type II error.**

Equal Variance t-Test in Independent Groups approach, like the Equal Variance Confidence Interval approach described earlier, is based on the following assumptions:

Random Sampling: Random sampling is not necessary as long as there is no bias in sample selection. However, obtaining a random sample provides the opportunity to generalize the results obtained from the sample to the population.

Independent Samples: Unless the samples are independent, the Equal Variance *t*-Test for μ_1 and μ_2 cannot be used.

Independent Observations Within Each Sample: If this assumption is violated, a *t*-Test with Equal Variance for μ_1 - μ_2 cannot be calculated.

Obtaining Samples from Normal Populations: If the population is not normal, an **Equal Variance t-Test** for μ_1 - μ_2 can be calculated if there are sample sizes to compensate for this anomaly. **Equal Variance t-Test** should not be calculated using highly skewed or few data.

Assuming that the difference in means is the same, less prevalent groups are more likely to be significantly different than more prevalent groups. This is because the error term is larger in more prevalent groups. Because of the prevalence of the data, the possibility of overlapping values makes it difficult to determine whether there is a difference between groups.

Assuming that the difference in means is the same, less prevalent groups are more likely to be significantly different than more prevalent groups. This is because the error term is larger in more prevalent groups. Because of the dispersion of the data, the possibility of overlapping values makes it difficult to determine whether there is a difference between groups.

The greater the variability (variance) within groups, the less likely it is that the difference between group means is significant. A situation where the standard deviation is too large relative to the mean is when there are very small or very large values in the groups.

Ensuring homogeneity of variances protects the research against **Type II error**. When the variances are not equal, there is less chance of finding the important **t-Test.** Thus, it can be falsely concluded that they come from the same population when they do not come from the same population.

With the help of SPSS for Windows, a statistical method that calculates the standard error differently and approximates the **t-Test** can be used when the variances are unequal.

In the equal variance approach, the variances of the population are assumed to be equal. How can this assumption be checked? As a rough measure, the following rule can be applied.

If,

$$0.5 \leq \frac{s_1^2}{s_2^2} \leq 2,$$

the variances of the population are considered to be equal (similar, homogeneous).

If s_1^2/s_2^2 is less than 0.5 or greater than 2, the population variances are equal.

SPSS evaluates the homogeneity of variances using **Levene's Test.** If the *p* value of Levene's test for homogeneity of variances is greater than the specified significance level, the hypothesis "Variances are equal" is accepted. Thus, it is determined that the variances of the experimental and control groups are homogeneous. In this case, the equal variance approach should be applied in comparing the two groups.

The Test of Significance of the Difference between Two Means with Equal Variance should not be used instead of the Test of Significance of the Difference between Two Means with Different Variances. Because the calculated p-value may not reflect what it should be.

The Test of Significance of the Difference between Two Means with Different Variances can be used instead of the Test of Significance of the Difference between Two Means with Equal Variances. However, in this case, the calculated p-value will be larger than it should be.

8.7.1.1 SPSS Application Example

A study was conducted to examine the factors affecting the outcome of Quality Control Department (QCD) activities. The proportion of products produced in 13 production facilities in an industrial zone that did not meet quality standards to those that were estimated by the QCD to not meet quality standards (defect rate) was calculated. A defect ratio of less than 1 indicates that there is less nonstandard production than predicted while a defect ratio greater than 1 indicates that there is more nonstandard production than predicted. Table 8.17 shows the defect ratios for eight production facilities with shortage of quality controllers and 5 production facilities without shortage of quality controllers.

Can Equal Variance t-Test in Two Independent Groups be used to test the null hypothesis that **"the population defect rate averages are the same in the populations with and without quality control personnel shortages"?**

Table 8.17. Defect Rates for Production Facilities.

Group 1		**Group 2**	
Quality Control Personnel Shortage		**No Quality Control Personnel Shortages**	
Facility No	**Defect rate**	**Facility No**	**Defect rate**
1	0.84	9	0.59
2	0.88	10	0.9
3	0.93	11	0.92
4	1	12	0.96
5	1.04	13	1.1
6	1.13	Average ± SS	0.89 ± 0.19
7	1.27		
8	1.58		
Average ± SS	1.08 ± 0.24		

The research question can be expressed in another way. The average defect rate of the group without quality control personnel deficiency (0.89) is smaller than the average defect rate of the group with quality control personnel deficiency (1.08). Is a difference of 0.19 between the groups a statistically significant difference? In addition to the appropriateness of the data, it is useful to evaluate the strength of the analysis before answering the research question. **In general, having eight subjects in the first group and five in the second group is not enough to ensure a reasonable power level of about 0.80.**

With an expected medium effect size (0.5), a significance level of 0.05 and a desired statistical power level of 0.80, a two-tailed *t*-Test requires 126 subjects, 63 in each group.

For a one-tailed test, at the same effect size, significance level and power level, 98 subjects are needed, 49 in each group. These sample sizes are taken from Table 1.5 on sample size in Chapter 1.

Since the defect rate of one facility does not give an idea about the defect rate of the other facility, the observations can be said to be independent. Although the histogram in Fig. 8.1 for the defect rates of facilities with a shortage of quality control personnel shows a skewed population, according to the central limit theorem, the data set is considered to be distributed close to normal since the sample is large enough to compensate for this skewness. The histogram in Fig. 8.2 for the disturbance rate of production facilities with no shortage of quality control personnel is consistent with the sample drawn from a normal distribution. Thus, since both groups of data are considered to be close to normal, **Equal Variance t-Test in Two Independent Groups** can be applied.

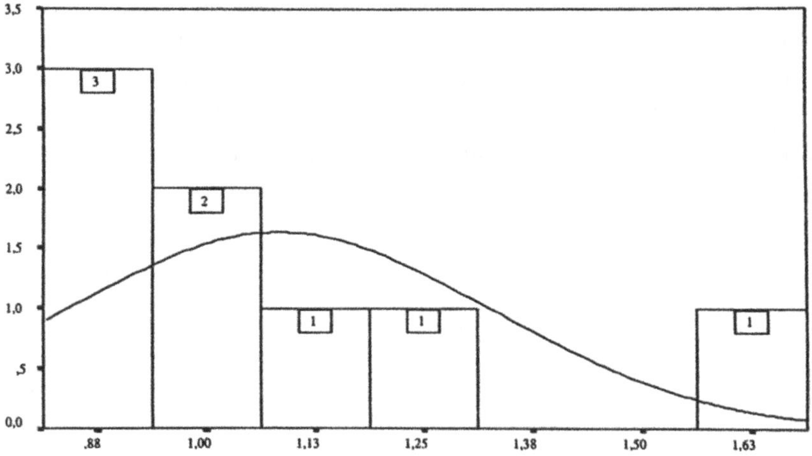

Fig. 8.1. Histogram of Data on Defect Rates of Production Plants With a Shortage of Quality Control Personnel.

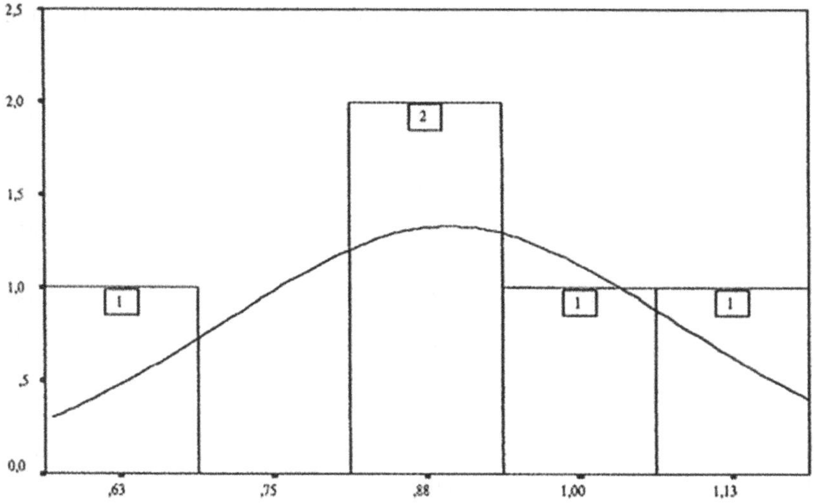

Fig. 8.2. Histogram of Data on Defect Rates of Production Plants Without Shortage of Quality Control Personnel Defects.

The fact that both groups are distributed close to normal makes it possible to apply the parametric test. However, as mentioned before, it is appropriate to work on a larger sample.

First, the data in Table 8.18 are entered into the computer using the SPSS data entry screen as shown in Table 8.19. Then, in order to obtain the Equal Variance **t-Test** result for μ_1 - μ_2, **"Analyze/Compare Means/ Independent-Samples T Test/Test Variable (defect)/Grouping Variable(group)/ Define Groups/Group 1(1)/Group 2(2)/Continue/Options/Confidence Interval(95)/ Continue/OK"** commands are selected, and the output in Table 8.20 is obtained.

8.7.1.2 Evaluation of SPSS Output

There are eight subjects in the first group and 5 subjects in the second group. The mean of the first group is 1.08, and the mean of the second group is 0.89. The relevant standard deviations and standard errors are given.

To check whether there is equal variance, S_1^2/S_2^2 $(0.24)^2/(0.19)^2 = 1.6$ is obtained, using standard deviations.

Since $0.5 \leq 1.6 \leq 2$, it can be assumed that the population variances are equal. This assessment can also be made by using Levene's test for homogeneity of variances. For this, the **Levene's Test** value in Table 8.20, which shows whether the variances are equal, can be used.

Table 8.18. Entering Defect Rates Data for Production Facilities Into SPSS.

	Defect	Group
1	0.84	1.00
2	0.88	1.00
3	0.93	1.00
4	1.00	1.00
5	1.04	1.00
6	1.13	1.00
7	1.27	1.00
8	1.58	1.00
9	0.59	2.00
10	0.90	2.00
11	0.92	2.00
12	0.96	2.00
13	1.10	2.00

Table 8.19. *t*-Test Results of Defect Rates Data for Production Facilities.

Group Statistics

GROUP		N	Mean	Std. deviation	Std. error mean
DEFECT	1	8	1.0838	0.24395	8.63E-02
	2	5	0.894	0.18703	8.36E-02

In **Levene's Test**, if the calculated *p*-value is greater than the specified α, the hypothesis "**Population variances are equal**" is accepted, and the **Significance Test of the Difference between Two Means with Equal Variance** is applied. Since the *p* value of this test is $0.465 > \alpha$ (0.10 or 0.05 or 0.01) significance level, it is decided that the variances are equal.

In other words, there is no statistically significant difference between the standard deviation of the first group (0.24) and the standard deviation of the second group (0.89). Thus, the assumption of homogeneity of variances is met, and **t-Test** with equal variances can be applied.

If the variances are equal, "**Equal**" is selected and if not, "**Unequal**" is selected and the relevant *p* value is read under "2-Tail Sig". In this example, since the variances are homogeneous, the "**Equal**" section is selected, and the *p*-value of

Independent Samples Test

		Levene's test for Equality of variances		*t*-Test for Equality of Means						
									95% Confidence Interval of the difference	
		F	Sig.	t	df	Sig. (2-tailed)	Mean difference	Std. Error difference	Lower	Upper
	Equal variances assumed	0.572	0.465	1.48	11	0.167	0.1897	0.1282	−9.20E-02	0.472
Defect	Equal variances not assumed			1.579	10.345	0.144	0.1897	0.1201	−7.70E+02	0.4562

Table 8.20. Amount of Unnecessary Expenditures by Marketing Personnel (TRY).

Trained	Not Trained
165	1,502
92	662
141	389
69	2,340
244	907
121	1,459
230	
82	
123	
134	

the **Equal Variance t-Test** is obtained as 0.167. Since the *p*-value is greater than 0.10 at the 0.10 significance level, the null hypothesis that the population means are equal is accepted.

In fact, the *p*-value is so large that we cannot reject this hypothesis at any reasonable level of significance. If the population means are equal, 10% of all possible samples would generate a t-statistic with equal variance with an extreme value of at least 1.48. In other words, if the means are equal, results like the one we obtained are not improbable.

At the 0.10 significance level, since we cannot reject the null hypothesis that the population means are equal, 0 is within the 95% confidence interval for μ_1 - μ_2 (−0.09; 0.47).

For $\mu 1$ - μ_2, **Equal-Variance t-Test in Two Independent Groups** and the **Equal-Variance Confidence Interval** are closely related. If the null hypothesis is rejected at any significance level, d_0 is not included in the confidence interval for μ_1 - μ_2

If the null hypothesis is accepted at any significance level, d_0 is included in the confidence interval for μ_1- μ_2. The hypothesis test and the confidence interval are consistent with each other. When the null hypothesis is rejected, a confidence interval is usually obtained to estimate μ_1- μ_2.

Point estimates, confidence interval estimates, and significance tests are usually correlated. The *p*-value for a null hypothesis value within the 95% confidence interval is greater than 0.05 while the *p*-value for a value outside the 95% confidence interval is less than 0.05.

8.7.2 Unequal Variance t-*Test in Two Independent Groups*

If the assumptions required by **Equal Variance t-Test in Two Independent Groups** are met, except for the assumption of equal variance, **Unequal Variance t-Test in Two Independent Groups** can be applied. This test requires the same assumptions for μ_1 and μ_2 as for the confidence interval with different variances.

As with **the Confidence Interval with Unequal Variance** approach described earlier, the Independent Groups *t*-Test approach is based on the following assumptions:

Random Sampling: Random sampling is not necessary as long as there is no bias in sample selection. However, obtaining a random sample allows the results obtained from the sample to be generalized to the population.

Independent Samples: Unless the samples are independent, the *t*-Test for μ_1 and μ_2 Unequal Variances for Two Independent Groups cannot be applied.

Independent Observations Within Each Sample: If this assumption is violated, Unequal Variance *t*-Test in Two Independent Groups for μ_1 - μ_2 cannot be calculated.

Obtaining Samples from Normal Populations: If the population is non-normal, but there are sample sizes that compensate for this slight skewness, then **Unequal Variance t-Test in Independent Two Groups** for μ_1 - μ_2 can be calculated. This test should not be calculated using highly skewed data.

As in the different-variance confidence interval process, the **Unequal Variance t-Test in Two Independent Groups** does not make the assumption that the variances of the population are not equal. **In other words, it does not assume that the variances are equal.** It simply does not require that the population variances are equal. In this case, when the population variances are equal, it is not erroneous to obtain a *t*-Test with **Unequal Variance t-Test in Two Independent Groups**. However, in a situation where the population variances are not equal, it would be erroneous to obtain a *t*-Test with Equal Variance in Two Groups. **If, for any reason, you believe that the population variances are not equal, do not use the Equal Variance t-Test in Two Independent Groups.**

The Significance Test of the Difference between Two Means with Equal Variance should not be used in place of the Significance Test of the Difference between Two Means with Unequal Variance. Because, in this case, the calculated *p*-value may not reflect what it should be.

The Test of Significance of the Difference between Two Means with Unequal Variances can be used instead of the Test of Significance of the Difference between Two Means with Equal Variances. However, in this case, the calculated *p* is larger than it should be.

In the approach with different variances, the variances of the population are assumed to be different. How can this assumption be checked? As a rough measure, the following rule can be applied. If:

$$0.5 \leq \frac{s_1^2}{s_2^2} \leq 2$$

the variances of the population are considered to be equal (similar, homogeneous).

If s_1^2/s_2^2 is less than 0.5 or greater than 2, the population variances are not considered equal.

SPSS evaluates the homogeneity of variances using **Levene's Test.** If the *p*-value of Levene's test for homogeneity of variances is less than the specified significance level, the hypothesis "Variances are equal" is rejected. Thus, it is determined that the variances of the experimental and control groups are different. In this case, in the comparison of two groups, the approach with different variances should be applied instead of the approach with equal variances.

As expected, **Differential Variance t-Test in Two Independent Groups** and the different-variance confidence interval for $\mu_1 - \mu_2$ are related. If, at a given significance level α, the null hypothesis is rejected, the different-variance confidence interval of 100% (1-α) for $\mu_1 - \mu_2$ does not contain the difference d_0. If, at a given significance level α, the null hypothesis is accepted, the 100% (1-α) confidence interval with different variance for $\mu_1 - \mu_2$ contains the difference d_0. The hypothesis test and the confidence interval are consistent with each other. **If the null hypothesis is rejected, a confidence interval with different variance is usually calculated to estimate $\mu_1 - \mu_2$.**

Point estimates, confidence interval estimates and significance tests are usually correlated. The *p*-value for the null hypothesis value within the 95% confidence interval is greater than 0.05 while the *p*-value for a value outside the 95% confidence interval is less than 0.05.

8.7.2.1 SPSS Application Example

In a study of a company's marketing department personnel, the amount of unnecessary expenditures made by 10 personnel who received a training on frugal behavior and six personnel who did not receive the training were determined within 1 year. These values are given in Table 8.20.

Can *t*-Test with Unequal Variances in Two Independent Groups be used to test the null hypothesis that "the difference between the average unnecessary expenditure amounts of the populations of marketing personnel who have undergone training and marketing personnel who have not undergone training is 0"?

H_0: The difference between the mean unnecessary expenditure amounts of the populations of marketing personnel who have undergone training and those who have not undergone training is 0.

or

$$H_0 : \mu_1 - \mu_2 = 0$$

The counter hypothesis can be formulated as follows:

H_A: The difference between the mean unnecessary expenditure of the population of trained and untrained marketing personnel is not 0.

or

$$H_A : \mu_1 - \mu_2 \neq 0$$

Since the amount of unnecessary expenditure incurred by one marketing personnel does not give an idea about the amount of unnecessary expenditure incurred by other marketing personnel, the observations can be said to be independent. The histogram of the group of marketing personnel who have undergone training is given in Fig. 8.3, and although it shows a slightly skewed population, according to the central limit theorem, the sample size is large enough to compensate for the skewed population, and it can be accepted that the distribution is close to normal.

Although the histogram in Fig. 8.4 for the group of marketing personnel who did not undergo training shows a skewed population, similarly, according to the central limit theorem, the sample size is large enough to compensate for the skewed population and the distribution can be considered to be close to normal. Thus, since the distribution of the two groups is considered to be close to normal, **Unequal Variance t-Test in Two Independent Groups** can be applied.

The near-normal distribution of both groups makes it possible to apply the parametric test. However, as mentioned before, it is appropriate to work on a larger sample.

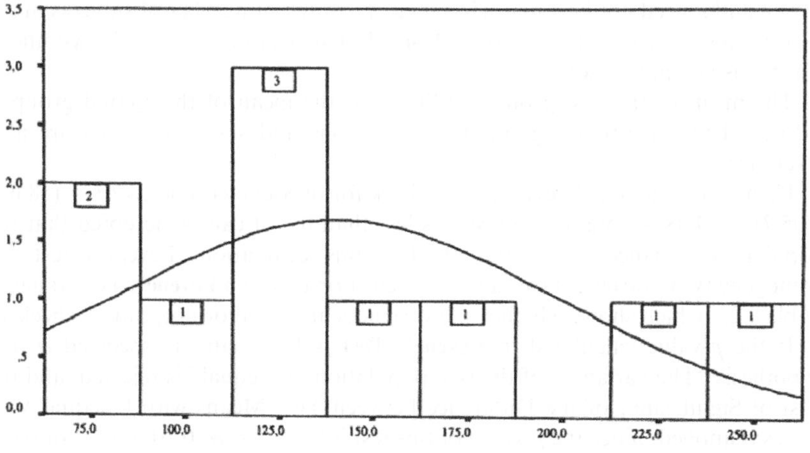

Fig. 8.3. Histogram of Data on Unnecessary Expenditures of Marketing Personnel Without Training.

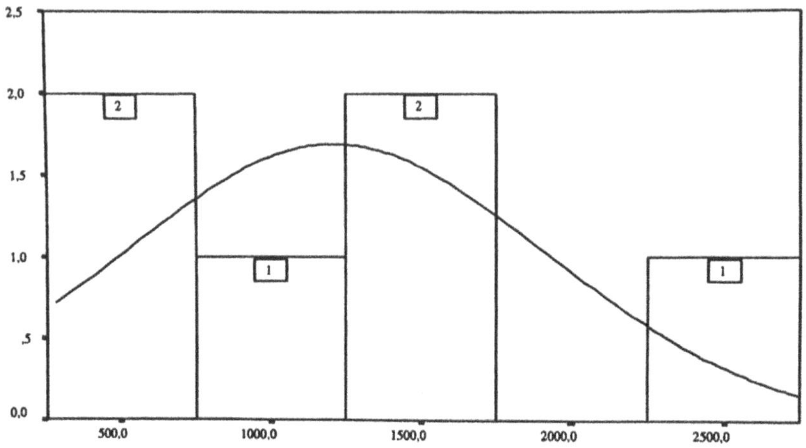

Fig. 8.4. Histogram of Data on the Amount of Unnecessary Expenditures of Trained Marketing Personnel.

First, the data in Table 8.21 are entered into the computer using the SPSS data entry screen as shown in Table 8.22. Then **"Analyze/Compare Means/ Independent-Samples T-Test/Test Variable (unnecessary)/Grouping Variable (group)/Define Groups/Group 1(1)/Group 2(2)/Continue/Options/Confidence Interval(95)/Continue/OK"** are selected to obtain the *t*-Test statistic for μ1 - μ2 with Differential Variance, and the output in Table 8.23 is obtained.

There are 10 units in the first group and 6 units in the second group. Sample sizes *n* and *n* need not be equal. However, the different number of subjects in the two groups increases the risk of a **Type II error** (rejecting the null hypothesis when it is actually false).

The mean of the first group is 140.1, and the mean of the second group is 1,209.8. The corresponding standard deviations and standard errors are also given here.

Using these standard deviations to check for unequal variance, $s^2/s^2 = (58.6)^2/(705.7)^2 = 0.08$ is obtained. Since it is less than 0.5, it can be accepted that the population variances are different. For this evaluation, Levene's test for homogeneity of variances can also be used. For this, the **Levene's Test** value in Table 8.23, which shows whether the variances are equal or not, can be checked.

If the *p*-value calculated in **Levene's Test** is less than the specified α, the hypothesis "The variances of the two populations are equal" is rejected, and the Test of Significance of the Difference between Two Means with Unequal Variances is applied. Since the *p*-value of this test is $0.0005 < \alpha$ (0.10 or 0.05 or 0.01) significance level, it is decided that the variances are different. **The difference of variances increases the risk of Type II error.**

Table 8.21. Entering the Data on Marketing Personnel's Unnecessary Expenditures Into SPSS.

	Unnecessary	Group
1	165	TRAINED
2	92	TRAINED
3	141	TRAINED
4	69	TRAINED
5	244	TRAINED
6	121	TRAINED
7	230	TRAINED
8	82	TRAINED
9	123	TRAINED
10	134	TRAINED
11	1,502	NOT TRAINED
12	662	NOT TRAINED
13	389	NOT TRAINED
14	2,340	NOT TRAINED
15	907	NOT TRAINED
16	1,459	NOT TRAINED

Table 8.22. *t*-Test Results of Marketing Personnel's Unnecessary Expenditure Amount Data.

Group Statistics

	GROUP	N	Mean	Std. Deviation	Std. Error Mean
UNNECCESSARY	Trained	10	140.1	58.63	18.54
	Untrained	6	1,209.83	705.736	288.116

In other words, there is a statistically significant difference between the standard deviation of the first group (58.6) and the standard deviation of the second group (705.7). In this case, since the assumption of homogeneity of variances is not met, **Unequal Variance t-Test in Two Independent Groups** can be applied.

Independent Samples Test

		Levene's test for Equality of variances		*t*-Test for Equality of Means						
									95% Confidence Interval of the difference	
		F	Sig.	t	df	Sig. (2-tailed)	Mean difference	Std. Error difference	Lower	Upper
UNNECCESSARY	Equal variances assumed	21.631	0	−4.881	14	0	−1,069.733	219.144	−1,539.75	−599.717
	Equal variances not assumed			−3.705	5.041	0.014	−1,069.733	288.712	−1810.059	−329.408

Table 8.23. Scores Received by Public Relations Personnel.

City A		**City B**	
Personnel No	**Points**	**Personnel No**	**Points**
1	7	13	15
2	6	14	14
3	4	15	17
4	11	16	16
5	16	17	16
6	4	18	16
7	10	19	14
8	6	20	12
9	9	21	14
10	3	22	17
11	13	23	16
12	5		

If the variances are not equal, the "**Unequal**" section is selected and the relevant *p*-value is read under "**2-Tail Sig**". In this example, since the variances are not homogeneous, the "**Unequal**" section is selected and the *p*-value of the **Unequal Variance t-Test** is obtained as 0.014. At the 0.05 significance level, since the *p*-value is less than 0.05, the null hypothesis that **"the difference in population means is equal to 0″** is rejected.

At the 0.05 level of significance, the null hypothesis that the population means are equal is rejected, and 0 is not included in the 95% confidence interval for μ_1 - μ_2 (−1810.06; −329.41). Here, we are 95% sure that μ_1 is smaller than μ_2.

8.7.3 Mann–Whitney Test

In the case of a data set that is too far from normality, **the t-Test of the Difference between Two Means with Equal Variance and the t-Test of the Difference between Two Means with Unequal Variance** cannot be applied in two independent groups. In this case, the **Mann–Whitney Test** is used to test that the two groups are the same. Another test that is equivalent to the Mann–Whitney test is the Wilcoxon Rank Sum Test.

H_0: The two populations are the same.

The two-tailed alternative hypothesis is as follows:

H_A: The two populations are different.

The Mann–Whitney test does not require a normal or near-normal distribution. However, it requires the following assumptions to be met.

Random Sampling: As long as there is no bias in sample selection, random sampling is not necessary. However, obtaining a random sample provides the opportunity to generalize the results obtained from the sample to the population.

Independent Samples: The Mann–Whitney Test cannot be applied unless the samples are independent.

Independent Observations Within Each Sample: If this assumption is violated, the Mann–Whitney test cannot be calculated.

8.7.3.1 SPSS Application Example

The employees working in public relations departments in two different cities of an enterprise were examined in terms of their behavior towards customers, and they were evaluated over 20 points. As a result of this study, the scores of 23 employees in total in both cities are given in Table 8.23.

A senior manager believes that the population of public relations department employees in both cities is the same in terms of treating customers.

Before applying hypothesis testing, normality analysis of the data should be performed. The histogram of the staff in City A is given in Fig. 8.5. According to the central limit theorem, the current sample size is large enough to compensate for the slightly skewed population and the **"approximate normal distribution assumption"** may be reasonable for these data.

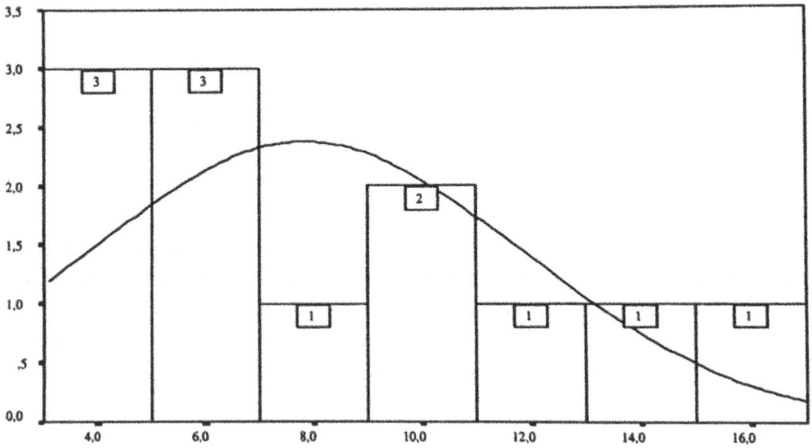

Fig. 8.5. Histogram of Data on Employees in City A.

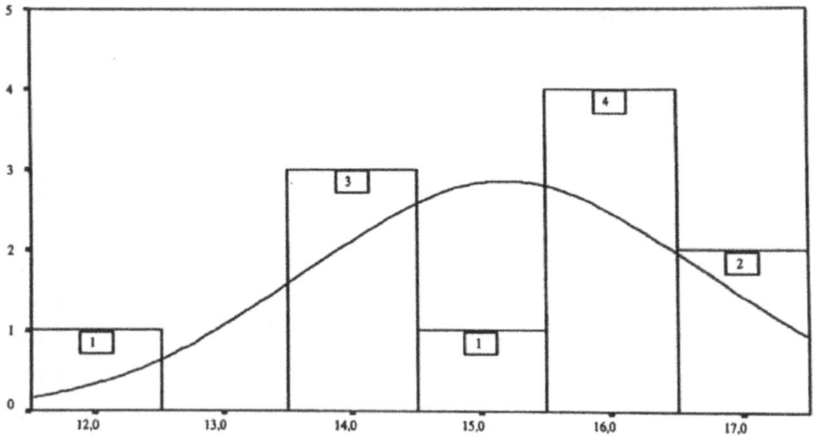

Fig. 8.6. Histogram of Data for Employees in City B.

However, as can be seen from the histogram for city B staff in Fig. 8.6, the data are far from normal. It is also seen that the number of possible different values in the premium group is very small. These are 12, 14, 15, 16, and 17. In this case, parametric tests cannot be applied because at least one of the populations is too far from normal. Instead, a nonparametric test, the Mann–Whitney Test, should be applied.

To apply the Mann–Whitney test in SPSS, the data are entered as shown in Table 8.24. Then, **"Analyze/Nonparametric Tests/Legacy Dialogs/2 Independent Samples/Test Variable List(score)/Grouping Variable(group)/Define Groups/Group1(1)/Group2(2)/Continue/Mann–Whitney U/OK"** commands are used to obtain Table 8.26.

When Table 8.25 is analyzed, it is seen that $p = 0.000$ is obtained. Accordingly, since there is a significance level of $p < 0.05$, there is a statistically significant difference between the public relations personnel in City A and City B in terms of the scores received according to customer behavior.

8.7.4 Paired Samples T-*Test for the Difference Between Two Matched Groups*

When the null hypothesis is to be tested in paired samples, *t*-Tests with Unequal Variance or Equal Variance in Two Groups cannot be applied. Instead, Paired Samples *T*-Test should be used.

Means can be compared in two paired groups by testing the null hypothesis, expressed in the following form:

$$H_0 : \mu_1 - \mu_2 = d_0$$

Here, d_0 is a number determined by the researcher, like p_0 and μ_0. However, since d_0 is usually taken as 0, the null hypothesis can be written as follows:

Table 8.24. Entering Sales Scores of Sales Personnel Into SPSS.

	Score	Group
1	7	City A
2	6	City A
3	4	City A
4	11	City A
5	16	City A
6	4	City A
7	10	City A
8	6	City A
9	9	City A
10	3	City A
11	13	City A
12	5	City A
13	15	City B
14	14	City B
15	17	City B
16	16	City B
17	16	City B
18	16	City B
19	14	City B
20	12	City B
21	14	City B
22	17	City B
23	16	City B

Table 8.25. Mann–Whitney Test Results of the Scores Received by Public Relations Personnel.

Ranks

GROUP		N	Mean rank	Sum of ranks
	City A	12	7.17	86
SCORE	City B	11	17.27	190
	Total	23		

Test Statistics[b]

	SCORE
Mann–Whitney U	8
Wilcoxon W	86
Z	−3.594
Asymp. Sig. (2-tailed)	0
Exact Sig. [2*(1-tailed Sig.)]	,000[a]

a. Grouping Variable: GROUP.
b. Not corrected for ties.

$$H_0 : \mu_1 - \mu_0 = 0$$

or

$$H_0 : \mu_1 = \mu_2$$

Here, μ_1 is the mean of the first cohort and μ_2 is the mean of the second cohort. The alternative hypothesis can be stated as follows when $d_0 \neq 0$:

$$H_A : \mu_1 \ \mu_2$$

The one-tailed hypotheses H_A: $\mu_1 < \mu_2$ and H_A: $\mu_1 > \mu_2$ are rarely used. The *t*-Test requires a ratio or interval form of measurement. However, as mentioned earlier, when the ordered data set has more than six categories, it can be treated as an interval measurement and used in the *t*-Test analysis.

The assumptions required by this test are the same as the confidence interval assumptions for μ_1 and μ_2 in paired samples:

- **Random Selection of Differences:** Random sampling is not necessary as long as there is no bias in sample selection. However, obtaining a random sample provides the opportunity to generalize the results obtained from the sample to the population.
- **Paired Samples:** If the samples are not paired, Paired Samples *T*-Test for μ_1 - μ_2 cannot be obtained.
- **Independent Differences:** Knowing one difference value should not give an idea about the other difference value. If the differences are not independent, Paired Samples T-Test for μ_1 - μ_2 cannot be obtained.
- **Selection of Differences from the Normal Population:** Ideally, the differences should come from a normal population. If the differences do not come from a normal population, but the number of differences is large enough to eliminate skewness, *T*-Test in Two Paired Groups for μ_1 - μ_2 is still applicable. Paired Samples T-Test should not be calculated using a data set of differences that consists of a few values and is highly skewed.

In order to apply Paired Samples *T*-Test, two paired samples should be transformed into a single sample of differences as in the paired confidence interval process.

The relationship between the test statistic and the corresponding confidence interval, which is always present, is also present between **Paired Samples T-Test** and the paired confidence interval. If, at a given significance level α, the null hypothesis is rejected, the 100% (1-α) confidence interval for $\mu_1 - \mu_2$ does not include the difference d_0.

If the null hypothesis is accepted, the 100% (1-α) confidence interval for $\mu_1 - \mu_2$ contains the difference d_0. When the null hypothesis is rejected, we want to calculate the confidence interval for $\mu_1 - \mu_2$.

8.7.4.1 SPSS Application Example

In a study on the training of staff working in the service sector, 10 staff were programmatically trained on how to treat customers.

The staff were given scores before and after the training (scores are out of 100). The scores of the staff before and after the training and their differences are given in Table-8.26.

Can **Paired Samples T-Test** be applied to test the null hypothesis that the average of the pretraining scores and the average of the post-training scores are the same? Here, all the personnel constituting the population are similar to the personnel in the study.

The differences between the scores before and after the training should be independent of each other. Knowing the difference of one personnel does not give an idea about the difference of the other personnel. Although the histogram

Table 8.26. Pre- and Post-Training Scores and Differences.

Personnel No.	Pretraining	Post-Training	Difference (Before-After)
1	65	85	−20
2	81	69	12
3	69	92	−23
4	42	69	−27
5	77	88	−11
6	69	88	−19
7	68	92	−24
8	69	77	−8
9	77	88	−11
10	58	96	−38

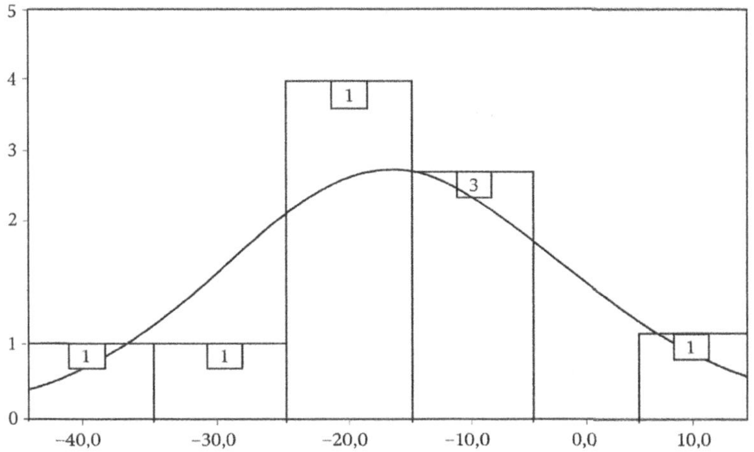

Fig. 8.7. Histogram of Differences of Scores Before and After Training.

of differences in Fig. 8.7 is skewed, according to the central limit theorem, the sample differences are large enough to compensate for the skewed population. Only the histogram of differences is analyzed here. Because paired samples do not give an idea about the distribution of differences. Thus, Paired Samples *T*-Test is appropriate for these data.

After entering the differences in performance status scores in SPSS as shown in Table 8.27, the output in Table 8.28 is obtained by selecting the **"Analyze/Compare Mean/Paired Samples T Test/Current Selections/Variable 1(before)/Variable 2(after)/Paired Variables(Before After)/OK"** commands to apply the Sign Test in Two Paired Groups.

Since the observed *p*-value (0.003) is smaller than the significance level (0.05), H_0, which states that the difference between the paired population means is 0, is rejected. Accordingly, a statistically significant difference was found between the scores obtained before and after the training. In other words, it can be stated that the difference between before and after the training is statistically significant.

Since H_0 is rejected, the confidence interval in two paired samples should be determined. 95% paired two sample confidence interval is obtained as (−26.5; −7.2) from Table 8.29. This estimate does not include 0. Thus, when both extreme values of the confidence interval μ_1 - μ_2 are negative, we are 95% sure that μ_1 is less than μ_2.

8.7.5 Paired Samples Wilcoxon Signed Rank Test

In cases where the data are far from normal, but symmetrical or close to symmetrical, the nonparametric "Wilcoxon Signed Rank Test" is used as an alternative

Table 8.27. Scores Before and After the Training and Entering the Differences Into SPSS.

	Before	**After**	**Difference**
1	65	85	−20
2	81	69	12
3	69	92	−23
4	42	69	−27
5	77	88	−11
6	69	88	−19
7	68	92	−23
8	69	77	−8
9	77	88	−11
10	58	96	−38

Table 8.28. Results of Sign-Test in Two Paired Groups.

Paired Samples Statistics

		Mean	**N**	**Std. Deviation**	**Std. Error Mean**
Pair 1	BEFORE and AFTER	67.5	10	11.138	3.522
		84.4	10	9.536	3.016

Paired Samples Correlations

		N	**Correlation**	**Sig.**
Pair 1	BEFORE and AFTER	10	0.158	0.663

to the parametric "Paired Samples T-Test". On the other hand, when the data are far from both normality and symmetry, the nonparametric "Sign Test in Two Paired Groups" is used as an alternative to the "Paired Samples *T*-Test". The nonparametric test is commonly applied when the data set consists of several different values such as 0, 2, 5.

Paired Samples Test									
		Paired differences							
					95% Confidence interval of the difference				
		Mean	Std. deviation	Std. error mean	Lower	Upper	t	df	Sig. (2-tailed)
Pair 1	BEFORE and AFTER	−16.9	13.47	4.259	−26.536	−7.264	−3.968	9	0.003

Table 8.29. Workers' Manufacturing Times and Differences (min).

Cashier No	Not under supervision	Under supervision	Difference
1	115	115	0
2	81	81	0
3	110	110	0
4	136	130	6
5	111	111	0
6	91	96	−5
7	118	118	0
8	97	102	−5
9	93	93	0
10	96	96	0
11	89	84	5
12	86	92	−6
13	99	99	0
14	99	97	2
15	113	113	0
16	127	131	−4
17	106	110	−4
18	111	111	0
19	91	91	0
20	96	97	−1
21	105	112	−7
22	93	94	−1
23	113	113	0
24	83	83	0
25	114	114	0
26	117	110	7
27	86	82	4
28	106	106	0
29	105	105	0

While the parametric **Paired Samples *T*-Test** uses the arithmetic mean for evaluation, the alternative nonparametric test uses the median for comparison.

Suppose there are two paired samples. These are transformed into a difference sample. To obtain the difference between two observations, one observation value is subtracted from the other observation value. With the observations of the first sample denoted by X_{1i} and the observations of the second sample denoted by X_{2i}, the difference for each pair is calculated as follows:

$$d_{1i} = X_{1i} - X_{2i}$$

We might want to test the null hypothesis that the difference of the population median is equal to a hypothesized value:

H_0: Population median difference $= m_0$.

The two-tailed alternative hypothesis is as follows:

H_A: Population median difference $\neq m_0$.

m_0, is a value determined by the researcher. Mostly, m_0 is taken as 0.

In order to apply Paired Samples Wilcoxon Signed Rank Test, the following assumptions must be met:

Random Sampling: Random sampling is not necessary as long as there is no bias in sample selection. However, obtaining a random sample provides the opportunity to generalize the results obtained from the sample to the population.

Independence of Differences: If the differences between observations are not independent, the Wilcoxon Signed Rank Test cannot be applied.

Symmetry of the Population with Regard to the Median: Ideally, a vertical line through the population median should divide the plot showing the distribution of the population into two equal parts. In other words, let us assume that the population median is m_0. Half of the observations in the sample are expected to lie above m_0 and the other half below it.

If the population is approximately symmetric, the Wilcoxon Signed Rank Test in One Group can still be applied. If the population is far from symmetrical, this test should not be applied.

Although the symmetry assumption is less important than the normality assumption, it is often neglected in research. The data to which this test is applied are skewed data. **If the data are highly skewed, this test should not be applied.**

8.7.5.1 SPSS Application Example

Let us consider a study that evaluates the time it takes workers to produce a part in a factory. Table 8.29 shows the differences between the time it takes 29 workers to produce a part under the supervision of the foreman and when they are not under the supervision of the foreman.

The researcher believes that the difference between the time it takes workers to produce the relevant part is 0. In other words, he believes that positive and negative differences are equally likely. The null hypothesis can be formulated as follows:

H_0: Population median difference = 0.

The two-tailed alternative hypothesis is as follows:

H_A: Population median difference *t*, 0.

Can the **Wilcoxon Signed Rank Test** be used here to test the null hypothesis? Random sampling was not used. However, this is not necessary as long as there is no bias. Since the difference of one worker does not give an idea about the difference of the other worker, the assumption of independence of differences is satisfied for these data.

The histogram in Fig. 8.8 shows that the production time differences data is close to symmetry. Thus, the assumption of being far from normality but close to symmetry is also met. In this case, Wilcoxon Signed Rank Test can be applied. Here, a significance level of 0.10 will be used.

After entering the manufacturing time differences in SPSS as shown in Table 8.30, the commands **"Analyze/Nonparametric Tests/Legacy Dialogs/2 Related Samples/Current Selection/Variable 1(notundersupervision)/Variable 2 (undersupervision)/Test Pair(s) List(notundersupervision undersupervision)/Test**

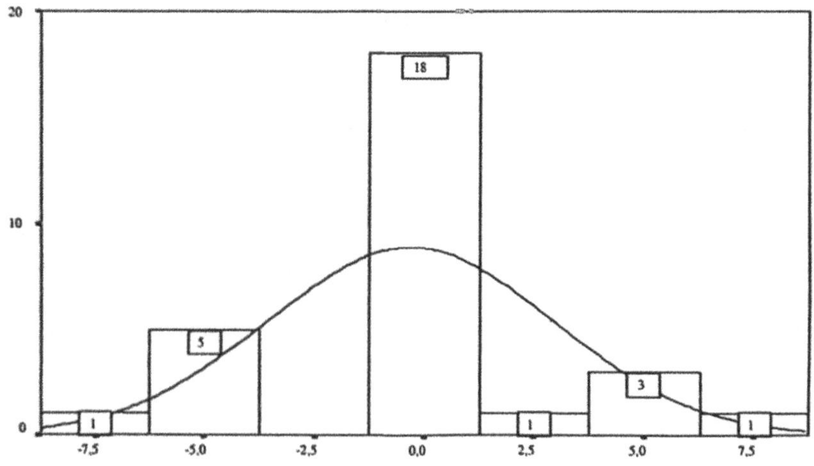

Fig. 8.8. Histogram of Manufacturing Time Differences Data.

Table 8.30. Entering Manufacturing Times and Differences Data Into SPSS.

	Not under supervision	Under supervision	Wilcox
1	115	115	0
2	81	81	0
3	110	110	0
4	136	130	6
5	111	111	0
6	91	96	−5
7	118	118	0
8	97	102	−5
9	93	93	0
10	96	96	0
11	89	84	5
12	86	92	−6
13	99	99	0
14	99	97	2
15	113	113	0
16	127	131	−4
17	106	110	−4
18	111	111	0
19	91	91	0
20	96	97	−1
21	105	112	−7
22	93	94	−1
23	113	113	0
24	83	83	0
25	114	114	0
26	117	110	7
27	86	82	4
28	106	106	0
29	105	105	0

Table 8.31. Wilcoxon Signed Rank Test Results of Manufacturing Time Data.

Ranks

		N	Mean Rank	Sum of Ranks
UNDERSUPERVISION	Negative ranks	5[a]	7.8	39
NOTUNDERSUPERVISION	Positive ranks	8[b]	6.5	52
	Ties	16[c]		
	Total	29		

a. UNDERSUPERVISION < NOTUNDERSUPERVISION.
b. UNDERSUPERVISION > NOTUNDERSUPERVISION.
c. UNDERSUPERVISION = NOTUNDERSUPERVISION.

Test Statistics[e]

	UNDERSUPERVISION – NOTUNDERSUPERVISION
Z	−0.456[d]
Asymp. Sig. (2-tailed)	0.649

[d]Wilcoxon Signed Ranks Test.
[e]Based on negative ranks.

Type/Wilcoxon/OK" are selected to apply the Wilcoxon Signed Rank Test, and the output in Table 8.31 is obtained.

Since the observed *p*-value (0.649) is greater than the significance level (0.10), H_0 is accepted. Thus, there is no statistically significant difference between the time taken by the workers to manufacture the relevant part.

8.7.6 Paired Samples Sign Test

If the differences are too far from both normal and symmetry, the Wilcoxon Signed Rank Test cannot be used to test the hypothesis about the population median difference. In this case, the Paired Two-Group Sign Test should be used to test the null hypothesis.

If the differences are too far from both normality and symmetry, the Wilcoxon Signed Rank Test cannot be used to test the null hypothesis about the difference in the population median. In this case, Paired Samples Sign Test should be used to test the null hypothesis.

The Sign Test does not make any assumptions about the shape of the distributions. **The only assumption required by the Sign Test is the independence of the differences.** If any of the differences are not independent, the Sign Test cannot be applied. Since the power of the Sign Test is very low, it should only be used when more powerful methods are not feasible.

In order to use Paired Samples Sign Test to test the null hypothesis, as with the Wilcoxon test, the two paired samples are first transformed into a single sample, which is the sample of differences.

The null hypothesis is usually tested against a two-tailed alternative hypothesis. Usually, m_0, set by the researcher, is taken as 0.

One-tailed Sign Test,

H_A: Population median difference $1 < m_0$

or

H_A: Population median difference $1 > m_0$

can be done using one-tailed alternative hypotheses.

8.7.7 SPSS Application Example

Let us consider a study on the implementation of a new reward system to improve the performance of employees in an organization. The reward system was applied to 29 randomly selected employees. Table 8.32 shows the performance status scores of the employees before and after the reward system (0 being the worst performance and 3 being the best performance). Can a sign test be used to test the null hypothesis that the population median difference is 0?

Table 8.32. Performance Status Before and After Reward System.

Personnel No	Before Reward	After Reward	Difference
1	2	1	−1
2	0	0	0
3	0	0	0
4	1	0	−1
5	3	3	0
6	1	0	−1
7	1	3	2
8	0	0	0
9	0	0	0

(Continued)

Table 8.32. *(Continued)*

Personnel No	Before Reward	After Reward	Difference
10	0	0	0
11	1	0	−1
12	1	1	0
13	2	1	−1
14	3	1	−2
15	0	0	0
16	0	0	0
17	0	3	3
18	2	3	1
19	2	3	1
20	3	2	−1
21	0	4	4
22	1	2	1
23	1	2	1
24	0	3	3
25	0	2	2
26	1	1	0
27	3	3	0
28	1	2	1
29	0	2	2

The following null hypothesis is tested using the Sign Test:

H_0: Population median difference = 0.

The null hypothesis is as follows:

H_A: Population median difference ≠ 0.

The assumptions required for the application of the Sign for a Group Test are the same as for the Wilcoxon Test for a Group. The difference here is that the data are very far from symmetry. Note in Fig. 8.9 that the data are far from normal and far from symmetry.

The Paired Samples *t*-Test cannot be applied here. This is because the differences data consists of only 0, 1, 2, 3, 4 values and data sets consisting of such a

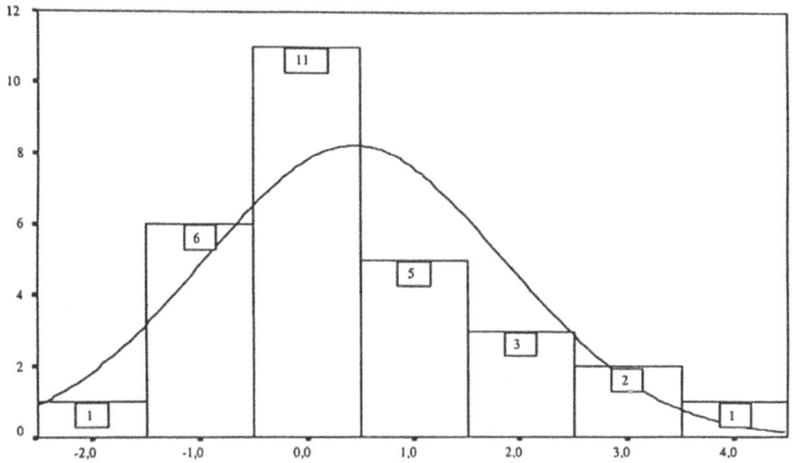

Fig. 8.9. Histogram of Signs of Performance Data Before and After Rewarding System.

small number of values are normally very distant. Since the symmetry assumption is not met, the Wilcoxon test cannot be applied either.

As a result of the data being far from normal, highly skewed and not symmetrical, the more powerful tests **Paired Samples t-Test** and **"Wilcoxon Signed Rank Test for One Group"** cannot be applied. In this case, **"Paired Samples Sign Test"** can be applied at 0.05 significance level.

After entering the differences before and after the rewarding in SPSS as shown in Table 8.33, the output in Table 8.34 is obtained by selecting the **"Analyze/Nonparametric Tests/2 Related Samples/Current Selection/Variable 1 (before)Variable 2(after)test Pair(s) List(before after)Test Type/Sign'OK"** commands in order to apply the Sign Test in Two Paired Groups.

Since the observed p value (0.481) is greater than the significance level (0.05), H_0 is accepted. Thus, there is no statistically significant difference between the performance of employees before and after the rewarding system.

Table 8.33. SPSS Entry of Performance Data Before and After Rewarding System.

	Before	After	Sign
1	2	1	−1
2	0	0	0
3	0	0	0
4	1	0	−1
5	3	3	0
6	1	0	−1
7	1	3	2
8	0	0	0
9	0	0	0
10	0	0	0
11	1	0	−1
12	1	1	0
13	2	1	−1
14	3	1	−2
15	0	0	0
16	0	0	0
17	0	3	3
18	2	3	1
19	2	3	1
20	3	2	−1
21	0	4	4
22	1	2	3
23	1	2	1
24	0	3	3
25	0	2	2
26	1	1	0
27	3	3	0
28	1	2	1
29	0	2	2

Table 8.34. Results of Sign-Test in Two Paired Groups.

Frequencies

	N
Negative differences[a]	7
Positive differences[b]	11
AFTER – BEFORE	
Ties[c]	11
Total	29

a. AFTER < BEFORE.
b. AFTER > BEFORE.
c. AFTER = BEFORE.

Test Statistics[e]

	AFTER – BEFORE
Exact Sig. (2-tailed)	0.481[d]

d. Binomial distribution used.
e. Sign Test.

References

Akgül, A. (1997). *Tıbbi Araştırmalarda İstatistiksel Analiz Teknikleri "SPSS Uygulamaları"*. Yükseköğretim Kurulu Matbaası.

Campbell, M. J., & Machin, D. (1990). *Medical statistics: A commonsense approach*. John Wiley & Sons.

Elston, R. C., & Johnson, W. D. (1994). *Essantial of biostatistics* (2 ed.). F.A. Davis Company.

Hulley, S. B., & Cummings, S. R. (1988). *Designing clinical research*. Williams & Wilkins.

Ingelfinger, J. A. (1987). *Biostatistics in clinical medicine* (2 ed.). Macmillan Publishing Co., Inc.

Munro, B. H., & Page, E. B. (1993). *Statistical methods: For healt care research*. J.B. Lippincott Company.

Norman, G. R., & Streiner, D. L. (1994). *Biostatistics: The bare essential*. Mosby.

Norusis, M. J. (1993). *SPSS for windows base system user's guide release 6.0*. SPSS Inc.

Özdamar, K. (1997). *Paket programlar ile İstatistiksel veri Analizi I, T.C. A.Ü. Yayınları No:1001, Fen Fak. Yayınları No:11, Eskişehir.*

Shott, S. (1990). *Statistics for health professionals*. W.B. Sounders Company.

Sümbüloğlu, K., & Sümbüloğlu, V. (1990). *Biyoistatistik* (Vol. 5). Baskı, Özdemir Yayıncılık.

Index

Printed and bound by CPI Group (UK) Ltd, Croydon, CR0 4YY

26/08/2026

14950698-0001